South County Studies

The Narragansett Glebe

SOUTH COUNTY STUDIES

OF SOME
EIGHTEENTH CENTURY
PERSONS, PLACES AND CONDITIONS
IN
THAT PORTION OF
RHODE ISLAND
CALLED

NARRAGANSETT

With an Introduction by Caroline Hazard
Compiled Largely from Letters
Now First Published
by
Oliver Wendell Holmes

Esther Bernon Carpenter

HERITAGE BOOKS
2010

HERITAGE BOOKS
AN IMPRINT OF HERITAGE BOOKS, INC.

Books, CDs, and more—Worldwide

For our listing of thousands of titles see our website
at
www.HeritageBooks.com

A Facsimile Reprint
Published 2010 by
HERITAGE BOOKS, INC.
Publishing Division
100 Railroad Ave. #104
Westminster, Maryland 21157

Copyright © 1924 Mary Carpenter

— Publisher's Notice —
In reprints such as this, it is often not possible to remove blemishes from the original. We feel the contents of this book warrant its reissue despite these blemishes and hope you will agree and read it with pleasure.

International Standard Book Numbers
Paperbound: 978-0-7884-3021-3
Clothbound: 978-0-7884-8364-6

Contents

	Page
PREFACE	vii
THE HUGUENOT INFLUENCE IN RHODE ISLAND *A paper read before the Rhode Island Historical Society, November 17, 1885*	3
JOHN SAFFIN, HIS BOOK	39
ANNALS OF NARRAGANSETT	
A SUNDAY IN OLD NARRAGANSETT	77
THE NARRAGANSETT GLEBE	92
THE WILL OF JAMES MacSPARRAN, CLERK	101
PARSON FAYERWEATHER	112
PARSON FAYERWEATHER'S WILL	122
THE WILLETT FAMILY IN RHODE ISLAND	132
THE WORLDLY GOODS OF A PURITAN	148
THE HELMES OF SOUTH KINGSTOWN	156
THE OLD FRIENDS' MEETING HOUSE	175
NEGRO SLAVERY IN THE COLONY OF RHODE ISLAND	195
TRADITIONS OF NARRAGANSETT SERVITUDE	211
THREE REPRESENTATIVE SERVANTS OF THE OLD TIME	222
A TRAVELLER IN OLD NARRAGANSETT	232

Contents

THE PIOUS DREAMER	248
SUNDRY SAVORY RECIPES TO CURE DIVERS DISEASES	255
AN OLD BOOK OF HOUSEHOLD MEDICINE	262
THE CONFLICT OF COLONIAL AUTHORITIES IN NARRAGANSETT	268
AN OFFICIAL PAPER OF 1727	274
INDEX	287

PREFACE

IT was in 1879 that Dr. Oliver Wendell Holmes wrote to Esther Bernon Carpenter: "I like to see you sailing in your own ship *à pleins voiles*, on your own course, a thinking woman, with strength as well as sensibility of fibre."

Ten years before, when she was a girl of only twenty-one, he began to write to her letters which she regarded as giving her the best lessons of her life, letters of encouragement, of criticism, of understanding, which put her in touch with the world of thought and literature. "I never know what you are going to grow to," he tells her later: "I have seen such effects from steady, long continued devotion to science and letters,— such skill, such erudition, that when I see in a young person assiduous and persevering application in addition to natural endowments I hardly venture to construct such a student's horoscope."

There are twenty-six of these letters from Dr. Holmes, beginning in 1869 and ending in 1886. He speaks in detail of her Essays or other papers which she sent him as they appeared in the *Providence Journal*. "If I were a millionaire," he writes, "I should have them printed on my private press (I should keep one of course) and I

Preface

cannot help thinking that the public must come to know you in some permanent form."

And who was Esther Bernon Carpenter, this girl, to whom Dr. Holmes wrote thus? She was born April 4, 1848, the daughter of Rev. James Helme Carpenter and Mary Hoxie Hazard his wife, and spent her earliest years in the old Willett house, a mile north of the South Ferry in Narragansett. The best blood in the country ran in her veins. Her great-grandfather, Francis Carpenter, inherited the old estate from his uncle, Francis Willett, son of Andrew, son of Thomas, first mayor of New York, who was thus her four times great-grandfather, and also the three times great-grandfather of Oliver Wendell Holmes.

John Saffin married Martha Willett, one of the daughters of Mayor Thomas Willett, and in 1692 built the house in which these families lived. Her great-grandmother Carpenter was Esther Helme, whose mother was Esther Powel, daughter of Esther Bernon, whose famous gold rattle, with its six golden bells and its whistle handle, belonged to one Esther after another, and thus came to her.

A quaint volume dated Boston, 1665, was among her earliest recollections. "Journals, letters, dialogues, dissertations on various grave subjects, from heraldry to theology, filled many

[viii]

Preface

pages of the strange old book which was so often my companion," she writes. This was "John Saffin, His Book," which Miss Carpenter embalmed in one of her most important articles. It is a folio twelve inches by seven, and about an inch thick, with excellent paper, now yellowed by time, but with the ink still black and clear, in the beautiful script of the seventeenth century when penmanship was an art. These with other heirlooms are safe in the care of the Rhode Island Historical Society.

The letters from Dr. Holmes speak in some detail of many of the papers contained in this volume—the Friends' Meeting House, the Helme Family, the Fayerweathers, the Historical Society study of the Huguenot Influence in Rhode Island. They also are the best indication of the ardent spirit that lived in that frail body. But the following extracts from them need no further words of mine.

Boston, Dec. 26th, 1869

MY DEAR MISS ESTHER: I shall take your letter as my text and preach you a little sermon — not a fault-finding one, you may be sure, but a sermon of encouragement, of good cheer, such as is fitting at this sweet season when the pillars of our churches are budding like Aaron's rod with fragrant evergreens and their vaulted roofs shaking with *Te Deums.*

Afraid, are you, my dear child, to send me this let-

Preface

ter? I never received a truer, simpler, sweeter one, nor one which I would more earnestly wish my children to read,— and I have had letters now and then from some of the great people of the earth, or —those I might be vain of, at least, as my correspondents. I only wonder what I have said or done to deserve such a tribute as you pay me. Nothing, nothing but speak a few kind words which any human creature with a few drops of mother's blood in his veins could hardly find it in his heart *not* to speak. No Christmas tribute has come home to me quite so nearly and so warmed my better nature. If I only deserved it.

You have written to me from time to time, never at superfluous length, as so many young people do, never insisting on perpetual answers to unending questions, but always, it has seemed to me, at the right moment, with a rare discretion, asking a few words of counsel when they were needed, telling me just enough of yourself to guide me in advising you, and, I think I can truly say of you, never writing an idle line, or one that you need remember with regret. And I have always answered you — none but a churl could do less — have given you a few brief hints and shewed a little human interest in you— what has that cost me? I sometimes think that in doing small favors we gain, ourselves, such an amount of selfish pleasure that it is almost like cheating to purchase our enjoyment so cheap. So when you thank me for these "best lessons of your life" I can only sigh and say, "Count it not a sin, my Taskmaster, if I have won the pleasure such words give, without paying for it."

All you tell me of yourself and your family is on the

Preface

whole most gratifying. For, in the first place you give me good news of your father, whose well-being must form one great element in your daily happiness. And there is a certain air of content — I do not mean that hilarity which is born with some people, but the content which has been fought for in many a daily contact and many a nightly vigil, — which is based in sacred trust, in self-conquest, in self-surrender. I am greatly pleased that your Rector is a man in whose human sympathies as well as his spiritual teachings you can trust. Every soul knows for itself what religious soil it grows best in. Refined and delicate natures, that find the wind of the open-air creeds too strong for them — that love the decencies and the dignity of a well-ordered service, are greatly attracted to the Episcopal church. I doubt if any of the protestant communions meet *all* the wants of many young persons, and those among the most devout and the most sensitive to religious influences, so well as this. To me the one great essential of every church is that it shall substitute nothing for "Our Father" of the Lord's Prayer, and admit no equivalents for *duty* and *character*. But your church has many large-minded and level-hearted men who I think are not very far removed from my opinion on this point.

Now as to your self-accusations. I know all about them — for I am one of the same kind. Fight them — fight them, heartily, cheerily. You and I shall never overcome them, quite, for they are constitutional with both of us. Your case is perhaps a little graver than mine, but I, your Doctor, tell you you are greatly improved — doing well, — so well that I have only to say

Preface

go on and do what to-day lays before you as well as you can, "As ever in the Great Taskmaster's eye," and avoid reproaching yourself, . . . *as a part of your duty.*

Boston, May 25th, 1873

As to the account of the Helme family, I read it all through from beginning to end and was exceedingly pleased with it—not because I recognized traces of your recollection of something of my own in it—but because it was an interesting family history, very well told. I have hardly any fault to find with it. One or two sentences were rather long, I thought, and might perhaps have been broken up to advantage. But I assure you it is a very creditable performance in a literary point of view, and shews a good taste and a discriminating eye for the points of narrative which would give you a good chance of success as a local historian. It is very pleasant to see the name and a fragment or two of a noble life which has passed away almost unremembered rescued by loving hands from oblivion. In this case I think I can see where you got some of those qualities which without meaning to flatter you I think—no, I feel sure you possess. It is a good thing to count a few strains of really, not conventionally, generous blood among one's ancestry.

Boston, Jan. 11*th,* 1874

I have just been reading the two articles on the "Old Friends' Meeting House" which you have kindly sent me. Although I thought I had my hands full, as my table is a litter of unanswered letters, I just threw all

Preface

out of the way to tell you before I touch one of them how much more than pleased I have been with these two charming papers. If I said my feeling was admiration it would not have exaggerated the truth. Your style is now formed and it is a really finished one, clear, graceful, sympathetic, not over-sentimental, and as far as I can see without affectation or pretence, one of which faults so many young writers conscious of their powers of expression sooner or later fall into.

I have not much to say to you now, but I hope you carefully preserve copies of all your contributions of the historical and biographical character, for they are far better worth preserving in a volume than most of the articles which are so embalmed. If I were a millionaire I would have them printed on my private press (I should keep one of course) and I cannot help thinking the public must come to know you in some permanent form by and by.

But remember in all this that I am your friend, and have a kind of personal interest in all you write, and must not allow myself to over-praise you. For all that, I can honestly say that I am surprised and delighted to find you choosing such excellent subjects and treating them in so finished and interesting a manner. You have often said I have helped you — don't you believe it — you have helped yourself, and would have learned from nature and men and women and books if you had never had a word of special counsel from anybody. But it does please me even to think you believe (though I tell you not to) that I have been of some kind of use to you.

Preface

Boston, Jan. 21st, 1880

All the communications to the paper you send me are good, but two interested me particularly, the two relating to the Fayerweather. In the first place I am always interested in an *inventory,* and you have unearthed a good one and related it in a very agreeable way—with just enough poetical side-light and incidental moral reflection to make the dough into bread by "raising" it with their mental yeast. But the Fayerweather interested me for another reason. About the time of my birth "Thomas Fayerweather Esq." was living in Cambridge. Just when he died I do not know, but I never saw one of the name, and the very existence of such a family in Cambridge was to me like a piece of mythology. My impression is that he or they lived in that famous row of old Tory houses, the same where Longfellow now lives, and the fine old English name with the Y in it sounded as if it came from the lord of some grand old manor in the Mother-country.

Well, after reading your two articles I went straight to the "little library" upstairs and took down two little pudgy, but venerable looking volumes—the Greek Septuagint of the Old and New Testaments. Well did I remember the name, but I was not sure of the exact date. On the first blank leaf I read

Abiel Holmes
The gift of Thomas Fayerweather Esq.

Whether this belonged to the library of your "Samuel Fayerweather, Clerk" or not I cannot say. If it did I suppose I ought to send it to the Corporation of King's

Preface

College, New York, with thanks for a century's use by borrower and apologies for detaining it so long.

Boston, Nov. 25th, 1885

I am delighted to hear of your reception at the Rhode Island Historical Society, and particularly pleased that you took up a subject in which I, like you, have an hereditary interest not through descent, however, but because my father wrote a "Memoir of the French Protestants" who settled at Oxford, with which as well as with Mr. Daniel's much larger history you must of course be acquainted. I felt sure long ago that you could make a reputation as an historical writer, and to say nothing of preceding papers this elaborate and admirable contribution to local, and I might add to general history, inasmuch as the story you tell relates to a great far reaching religious movement—your contribution, I say, amply proves your fitness for the noble task of conservation of that which is best worthy of memory in the past. It gives me really a thrill of pleasure to see how you are redeeming the promises of your earlier girlhood.

Boston, Feb. 11*th,* 1886

I do not write because I feel obliged to, but to thank you for the two newspaper extracts you have just sent me. I was reading the Aeneid when they came, and much interested in that old story. I laid my Virgil down to look at the E. B. C. article, and before I knew what I was about I had read the whole article. Pretty well, to beat P. Virgilius Maro!

Preface

Miss Carpenter lived a secluded life in a small village, for after the early years near the sea, Wakefield was her home. But to her the quiet country echoed with voices from the past, voices demanding utterance. "The gray walls of familiar homesteads fast crumbling under the touch of time plead for a longer continuance in our kind recollection," she writes. It is to fulfil such a desire that friends of hers and lovers of the past in Rhode Island have made possible the publication of this book. Not in vain shall the voices she heard cry to her, "Child of our race, kindle again the fire on our deserted hearth. By all the memories of thy childhood forget not thine ancient heritage. Let it perish not, but endure to be our memorial upon the earth. When it is gone what shall remain to tell of us, and the pleasant places where we dwelt and the lands we called after our own names!"

C. H.

Peace Dale, November, 1923

South County Studies

THE HUGUENOT INFLUENCE IN RHODE ISLAND

THE principal anniversary in the course of the greatest national persecution in modern history was observed thirteen years ago, at the three hundredth return of the memories of the martyrdom of St. Bartholomew's Day, that "bloodiest picture in the book of time." The massacre of that day was the severest blow ever struck at religion under any name, and in the sorrowful words of the devout Catholic and brilliant thinker, Chateaubriand, "gave to philosophical ideas an advantage over religious ideas which has never since been lost." The courtly instigators of that crime, and the brutal executors of their will, alike believed that they had well-nigh extirpated the heretics. And Louis XIV was convinced that in affixing his signature to the Revocation of the Edict of Nantes he should extinguish the very name of heresy in his dominions. But the spiritual forces which brought about the Reformation, with its final corollary, religious freedom, were working out results which in their ultimate course could neither be arrested by persecution nor limited by toleration. Kings and statesmen, priests and nobles, could direct the cumbrous machinery of the state and the law against the visible manifestations of heresy, but they could not cope with the finer agencies of thought and conscience, and the soul of the heretic was an unshaken citadel.

The Huguenots of France who first began to be generally called by that name under Charles IX, were destined to carry it to distant countries, and to make it an honored title to the latest generation. Colonization had been attempted even before the great massacre of 1572, and the brief period of toleration, under that honest soldier and clear-sighted man of affairs, Henry VI, was quickly followed by the oppression of more than half a century, culminating with the infamous dragonnades, the results of which, in the multitudes of forced conversions, furnished the pretended warrant for that Act of Revocation which, in 1685, drove hundreds of thousands of loyal and home-loving Frenchmen into exile.

With the fall, in 1628, of La Rochelle, the historic Huguenot city, "the Religion" ceased to be coupled with the strife of civil factions, many of the great nobles deserting a cause that could no longer serve their party interests. The Reformed Church, thus tried by adversity, was to be still further purified by persecution. Those who endured both these ordeals, and remained true to the reformed doctrines, were recruited from the intellectual and the industrial strength of the nation. First may be named a group of noble families of ancient distinction, who were still loyal to the Protestant faith. With them stood the leading merchants and manufacturers of the kingdom; and they were followed by the more intelligent artisans, peasantry, and seamen. With the Huguenots, as in the case of the Jews, exclusion from all the ambitions of civil and political life had resulted in the concentration of their abilities upon the practical interests of business. French trade and manufactures flourished in heretic hands. One-third of the trade of the country was conducted by the Reformed. In silk weaving, glass manufacturing, as fabricants of jewelry and pottery, and in many other branches of the finer industries, they were eminent for their ingenuity and taste. In agriculture, wherein, as the good sense of the French nation has always acknowledged, lies the true wealth of a people, they were especially diligent and successful. A refugee in Boston in 1687 is surprised at the careless husbandry of the English, *qui sont beaucoup fénéans*, and are proficient only in raising their Indian corn and cattle. No small number of the French seamen, and those confessedly of the best type, were of the Reformed religion. In departing from the able policy of Richelieu and Mazarin, and causing the Huguenot emigrations, the government of Louis XIV disorganized the great middle class of the kingdom, and impaired the chief resources of national prosperity.

When the time arrived for the multitudes of Frenchmen, natives of separated provinces, members of different classes and belonging to diverse callings, but all united as confessors of a common faith, to decide between recantation and expatriation, the stern choice was firmly made. In a moment, as it were, by the power of a noble impulse that warmed the hearts and nerved the wills of the tens of thousands of " the Religion," France was abandoned for a refuge beyond the seas. Then began such an exodus as the civilized world had never seen. The expulsion, early in the same century, of the Moors and Jews from the borders of Spain could scarcely afford a parallel to the decree by which the Most Christian King drove his Protestant subjects from the heart of his kingdom into perpetual exile. As the children of Israel departed in haste, taking with them their yet unleavened bread, so it is told, in the homely story of a refugee family, that they fled at a sudden warning, leaving "the dinner on the fire." These also left all and followed Him, their Divine Master, as truly as those who left houses and lands, for His name's sake.

The emigration was from the most distinguished provinces of the kingdom. From proud Normandy and ancient Bretagne went the descendants of the Crusaders, to begin a holier pilgrimage than that on which their ancestors had departed centuries before. From Saintonge, the early seed plot of the Reformation in France; from the Lyonnais, the seat of Protestant industry; from sunny Champagne and stately Dauphiny; from romantic Languedoc and fair Lorraine; from Touraine, Berry, and the Orleanais, copiously watered by the veins and arteries of the noble Loire; from Poitou, rich in ancient memories; from the Isle de France and the capital of the kingdom; from Guyenne, the fruitful; from the inheritance of the Counts of Foix; from Picardy and Maine; and above all, from Aunis, the faithful province, with its Huguenot stronghold, La Rochelle, "proud city of the waters," from town and hamlet, from chateau and cottage, from hill country and islet, from the seaboard and from the interior, from the north, east, and south of France, the fugitives, eluding the strictest vigilance of the watchful guards stationed on the frontier, escaped in multitudes to their distant refuge among a people of an alien race and a foreign tongue.

What elements of mind and character did they bring to the formation of the complex nationality which, in the last two centuries, has been developed in the maturing of the American Republic?

Huguenot Influence in Rhode Island

It has never been denied that the emigration wielded a greater influence than might have been expected from its mere numbers. The qualities of its members were, indeed, of a shining order to have irradiated our history with that long, bright track of light which we are now following to its origin in the dawning of the Reformation.

Though Lefèvre is called the father of the French Reformation, Calvin, as its tutor and governor, formed its character and shaped its destinies. Geneva dominated La Rochelle. Calvinism, originating in the demand of the logical French mind for a definite theology, was, in the severities of its discipline, a more wholesome training for the people of the Gallic race, natives of a smiling country, strong in *le bon sens* against the promptings of fanaticism, and sustained in all reverses by an inexhaustible cheerfulness, than to the moulding of the morbid and gloomy Saxon, whether brooding in the mountain retreats of the Covenanter or battling with the assaults of the stern climate in which the Puritan met an unrelenting foe. No superstitious terrors or cruelties mar the civil record of the Huguenots. During the wars of "the Religion" they fought in self-defence and with few violations of the laws of civilized warfare. In retaliation for massacres they repeatedly committed acts of iconoclastic impiety, and this is a reproach from which even the sober blood of the Netherlanders is not free. But it may be said of them as a people, that though tried by the refinements of persecution, suffering in the separation from their children, goaded by the violence of a brutal soldiery, transported like criminals, enduring as galley-slaves the severest labor that can be performed by man, or driven into hopeless exile, they still remained confessors, and did not degenerate into fanatics. In them the best type of the national character asserted itself, blending with its kindred traits in Protestant England and America, and within the scope of its immediate influence, subduing the asperities of a race that was ruder in the etiquette of its pleasures than the more gentle people had been in the chivalry of its warfare. The sudden and secret departure of the exiles constituted a phase of history that was to be repeated little more than a century later, in the flight of the *émigrés*. But the priests and the nobles who composed the proscribed classes of the Revolution brought to England no such accession to her moral or material wealth as was furnished by the Huguenot manufacturers and artisans of the intelligent middle class. The character of the refugee contribution to the strength of the English people was chiefly industrial. In America the Huguenot name has been especially identified with political ascendancy. By a fulfilment under favoring conditions of national aspirations analogous to that which was seen in the founding of the democracy of New England, long before English liberties were secured by the Revolution of 1688, the immediate descendants of expatriated Frenchmen, by their share in our struggle for independence, anticipated the rising of their countrymen, the *tiers état* of France, with whom originated the Revolution. In summing up all these phases of nationality, either industrial, political, scholarly, social, or religious, it is enough to say that intellectuality is the note of Calvinism. French Protestantism owed its early development to the results of the Humanist culture, chastened and systematized by the logic of Calvin, who may be styled the Apostle to the intellectual; and wherever we trace the influence of his teachings, whether in discipleship, under the skies of antique France, or in the revolt of modern New England, we recognize the workings of Renaissance scholarship and Calvinistic thoughtfulness, as in the reactionary types which to-day are reproached as cultivating a mere intellectualism, or even as Pagan, by those religionists who jealously profess a more full-blooded creed, and engage in a heartier worship. But though the French Calvinist, by his moral elevation, represented the most dignified type of French character, he was not of the school thus indicated by the poet of Puritan antecedents:

> "Severe and smileless, he that runs may read
> The stern disciple of Geneva's creed."

Like the Puritans, the Huguenots sang psalms, and were diligent Bible students. Like them, they chose the names of their children from the Scriptures rather than from the calendar of saints of doubtful associations. The analogy of their sufferings under the Bourbon Ahasuerus with those of the Jews of old time, as related in the Book of Esther, was constantly present with them, and no name was oftener given to their daughters than that of the Jewish heroine. The name of Samuel, the early called, was so often used among them in pious memory of youthful devotion as to provoke the scornful notice of their opponents. But, unlike the New Englanders, they cultivated the amenities of life, in cheery and kindly social observances, in delicacy and refinement of manners, and in taste for music and the arts.

In engraving, ceramics, painting, and sculpture, and in the walks of science, scholarship, and literature, they furnished examples of exceptional ability and skill. While civil war was raging, in 1574, the theatres of La Rochelle were frequented, as those of Paris were in the Reign of Terror, more than two hundred years later. And the play which divided the attention of the Rochellese with the interests of the war was the work of a Huguenot woman, afterwards known in the long history of a desperate strife as the heroic Duchesse de Rohan. Creeds and systems cannot extinguish race characteristics, and these Puritans of France kept Christmas and Easter, used a ritual, and in exile readily conformed to the Church of England, who numbers on her long list of worthies some of their most valued sons.

One distinction between the fugitives of La Rochelle and the Pilgrims of Leyden cannot be overlooked — the former fled from persecution in its severest form; the latter did not; and, praiseworthy as was that motive of their departure from Holland which prompted them to preserve and transmit their English nationality, the Puritan emigrants cannot command those deeper sympathies which respond to the story of the Huguenot exiles.

The merciless fate that banished the fugitive from his home and country pursued him, in various forms of misfortune, in his flight to distant refuges. England and Holland afforded peaceful asylums. But treachery undermined Coligny's colony in Brazil, and Spanish and Portuguese hostility completed its ruin. The Floridian colony was soon extinct in the blood of those Spanish massacres which the tourist learns to associate with the antiquity of St. Augustine. By the triumph of the Jesuits, the heretic was expelled from Acadia and Canada; and France was arrested in the career of colonial empire. In her Protestant population she possessed her most valuable material for the work of colonization. The Huguenots were of the prosperous class that emigrates only under the stress of some extraordinary motive, such as was supplied by the pursuit of liberty of conscience. But this means of escape was denied to them; for the persecution long rife in the kingdom was finally carried into the far Antilles; and the Huguenot, already an emigrant for his faith to these remote dependencies of the French crown, became a fugitive to the English colonies. By a system which illustrated the irony of cruelty, the Protestants were now sent in forced emigrations to the Antilles, transported like convicts to be sold into peonage to the Roman Catholic planters. As in the history of the Inquisition, which mocked the hopes of the converts to its terrors with a pious death, inflicted on them as penitents, and not as heretics, so among the Huguenot victims the recanting and the constant were shipped together from French ports to a fate more dreaded than even the slavery of the galleys, of which Victor Hugo has given so fearfully vivid a picture in his recital of the sufferings of *les forçats*. Only in escape from the tortures of the West Indies to the haven of the nearest Protestant country could the hunted exile find security. And here, too, his unhappy destiny awaited him in the earlier experiences of his settlement in our Eastern, Middle, and Southern colonies, for the fever of Carolina, the savages of the New Netherlands and of Massachusetts, where they were incited by Jesuit craft to the Oxford massacre, were deadly foes. No more touching story is written in our colonial annals than that of the sorrowing exiles of New Oxford, homeless for the second time, departing in tears from their church in the wilderness, and from the graves of their dead.

But in Rhode Island, the retreat of the persecuted, and in Narragansett, the seat of the friendly tribe that welcomed the exiled founder of the colony,—here, assuredly, the wanderer must find repose. It was not so. Even here he tasted again of the bitterness of exile, and once more took up the burden of his griefs, a homeless man.

The cause of his expulsion from the little territory, of which our local tradition relates that he chose it for its fertility, as hoping to find in it an Eden of fruitfulness and peace, was, according to the researches of the late Elisha R. Potter, one of those disputes over conflicting land titles which so often sowed thorns in the path of our pioneers. The designing Atherton Company, through its London agents, secured these unsuspecting emigrants as settlers of territory which nearly ten years before had been parcelled out by the Rhode Island Assembly to the proprietors of East Greenwich, under which name the new township was already known. More than forty-five families left London to sail for New England in 1686. The leader of the expedition was a nobleman, and among the emigrants were the pastor and the physician of the future colony. Its annals are short and simple indeed, for in five years the settlement was broken up and almost every family had left Rhode Island.

Huguenot Influence in Rhode Island

The members of the Atherton Company had obtained their large Indian grants partly by means of frauds, which led Roger Williams (who refused to interpret for them, on their first coming into Narragansett as representatives of Connecticut) to denounce their greed for land, as "one of the gods of our New England, which the Eternal will destroy." The various colonial and individual claims to the Narragansett lands were still pending, while the claimants awaited the decision of the Crown, when the refugees entered this doubtful region as settlers. They were first assigned to a tract six miles square, lying west of Wickford, the Newbarry Plantation, probably so called after Walter Newbarry, a Rhode Island member of the Council of Governor Andros. But it was rejected by these emigrants from the Rochellese seaboard as lying too far from the ocean, and another site was occupied, then, as now, principally included in East Greenwich and still identified as Frenchtown, where the excavations made for nine of their temporary habitations may still be traced, chiefly grouped about the spring, around which they planted their orchards and vineyards.

And now we pause on the eve of their settlement to consider the character of the new surroundings in which they found themselves, after nearly a twelvemonth of the homeless journeyings of exiles. Two centuries from the crowded years of the ancient civilization of France! Two hundred years from the brief story of the American colonization! We go back to the rude beginnings of our colonial life, to find it confronted in strangest contrast, by the finest qualities of European maturity. In 1686, Roger Williams had been dead but three years. Louis XIV was yet to live nearly thirty years to see the injury wrought to his kingdom by his unrighteous enactment. James II was in the first year of his short and turbulent reign, during which, under the administration of his colonial representatives, the early names of the townships in the King's Province were temporarily changed, in petty conformity to that arbitrary policy which was arrested by the New England Revolution of 1689. The political state of Narragansett was so wretched that Kingstown, in consideration of the disturbances of the country, had lately obtained the remission of her tax. Her chosen deputies to the Assembly had for several sessions refused to serve. All these troubles arose from the strife of colonial jurisdictions, and from the conflicting claims to individual holdings. Both Connecticut and Massachusetts were territorial claimants in Narragansett; the latter colony having formally annexed Westerly to her County of Suffolk. The disputed land claims in Narragansett, as set forth by Roger Williams eight years earlier in a quaintly graphic paper, were no fewer than fifteen. Ten years had passed since King Philip's War, but the country had not yet recovered from the devastation wrought by the attacks of the Indians and the quartering of the troops of the United Colonies. Bull's Block-house, and the other burned buildings of the settlers, had not been replaced; and the agriculture of the Narragansetts had ceased with the destructive blow suffered by the tribe in the battle of the Great Swamp Fort. The unsettled state of a country, the ownership of which had been long and hotly disputed, and which finally had been the seat of Indian warfare, as well as of border frays, may be indicated by the fact that the date of 1686 is still eighteen years earlier than that of the pilgrimage made in 1704 by the resolute Madam Knight, from Boston to New Haven, passing through Narragansett, and meeting in the course of her undertaking with such difficulties and dangers as embellish this journey of two hundred miles with more adventures than a woman would now encounter in making the tour of the world. "The French doctor," mentioned by her (Dr. Pierre Ayrault, of the Frenchtown settlement), figures in her narrative as nearly the only reminder of that civilization of which she took leave almost at the beginning of her travels in her visit at Dedham, to "Mr. Belcher, the minister of the town." One incident of travel related by her is the passage of a river, since identified as running south of East Greenwich. She says: "The post told me there was a bad river we were to ride through, which was so very fierce a horse could hardly stem it." On reaching it, "I perceived by the horse's going we were on the descent of a hill which, as we came nearer to the bottom, was totally dark with the trees that surrounded it." But "I knew by the going of the horse we had entered the water." Having crossed, giving the reins to her horse, as bidden by her guide, "he then put on harder than I with my weary bones could follow; so left me and the way behind him in the dolesome woods." These descriptive touches show us that the conditions of pioneer life in Narragansett were, as the writer says of the experiences of her journey, "enough to startle a masculine courage."

The fertility of the land was the chief advantage enjoyed by the Huguenot settlers. In this temperate climate their favorite gardens and orchards would flourish abundantly. Nowhere in Rhode Island does the wild grape grow in greater profusion than here; and the scions of the mulberry trees of their projected silk culture are still cultivated in Frenchtown. But, in the words of the Psalmist, "A fruitful land maketh He barren, for the wickedness of them that dwell therein"; and the dispersed settlers, in their ignorance of any well-established prior claim to the land, must have believed it a wickedness to drive them from the fields they had diligently tilled and planted. How severe must have been the hardships of exile from the oldest of European civilizations to the struggles of colonial existence! How rude the transition from the courtly scenes in which some of the emigrants had moved to the stern solitudes of Narragansett! The strange contrasts in their experiences did not pass unnoticed by their fellow-colonists. In the manuscript diary of John Saffin, of Bristol, one of the three "Proprietors of the Narragansett Country," who signed the articles of agreement with "the French gentlemen," may be traced certain indications of his indignation at the story of their wrongs and his hearty hatred of their royal oppressor. "The king of France is so absolute that his will is his law. . . . The mere impost of salt throughout France is said to amount to two million of pounds sterling, the poor people being forced to take yearly such a quantity they know not how to use at the King's excessive rates." And further: "It is affirmed and taken for a certain truth that the French King's own table stands him £500,000 yearly, besides the Dauphin and the Queen's expenses at

Huguenot Influence in Rhode Island

court, and in pensions yearly, at home and abroad, seven millions of money. And the French clergy are believed to possess thirty millions of yearly rent which they pay to the King." Thus far our diarist, whose homely record impresses us with the arrogant luxury of a court, the abuses of which had become matter of reflection with an obscure provincial in a foreign colony. His bare rendering of the "certain truth" brings before us the Grand Monarque, the dispenser of the wealth of the nation in pensions among the tools of his policy "at home and abroad," and especially at the English court, no less strongly than his figure is displayed in the brilliant narrative of Macaulay, whose rhetoric but enhances the original force of the facts. Where in all the circuit of human affairs could the moralist find the antithesis more sharply drawn between the splendors of sin and the sufferings of the righteous, than in the opposite fortunes of the Most Christian King and his unhappy subjects? As we have seen, the power and opulence of "Lewis, ye French King," had penetrated even the obscurity of Narragansett

> "With far-off glories of the Throne,
> And glimmerings of the Crown."

And the keen distresses of these exiles from persecution had gained a hearing even from Andros, whom Puritan narrators have depicted as the tyrant of New England annals, but who lent a merciful ear to the prayer of the refugees, ordering half the hay mown on the meadows of which the holding was disputed between the old and the new settlers, to be "for the use and benefit of the said French families, who, being strangers and lately settled, are wholly destitute, and have no other way to supply themselves." Such were the contrasted conditions of royalty and exile. But the earthly honors of Louis could afford him only a corruptible crown, while

> "The memory of the just
> Smells sweet, and blossoms in the dust."

The giving of this considerate order by Governor Andros, and his neutrality in the conflict of possession, could not provide against the difficulties of an imperfect title. To review the controversy over the jurisdiction and occupation of Narragansett would, as Updike said, require a volume. But the nucleus of the annoyances experienced by the Huguenots lies in the fact of their making claim to lands which in 1677 had been granted to actual settlers. Had they taken up some of the vacant lands of Narragansett, the difficulties attending the adjustment of the rights of the Crown, and the proprietorship of the Atherton Company, might have been as slight as the colonists had expected them to be. They seem never to have known that Rhode Island, by the act of her Assembly, had committed herself to the protection of the earlier settlers; nor to have taken account of that Colony as a party, and an active one, in the controversy. It is true that all parties were nominally awaiting the decision of the Crown in respect to the opposing claims of Rhode Island and Connecticut; but Rhode Islanders were by no means disposed to tarry for the slow processes of a conclusion concerning which they cherished an assurance, eventually to be justified, that it would prove favorable to their rights. They were first in possession, and they vigorously enforced their claims. The Huguenots, lacking any effectual support from Connecticut, and finding no hope in the intricacies of the law and the administration of a foreign country, the language of which was but imperfectly understood, but interpreting only too plainly the signs of violence and hostility in the effacing of their boundaries, the blocking of their highways, and finally in personal assaults, quietly withdrew from the debatable land. The East Greenwich and Kingston settlers seem to have asserted their ownership by the arm of flesh rather than by the arm of the law. It was perhaps too much to expect of their magnanimity that they should show moderation in the defence of rights which they regarded as outrageously violated; and we cannot be surprised at their disorderly behavior, in view of the fact that they evidently belonged to that class of society which knows little of self-control. The long period of border warfare over the disputed lands of Narragansett had developed the natural lawlessness of persons for whose conduct the better order of settlers were not responsible. "Many of the English inhabitants," says Dr. Ayrault, in his remonstrance to the Commissioners of the Colony, "would have helped us, but when they used any means therein they were evilly treated." When the war between France and England was impending in 1689 the Huguenots suffered serious annoyance from the rude search for arms made among them, without legal warrant, by their turbulent neighbors; but such of the English as were of better nurture joined the French in making formal complaint of this treatment; and the refugees, by obeying the order of the Rhode Island government, and taking the oath of allegiance to the British Crown, secured themselves against further molestation.

It was a fair promise of colonial prosperity that was dissipated with the expulsion of the refugees. Each family was entitled to 100 acres of upland, besides meadow land in proportion. The price was to be £20 the hundred acres, if paid immediately, or £25 if the payment were deferred for three years. The pastor's endowment consisted of 150 acres. One hundred acres were set apart as glebe land; and fifty acres were allotted toward the support of a schoolmaster. A church was built, in which, to quote the touching expressions of Ayrault, "we could enjoy our worship to God, . . . it being a very wilderness country." This little church was destroyed by persons unknown to posterity, but charitably characterized by Ayrault in terms much below the severity merited by the offence as "the vulgar sort of the people."

Five hundred French families, we are told, would have come to join their countrymen in Narragansett, but it was not to be the fortune of the French emigrant to America to found a lasting, vigorous, and homogeneous colony, save in that province which has been called "the home of the Huguenots," and in which the sheltered flowering of the transplanted French character has been apparent in the social supremacy and the generous traits of the Carolinian. The researches of the Rev. Dr. Charles W. Baird, as given in his history of the Huguenot Emigration to America, have unveiled the few facts in the story of the dispersed colonists that can now be ascertained. Natives of La Rochelle, and of Normandy, of Saintonge, Poitou, and Guyenne, they were finally scattered among the several colonies already entered by their countrymen and brethren. The greatest number went to New York; others removed to New Rochelle, South Carolina, Boston, and Oxford. But Pastor Carré, born in the faithful Protestant Isle de Ré, which lay under the protecting shield of La Rochelle, a Genevan student of the academy founded by Calvin, the former minister of two congregations in France, and now in the fortieth year of his useful life, passes out of ken, with the dispersion of his flock. The local tradition of the pastor of the Oxford colony is preserved by the beautiful outlines of Bondet Hill, but no trace remains of the brief residence in the Narragansett country of this European scholar and man of gentle nurture. Two families only, of those named on the authorized list of the original settlers, remained in Narragansett. Möise Le Moine (the name being now corrupted to Mawney) retained the farm still held and occupied by his descendants, and on which are found the principal evidences of the French settlement. Dr. Ayrault also continued to hold his lands, being, as he says, "persuaded by many to stay," doubtless because of his usefulness to a community in which, to quote his own words, he had been "a help to raise many from extreme sickness." A third settler, Julien, removed to Newport.

Though, perhaps, an idle speculation, yet it is one upon which the annalist pensively dwells, that represents the results of the growth of a large and flourishing Huguenot settlement in our borders, as they might have been felt in the greater prosperity and finer culture of Narragansett. From the character of the actual settlers we may judge of such as were to have been added to their number; and the names of De Marigny, the Norman noble, Carré, the learned pastor, and Ayrault, the able physician, are guarantees of the high order of the moral and social elements of the colony. With these leading members were fitly joined Beauchamps, of a family which still remained among the faithful few in Paris, so long the centre of Romanist fanaticism and cruelty. He became one of the successful merchants of Boston, and removed to Hartford, where his descendants are now living. There were besides, in the list thus suggestively labelled in the British State Paper Office "Mapp of the French refugee Gentlemen who are all turned out by the Road Islanders," the names of the two Davids, scions of one of the best families of La Rochelle. Allaire, afterwards a Boston merchant, was also of that city, and belonged to a family even then long tried in fidelity to the reformed religion, and to this day still true to its cause. Collin, another member of the Rochellese gentry, became the ancestor of a well-known Connecticut line. Grazillier was, in later years, one of the leading members of the Huguenot colony in New York. Tourtellot, of Bordeaux, was connected with some of the chief refugee families. Legaré belonged to the family of that name which has won intellectual and social distinction in Charleston, South Carolina. Barbut and Grignon were to be known as elders of the French Church in Boston. These colonists, with others of no slighter respectability, were unfortunately lost to Rhode Island, and their energies and influence were expended in the building up of other communities. Had they been able to make Narragansett their home, it would certainly have become the seat of a civilization in many respects superior to that which has as yet penetrated some of the interior regions of our State. Beginning with the earliest requirements of a newly settled country, they would have pursued their diligent and painstaking system of agriculture until their orchards and vineyards had enriched the plantation with the fruits of their patriarchal toils. Their simple gayety and social refinements would have brightened the savage gloom of the wilderness. Their "songs of lofty cheer," the psalms which they suited, not only to the stated hours of devotion, but to the daily round of duty, would ring out, as in the happier years of "the Religion" in France, from field and garden, from the workshop and the shallop. Their school would keep alive the traditions of classic learning, and inculcate those gracious lessons of courtesy and reverence by which their own youth was formed, in their old home. And then, rising to the highest need of their natures, their spiritual aspirations must find expression. To their rude church in the clearing they devoted their first labors:

> "Scarce steal the winds that sweep his woodland tracks
> The larch's perfume from the settler's axe,
> Ere, like a vision of the morning air,
> His slight-framed steeple marks the house of prayer.
> . . . .
> It sheds the raindrops from its shingled eaves
> Ere its green brothers once have changed their leaves."

Here they came to receive from the hands of their faithful pastor the ministrations of the altar and the font. Here they fervently repeated their pious ritual, and hither, if death visited them during their stay in our coasts, they came to chant a funeral psalm. Here was kindled a pure spiritual light—not the fierce and short-lived flame of fanaticism, but a mild glow that might have shed its sacred cheer upon many a Rhode Island home. But the fair prospect soon faded, and the Huguenot settlement was added to the long list of dispersions which belong to the history of colonization. No evident trace of their sojourn remains, and nothing has been supplied by any appeal to the motive of sympathy for their misfortunes. Rhode Island has done a tardy justice to the memories of her great sons; and has even given a monumental form to her gratitude toward the Indian benefactors of the infant colony; but not the humblest memorial points out the spot once dignified by the pure home life and sacred to the worship of the Huguenot exiles. Few of the present generation have heard their story, or can appreciate the regretful suggestions of interest and sympathy that are recalled to others by the homely and provincial name of Frenchtown.

There was to be no focus of Huguenot influence in Rhode Island, and the names associated either by record or by strong presumptive evidence with Huguenot ancestry, and which chiefly appear in their noted representatives, at a later date than the founding of the short-lived Narragansett colony, such as the historical name of Decatur, with Papillion, Pineau, Lucas, Ballou, the ancestor of Garfield, Grennell, founder of the mercantile family of the brothers Grinnell, Ganeau, Marchant, Jerauld, and others, are isolated instances of national traits which were never so combined as to give character to any one community.

But the religious interests of Rhode Island were to be in no small degree moulded by the zeal and energy of one whom Dr. Baird characterizes as perhaps the most remarkable of the Huguenot emigrants to America. Not to honor an individual, however worthy, have tributes repeatedly been paid to the memory of Gabriel Bernon. But the place which he fills in colonial annals, and especially in the religious history of Rhode Island, justly entitles him to rank as the representative of the Huguenot character and influence in this State.

Nor is it from motives of family interest, nor even as presenting interesting features of a picturesque family history, that reference is made to his origin and associations. The analysis of the Huguenot type in New England must be preceded by the study of the typical Huguenot family in La Rochelle, the capital of "the Religion," the "Geneva of the West." In art we find no figure of heroic stature without its cloudy background of ancestral prototypes. To define the hereditary qualities which Bernon received and transmitted, we must know the stock whence sprang this vigorous offshoot.

The Bernons are identified with La Rochelle, where they have been seated for centuries, but their remote history, as traced by Dr. Baird, relates their descent from a younger branch of the Counts of Burgundy. In this province the family originated, and its fortunes have been known and celebrated from the earliest ages of the French monarchy. The house of De Bernon is numbered in the lists of crusaders, and the name of Bernon is mentioned in Froissart's chronicles. In the sixteenth century the Bernons contributed to the ransom of the sons of Francis I, held as hostages in Spain after the battle of Pavia, and they aided Henry IV in his struggle for the crown, sending him a sum of money by the hands of Duplessis Mornay. They held the manors of La Bernonière in Poitou, and Bernonville on the Isle de Ré. An official claim to nobility among the Bernons of La Rochelle (the lineage of this branch being traced to an early date in the thirteenth century) was founded on the antique usage which conferred rank upon the mayors of the city and their descendants in perpetuity. This civic honor was often held by members of the family. When the golden book of the French Noblesse says, "The house of Bernon has formed alliances with some of the most illustrious families of the kingdom; it has rendered military services that have not been without distinction; it counts among its members superior officers of the greatest merit, both military and naval; and it has had several chevaliers of the Order of Saint Louis"; it simply sums up the facts which may be gleaned from the Bernon genealogy, compiled a century ago.

Such was the record of a family which, according to the Genealogical History of Poitou, had always been flourishing and distinguished before embracing the Calvinist heresy. "I might have kept my property and my quality," wrote the exiled Gabriel Bernon in his old age, "if I had been willing to submit to slavery." The pride of resolute will in the De Bernons, which had sustained them as knightly crusaders for the faith, and, in later times, as true followers of Henry of Navarre, was a trait that, purified by adversity and persecution, shone out in the firmness of the confessor or the constancy of the saint. The family narrative, as followed to a later date than that of the emigration, shows that the sons were zealously attached to the creed of the fathers. From the Revocation to the Revolution, or through the eighteenth century, and until France enjoyed freedom of conscience, the home of the Bernons was the centre of the Reformed religion in La Rochelle. Here secretly, but continuously, were held those Protestant services which the Government tacitly tolerated, with a consideration which probably would not have been shown to heretics of slighter distinction. These were the surroundings and the antecedents from which Gabriel Bernon separated himself in loyalty to his faith and in obedience to his conscience. He could not be less than true to the example of a father who, when he, with other heads of families, was summoned before Arnou, the military governor, after the first quartering of the dragoons upon them, and bidden to choose between ruin and recantation, exclaimed: "Sir, would you have me lose my soul? for it is impossible for me to believe in the religion which you command me to accept." "Much do I care," was the reply, made in the characteristic spirit of military insolence and sordid worldliness, "whether you lose your soul or not, provided you obey." This André Bernon derived his name from the first of his ancestors enumerated in the genealogy drawn up in 1782, by M. Joseph Crassons, and beginning with the year 1545, a date six generations later than that with which authentic records begin the history of the Rochelle branch. This paper, which now piques the interest with its inevitable blanks and omissions, and again displays a redundant fullness in its title-rolls and its hints of antiquarian zeal and family pride, is like some ancient and faded tapestry, showing dagger-rents and dusty folds in its hangings, but still a proud relic of antique story. From its records we gather that the Bernon lineage, in its different branches, and by the brilliant alliances of its daughters, has been illustrated, among its representatives and connections, by chevaliers of St. Louis, mayors of La Rochelle, naval and military officers, merchants and bankers, government officers, seigneurs, canonesses, grand seneschals of La Rochelle, holders of high places at court, nuns of the La Rochelle convents, colonists (evidently Protestant) of St. Domingo, Martinique, and New York, members of the learned professions, prefects, barons, military governors, civil engineers, pastors of the Reformed faith, marquises, viscounts, counts, consuls, and a manufacturer of glassware, this industry being one of the distinctive Huguenot callings. Among its semi-historical figures are such as the son of the house who was killed "at a siege in the Indies," one who fell at Fontenoy, another who was physician to Monsieur, brother of Louis XIV, and afterwards the Regent, and Benjamin, father of Peter Faneuil, of Faneuil Hall memory.

Against this rich background of courtly associations the severe outlines of the self-denying life of Gabriel Bernon, the fugitive for conscience' sake, are defined in a simple dignity. Although forty-one years old at the time of his flight, soon after the Revocation, his life was to be prolonged for half a century of the experiences of exile, until his ninety-first year. Recalled to his native La Rochelle from his mercantile affairs in Canada by the decree which excluded the Reformed from the colonies, he was incarcerated for several months in the gloomy Tour de la Lanterne, where prisoners of state were confined. A memorial of his imprisonment is still preserved among his descendants. It is a psalter of the version of Marot, given him by a fellow-prisoner; and is of that minute size in which Bibles and psalters were often issued from the press of Geneva or Amsterdam, in order that they might be thus more readily concealed by those colporteurs whose pious mission is touchingly described in one of Macaulay's Huguenot ballads, and by the readers among whom they were distributed. Such also is the tradition respecting the use of this volume by the prisoners, who hastily secreted it at the approach of their jailer. Most of these editions were destroyed at the public burnings of heretical books in France; and very few copies are known to be extant in America.

On his release, due probably to the intercession of relatives who were numbered among the *nouveaux convertis*, he escaped to Amsterdam, where he was soon joined by his wife and children, and thence to London, where he obtained a certificate of denization. While there, the project of the Oxford settlement affected him as an inducement to execute the plan of emigration to New England, to which he had given expression after the signing of the Revocation, in the eventful month of October, 1685, by a letter to a Boston correspondent.

In 1688 he arrived in Boston, where he became a member of the French Reformed Church. He soon entered upon various enterprises of trade and manufacture, such as proved to be of difficult and costly development, under the new conditions of colonial immaturity which formed his surroundings. His leading motive in these numerous undertakings is believed to have been that spirit of fraternal benevolence which so prevailed among the exiles as to be recognized in the different colonies as a Huguenot trait, and which closely united him to "our refugee brothers," as he styled his co-religionists. The manufacture of wash-leather in the *chamoiserie* which he established at Oxford, and the making of hats at Newport, as promoted by him, may be named among instances of his systematic provision for the employment of artisans some of whom had emigrated as under his protection. He twice returned to London on errands intimately connected with the promotion of colonial industry. After a residence of nine years in Boston, during which occurred the attempt toward settling Oxford, in which he took the leading part, paying the passage of the emigrants, and building the fort against the Indians which has lately been restored, he came to Rhode Island, which for nearly forty years, and until his death, was to be his home. For eight years he was a resident of Newport, which doubtless attracted him by its rising commercial importance, but more especially by that atmosphere of religious freedom which made it a fitter residence than Puritan Boston for a man of independent mind. Some of his near connections had been settlers of Frenchtown, and one former member of that colony, Daniel Ayrault, became his business partner in New-

Huguenot Influence in Rhode Island

port. He was also associated with him in the petition originating with Bernon and headed by him, for the sending of a clergyman of the Church of England as a missionary to Newport. This, with like appeals from other colonies, led to the organization, two years later, in 1701, of the Society for the Propagation of the Gospel in Foreign Parts. Thus Trinity Church was founded in Newport. Bernon resided in Providence from 1706 to 1712, when he went to Kingstown, where the ruins of his house were still to be seen, a generation ago. Here he was active in the formation of St. Paul's parish. In 1718 he returned to Providence, where he contracted a second marriage, with a lady of that town, and becoming closely identified with its interests, continued to reside there until his death in 1736.

His Providence house, which stood till about 1875, was nearly opposite the old St. John's Church, beneath which he was buried. He had been its founder, having made a journey to London in his eighty-first year, his third visit to that capital since his emigration, to secure the services of a missionary as rector of this venerable parish, which is to-day distinguished by the same earnest Protestant spirit that marked the influence of the Huguenot refugee, "to whose untiring zeal," in the words of Arnold, the historian of Rhode Island, "the first three Episcopal churches in the colony owed their origin."

What were the results of this long, active, and useful life of untiring and versatile energy? Gabriel Bernon engaged in almost every branch of colonial traffic, spending £10,000 in trade; he made himself the owner of a great landed estate; he labored toward the founding of a Huguenot colony; he undertook tedious journeyings by sea and land, and, in the pursuit of these varied interests, he met the persons most distinguished by birth, position, or talent among his contemporaries. In a word, he toiled long and faithfully in the round of his duties as a citizen, yet was denied the fruition of that success which should have been the reward of his abilities and his public spirit. His private interests were not served by the manufacturing schemes upon which he entered with a confidence and an enterprise in which he anticipated the merchants of a period of more developed resources. He failed in his endeavors to release the colonies from such restrictions on home-trade or inter-colonial traffic as his intelligent son had complained of in the relations between Acadia and Massachusetts; and he could not obtain any encouragement for new industries among the colonists from the parent country. The home government was too suspicious of colonial independence to favor any schemes looking toward colonial prosperity, and Bernon lived an age too early for the dissemination of ideas which were yet to find their place in the slowly maturing science of political economy.

The study of this life, of which, in its material sphere of activity, we are often constrained to write "failure" upon the promise of many brave hopes and efforts, may suggest the question whether it left any lasting influence beyond that of the lesson which a virtuous example communicated to contemporaries and descendants. What special work was accomplished by this representative of the Huguenot mind as an element in the evolution of Rhode Island civilization? Many aims and

Huguenot Influence in Rhode Island

endeavors of eager and restless spirits leave but little impress on a community like ours. The renewing processes of assimilation and circulation can be traced in the body politic no less clearly than in our physical life, and our State has not the same component parts as the Colony of our ancestors. The Rhode Island of the present is not the Rhode Island of the generation that has just passed away, and, if we are to anticipate the changes that are already indicated, it will not long be the Rhode Island of even a short term of years ago. Then can there be truth in the claim that there still exists in the Rhode Island of to-day an appreciable influence emanating from a single mind, the activities of which belong to the record of a buried past? Can the agencies that controlled the nurture of the infant Colony still be felt in the matured manhood of the State?

The answer is found in the recognition of the higher quality of the work to which this typical Huguenot devoted his best energies. "Every man's work shall be made manifest; for the day shall declare it." To this faithful worker long since came the fulfillment of the promise, "If any man's work abide, which he had built thereupon, he shall receive a reward"; for he built, in his noblest undertakings, not as for his own honor or advantage; not upon perishable foundations; but upon the indestructible religious element of our nature.

The persecuted exile from far-away Rochelle, buried beneath the ancient church of the parish, which is his enduring memorial, brought to the service of his adopted country a religious fervor that was untinged with fanaticism or bigotry. His great benefaction to New England and the colony with which he identified his interests, saying warmly, in his Boston correspondence, "I am for Rhode Island," was the introduction of the worship of the Church of England. As one of the chief instruments in bringing about the formation of the Society for the Propagation of the Gospel, his memory is associated with an influence as far-reaching as the wide-spread missionary work of that Venerable Society. As the founder, among laymen, of the Episcopal Church in this State — a church named by the voice of one alien to her communion, "one of the grandest of the Christian sisterhood," and recognized by an eminent jurist of Puritan antecedents and spirit as "one of the few of those conservative forces so essential to the welfare of our country" — his name must be honored with the gratitude due to a benefactor. This is not the homage of the Churchman, for which the present occasion affords no fitting time or place. It is simply the calm judgment of the citizen, recognizing the value of the mission of charity and comfort, of education and elevation in which this sacred organization has its part, sharing in the work of reaching the sordid life of our manufacturing towns, and penetrating the homes of labor with the lessons of practical helpfulness, and the teachings of the Christian ideal.

Other proofs of the conservative tendency of the Huguenot influence are found in the instances of *tenacity of tradition*, in the families of Huguenot descent. The peculiar veneration with which they regarded the memory of their expatriated ancestors led them to cherish an honorable pride in virtuous antecedents, and to treasure up every material or verbal reminder of the days of persecution with a pious care that was joined

Huguenot Influence in Rhode Island

with a meritorious zeal for the furtherance of historical and genealogical researches. Their interest in the facts of family records long anticipated the energy in that work, of which the present time affords instances of almost daily occurrence. Rhode Islanders in general were too long neglectful of the tribute of regard due to the memory of a virtuous ancestry. Judge Potter said, not long before his death: "When, many years ago, the writer was collecting material for the 'Early History of Narragansett,' published in 1835, it was with the utmost difficulty that the materials could be obtained for the few pages of family history contained in that work. Few families had preserved any family records, and few seemed to care about them. And most of this information in that work was obtained from the records with a good deal of labor." Among the few who readily contributed to that valuable collocation of materials for history were the Huguenot families of Rhode Island, to one of which, as is well known to our genealogical students, Judge Potter, the early leader in our State in this species of research, belonged. Nor is it needful to name the late president of the Rhode Island Historical Society to recall his memory to listeners who were instructed by his bold analysis of the elements of colonial history, or to friends who loved to trace hereditary merit as reflected in the traits of the true son of a worthy ancestor.

The general commemoration of the two hundredth anniversary of the Revocation of the Edict of Nantes may be thought to have come a century late. But it would have lacked some qualities of its full significance had it been earlier observed. True, a harvest of memorials and recitals might have been garnered in 1785. Pardon Mawney, of the Le Moine line, to whom we owe the scanty traditions of Frenchtown which reached Judge Potter through an intermediate link in the chain of descent, was then in the prime of middle life. Born in 1748, and having personal knowledge of the emigrants, how readily he could have answered those questions which we now vainly ask from lips on which "the mossy marbles rest"! Mrs. Seabury, granddaughter of Gabriel Bernon, relict of the Rev. Samuel Seabury, and stepmother of the first Bishop in America, who, coming under her influence in early childhood, owed to her Christian nurture the principles by which his maturity was guided, then past her three score and ten, was yet to live until the last year of the eighteenth century and the eighty-seventh of her age. Among survivors of their generation like her lingered a fund of traditional knowledge which perished with them. But it was no time, in 1785, for the independent State to review her colonial history. The questions of the present were too engrossing, the outlook into the future was too momentous, for the revival of the lessons of the past; and thirty-seven years elapsed before the formation, in 1822, of the Historical Society, charged with the duty of preserving the annals of Rhode Island. Indeed, it would have been too early in the eighteenth century to celebrate an era of religious freedom in France. So late as 1773, a Protestant minister, La Brie, was apprehended for exercising his vocation, the civil rights of the Reformed dating only from the time of the Revolutionary legislation, when the power of the church was prostrated, and a new class of refugees, the

Huguenot Influence in Rhode Island

émigré priests, were escaping from the country by stealth and in dread of persecution, as the heretics had taken their flight in 1685. Nor was the time ripe, in the year 1785, for the full estimate of all that our State and country owes to the merits of this class of her founders. The second centennial brings the fitting opportunity for the judgment of a generation taught of national experience, rich in a culture such as colonial scholarship could not command, and armed with those methods of critical study and original research with which only the analysis of historical sequences should be attempted. The time has arrived for the summing up of the debt which American nationality owes to the Huguenot character.

But if, ceasing from the retrospect of the buried century, we lift up our eyes and meet the century to come, we pause with some touch of the wondering awe of childhood, before the promise of a future which must hold even greater gifts than such as are the heritage of the present. What revelations in science, what prospects in the arts, what wealth of culture, what energy of scholarship, what purity of reform in the national life, what development of the unsunned riches of this new continent, what elevation of manners, and what enlargement of human sympathies float before us! There, in the distant vista, are the treasures awaiting our successors to the perpetual hope of that golden age which always precedes and follows the present. The coming century with all its substantial possessions, and all the glory which our imagination lends it, rises upon us in a power that stills our busy employments and hushes our too eager voices. In its silent presence we keenly feel the poor and petty nature of very many of our judgments and the inanity of our activities. Yet one word may be firmly spoken, here and now, in the assurance that the verdict of the future will but confirm its foundation in immutable truth. It is a word of prayer to

> "Our fathers' God, from out whose hand
> The centuries fall like grains of sand,"

to whom arises no purer petition than that He would keep us steadfast in the faith of our righteous fathers, that faith in the supremacy of honor and conscience, of truth and loyalty, by which they lived bravely, and died peacefully, leaving in the name of Huguenot an inheritance in which their descendants cherish the presence of an ideal, and their country guards the incalculable wealth of an historical inspiration.

JOHN SAFFIN, HIS BOOK

THE name of Saffin declares itself to be of other than Saxon derivation, and is thought to have a Norman origin. Its New England associations have been strictly Puritan, and whenever it appears in Rhode Island annals, it stands for that measure of influence which Massachusetts communicated to our Colony. If we may indulge a taste for the picturesque in historical retrospect so far as to personify the elements that mingled in our early colonial life under the aspect of figures in a dramatic scene, we shall recognize in the Rhode Island of more than two centuries ago a vigorous infant, sprung from a hardy stock, and we shall naturally conceive of the influence which formed the future State under the homely image which furnishes a summary of the ingredients of the caudle posset. The infant Colony, born to the heritage of poverty and exile, and reared with but scant counsel from aristocratic, ecclesiastical, or scholarly authorities, was nurtured upon a potion for which English tradition supplied the formula. But it was freely diluted with pure water from the Founder's spring, and it was steeped over the pioneer's camp-fire, at the edge of the unbroken forest. The friendly Indian brought to it his offering of wholesome roots, of which the evanescent woodland aroma exhaled gratefully. The Quaker salted and stirred the mixture with benevolent care; the Huguenot piously mingled with it the rare gift of a few drops of wine from the sacred chalice; the Churchman, newly arrived in the Narragansett wilds, rose up reverently to say grace over it; then the Puritan, roused to wrath by the spirit of independence and fraternity uniting this pacific group of fugitives, suddenly strode forth among them, from the lowering shadows of the forest, and, sternly thrusting them aside, cast into the decoction a handful of bitter herbs. The subtle infusion crept into the colonial veins, and lingers yet in the circulation of that body-politic whereof we are members. But by virtue of the timely spell pronounced by the Father of the Colony, providing for the authority of the magistrate "only in civil things," the harshness of the controversial rancor was forever allayed; so that, despite the clash of Puritan bitterness in our colonial loving-cup, all the coming generations might drink from it, undismayed. The characteristic temper of Massachusetts towards Rhode Island is illustrated by some phases of the life of John Saffin, a typical Puritan. Puritan types have become fixed in our conceptions of such figures as are familiar to us either under the historical or poetical touch — stern leaders of our mythical age, or potent by the genius of our great romancer. Seldom do we meet with the sincere rendering of the life of an obscure but representative Puritan, unknown to history, unidealized by tradition. Searching the records that most vividly reproduce for us such a man, his class, and his times, is assuredly a work that needs no justification under a system of historical study which, in the modern spirit of inquiry into the social conditions of the colonists, has unveiled the Sewall diary.

John Saffin, who was born in 1632, belonged by nativity and family to "the County of Devon," England, being the eldest son of Simon Saffin, merchant, of

Exeter, and Grace his wife, only daughter of Mr. John Garrett of Barnstable. We first hear of him in Scituate, Massachusetts, when but ten years old. Apparently he lost his father early in life, and almost the only glimpse of his mother is afforded by one of her letters, received by him in his twenty-second year, but copied out by him with great reverence after he had reached middle age. His preface to it runs in a strain of true filial piety, albeit he winces slightly at the necessary recognition of a step-father. "A copie of a pathetical, pious, Instructive Letter, written by my own Dear and Hon'd Mother, Mrs. Grace Saffin, alias Ellsworth: her own handwriting: w'ch being worn allmost in pieces, I for its singular worth here Revived it:

London, March first, 1654

DEAR SON,

Three Letters I received by Mrs. Winslow, whereby I perceive you are going a Voyage for Virginia: I cannot but admire at God's Love and Mercy, both to me and mine that he doth look upon us in all Estates and conditions wheresoever we are, Either far or near."

The mother's pious meditations flow on, as in the familiar cadences of the Prayer Book, or as caught up and echoed directly from the rhythm of the Psalmist. Her notes of praise are in tune with his harmonies, and her prayers rise on the wings of his words. This, and a second journey to Virginia, which Saffin made a few years later, were doubtless commercial ventures, for he is described as a merchant, though he must have had some legal training to fit him for the positions to which he rose. His mother fervently exhorts him to "rest on Him that heard our prayers, and left us not to the will of them that would have trodden us down, and cryed there is no help for us: But the Lord was seen in the Mount when man rose up against us." Saffin notes in the margin, with a literalness that brings the seventeenth century almost within our touch, "This was in the civil war, between the King and Parliament. J. S." Mrs. Ellsworth again refers to the past, in closing: "Now for myself I bless God I have a Comfortable Subsistance, and more than I did expect I should have had, in regard to the troubles of War we have had among us, wherein few were sure of Enjoying what they had, so that I may say with Jacob hitherto hath the Lord helped me and mine. Blessed be his holy Name." The tone of the mother's letter, intense in the solemnity of its appeals, even rising to the adjuration, "I charge you upon my Blessing that you labour after the knowledge of Christ," indicates the quality of the spiritual atmosphere breathed by the son and prepares us for that proof of young Saffin's gravity and stability which appears in his election as a selectman of Scituate in his twenty-first year. Further testimony to this effect is found in a paper drawn up and subscribed by two of his townsmen, at his request (probably with a view to his settlement in Plymouth), and stating that "we have known him ever since he was about ten or twelve years old, . . . during which time his carriage was sober and civil, yea very commendable, and we do not know neither have hard of any carriage of his that could be a just blame unto him, nor did we ever p'ceive that he was at all edicted to keepe company (according to the common acceptation) but allways observed him very prudent in his carriage and wary whome he consorted with, always companinge with the better sorte, and every way demeaninge and carrying himself as inoffensive, and as became an honest man."

A young man of such maturity of character and such dignity of manners soon found favor even with a father-in-law so exacting as the Worshipful Thomas Willett, a magistrate of Plymouth, and the first mayor of New York, who ordered by his will that if any one of his sons should marry without the consent of a majority of the five executors, he should by that act forfeit his inheritance. John Saffin, in his twenty-sixth year, married Martha Willett, one of the magistrates officiating, on a Friday, as he notes, evidently in the spirit of Puritan protest against any fast day of ancient appointment. On a Friday, also, he sailed for Virginia the next year, in a ketch bound from New London, probably in accordance with the vessel's horoscope, since in such cases the superstition of the sea revoked its laws. After twenty years, his wife died, and the last survivor of his eight sons died in London, aged twenty-three. In Boston, of which town he had been a freeman since 1671, he married Elizabeth, widow of Peter Lidgett, Esq., a merchant, by whom she had been named executrix of his will, being described as "the well beloved wife of my youth." The ceremony was performed by "the Worshipful Joseph Dudley." Mrs. Saffin became an invalid and was "sundry years Bedrid, and some part thereof Distracted, but came to herself againe before She Dyed." Saffin, now aged fifty-six, married an heiress, Rebecca, the young daughter of his contemporary, Rev. Samuel Lee, and granddaughter of a wealthy London citizen. The marriage was performed by a minister. Among the Puritans as with other colonists marriages were frequent, and the intervals of widowhood were brief. In their revolt from the Catholic interpretation of Christianity, and their literal following of the Old Testament, their asceticism, parting with the mediaeval type, became wholly Hebraistic in its regulations. Their esteem for marriage was absolutely Jewish, and their records, crowded with marriages, remarriages, and intermarriages of family connections, suggest the solidity of a densely woven web of life, in which the cutting of one thread is felt throughout the fabric.

Saffin's life is naturally divided into two periods, the first marked by his prominence in the affairs of Boston, and the second by his retirement to "New Bristol." He had lived in Swansea, Massachusetts, being numbered in the first rank of that unique New England community, which was divided into patricians and plebeians, with inhabitants of middle standing. His manuscript record opens thus: "Memoriam. That in the beginning of November, Anno 1665, I was joyned to the first Church in Boston, God in mercy make me faithful to his covenant." A long letter to his "Hon'd and Beloved about to be Brethren," written four years later when the Old South was founded by separation from the First Church, breathes a more moderate spirit than that by which he was afterwards known, but lays no slight emphasis upon his individual opinions. Still, he is resolved not to secede from the Church, quoting the opinions of certain of "the Reverend Elders of New England," in support of his position, and using the words of one worthy, who says of such divisions that " they are as Weights that Sinke and as Darts that Strike through my very Soul." "Thus Hee." The letter is marked by that vigor of which the writer has left many similar examples. Saffin was one of the two "overseers" (as executors were then styled) of the junior Endicott's will, proved in 1666, and in 1676, not long after the Narragansett Swamp Fight, he was the bearer of a letter from the Massachusetts Council to the Rhode Island Government, demanding the delivery of Indians that "lie skulking in the woods," the tone of the message implying that Rhode Islanders were culpably lenient with the savages. In 1678 he took a prominent part in the elaborate funeral ceremonies of Governor Leverett, carrying one of the banners displayed in this first mortuary pageant which Puritan rigor had allowed. As the representative of the heirs of Thomas Willett, and as an independent proprietor, his name repeatedy appears in the records of the Atherton Purchase, and he was one of the three Narragansett proprietors who, in 1686, assigned to the Huguenot refugees the Newbarry tract, west of Wickford, and who, upon their objection to it, as too far from the sea, granted them that portion of East Greenwich still known as Frenchtown. He had long been involved in that controversy over the possession of the Narragansett lands which very nearly assumed the proportions of border war.

In 1679, upon his conviction, at Newport, of upholding a foreign jurisdiction (that of Connecticut), the worthy Boston merchant experienced the fate of a very Shylock. Not only were his lands pronounced "confiscate unto the State of Venice," or her modern representative the indignant republic of Rhode Island, but he was, with superfluous severity, also fined and imprisoned. Saffin's resentment afterward inspired a rhymed address to the newly appointed Governor Bellamont, whom, of course, "Heaven hath sent to be a Sun in this our Firmament." Adopting the fraternal style of the Colonists of the Bay in saluting those of the Plantations, he brands them as "false perfidious, vile Rhode Islanders." The lapse of twenty years had not cooled the poet's wrath. Again he bore a part in this colonial drama, when, in 1683, he, with other adherents of Connecticut, sustained their claims before the King's Commissioner at Wickford, on that memorable occasion when the Rhode Island Legislature, assembled within a mile, redeemed its offended dignity by sending out the "sergeant general" with his trumpet, at the head of a troop of horse, who, by loud proclamations, or as the Commissioners plaintively allege, "in a riotous manner," warned them against holding a court in that jurisdiction. This blowing of horns around that miniature Jericho, the contumacious hamlet of Wickford, failed to bring the besieged to terms of surrender; and Saffin once more paid an official visit to Narragansett when Dudley, in 1687, at his court held in the Smith Blockhouse, recognized the King's Province.

In Boston Neck, North Kingstown, he built in 1692 the house which was standing until 1872. This estate, which he is said to have occupied for three years, descended from him to the Willetts and from them to the late Willett Carpenter and his heirs. Here his individuality found expression in the massive chimney and wide hall that testified to his right English spirit, and the Scriptural tiles, crannies, and cupboards that illustrated his literal Puritanic beliefs and his labored quaintnesses of taste. It has been said that nothing so clearly marks the progress of the human mind as the changes in architecture: and in the typical homes of the colonists the buried seventeenth century still communicates with us in tangible signs of timber and stone. Saffin could not escape that moral contagion of the slave-trade which left its blight on some of even the most exalted minds of his time. His letter in behalf of himself and other merchants, one of whom, Edward Shippen, was a Quaker, shows that more than two hundred years ago the wealthiest Bostonians were concerned in this traffic, while Rhode Island was as yet strongly opposed to it. The owners inform Mr. Wilstead, the master of one of the smaller vessels, that their ship Elizabeth, sent out the last year for Guinea, may be expected to touch at Swansea on her return. But the Rhode Islanders "understand thereof, and all give out there to leave her." Wilstead is to "Gayne ye entrance of that haven" ostensibly for fishing, keeping his men ignorant of his real design. He must speak with Warren, the returning captain, giving him the enclosed letter, and directing him to change his course to Nantasket, where Wilstead is to "take in such negroes, etc., as he hath of ours, and come up in the night with them, giving us notice thereof with what privacy you can, and we Shall take care for their Landing." Nothing must be suffered to hinder the meeting with Warren, "w'h is the needful at present."

Saffin, though closely associated with Judge Sewall

in official and intimate relations, was no convert to his more humane views, but printed an answer to Sewall's paper against the slave-trade. Yet in 1694 he granted a "Deed of Freedom" to one of his slaves, provided that he should continue to serve Mr. Saffin's tenant at Bristol for seven years, after which the instrument should take effect. He carefully states his motive, as "one's love to and for the Incouragement of my Negro man Adam to goe-on chearfully in his Business." At the end of this Hebrew term of servitude, Adam would be required to fulfil the condition that he "Doe-behave and abase himself as an honest true and faithfull Sarvant ought to Doe." Saffin's conscience was not more callous than that of the mass of his contemporaries, whose humanity was subject to the limitations of the age. Strange and devious are the ways of custom and prejudice wherein the little souls of men grope through their accepted round. The hand that signed this letter, authorizing the most cruel of all legalized schemes of wickedness, was the same that records many a righteous groan at the tragedy of St. Bartholomew's Day, or the corruption of the Papacy, with an "O Abominable," "O Luciferian." When he reverently transcribed his mother's solemn exhortations, did he never apply them to the standards of his daily dealings, or did they pass unrecognized, as no more than a strain of pious and pleasing sentiment? "Labour for an Interest in Christ," she pleads, "and you have all, he is Riches; then the Blessing of the Lord will be upon you in your going out and coming in, Buying, Selling, and all that you set your hand unto." A mother's sacred tenderness, a son's deep affections, and the religious devotion of both, fail to reach any purer ideal than such as emanates from the dark spirit of the age, revealed in the pastoral example of Cotton Mather, who held his slaves, and never raised his all-powerful voice against the traffic in human merchandise.

In 1684 the last formal claim made by the Indians to the site of Boston was extinguished, the town taking a deed from Sachem Charles Josias to sundry of the "proprieted inhabitants," of whom John Saffin was one. From 1684 to 1686 he was returned as a deputy to the General Court, and in the latter year his abilities obtained for him the place of Speaker of the House, which he filled until the arrival of Andros, being at that time one of the Governor's Council. The protest of the Assembly against the new government was addressed to Dudley and his Council, having been "taken by me J. S.," as he relates in his note-book, "passed by the whole Assembly, and so Entered by Record." In this paper the members complain that they are not officially recognized, and protest against the abridgment of the colonial liberties, implied in the new commission. They "cannot give assent thereto, yet hope Shall demean ourselves as true and loyal Subjects to his Majesty and humbly make our Addresses unto God, and in due time to our gracious Prince, for our relieff." Saffin calls this the "last reply" of the Court to Dudley. Five days later the change was officially announced, being generally accepted with a resignation to which the harsh spirit of Saffin could not readily conform. He was one of the confidential committee of three appointed to receive from Secretary Rawson all papers relating to Indian titles, and all referring to the negotiations for keeping the charter; the mass of the state papers having been delivered up to Andros. A year later Saffin counselled submission to the new government in his letter despatched to his friend John Allen, the Colonial Secretary, at Hartford, and which is preserved in the files of the State Department. He anticipates the abrogation of the colonial charters, and fears that "they that stand out longest will fare the worst at last." Rage furnishes weapons, saith Saffin, saying it, however, in a learned language, with scraps of which he ever loved to adorn his pedantic pages. But his immediate anxiety is lest Connecticut should "adhere to the West." This expression refers to the designs of Governor Dongan, who was taking all means to secure the charter, in the hope of annexing Connecticut to New York. Should this happen, "you will be an undone people," exclaims Saffin, "for you will part with your best grounds." This letter was doubtless sent as an antidote to the bane contained in the official one from Andros with which it went, requiring the surrender of the charter, and commending Randolph, as worthy of confidence.

The General Court being abolished, Saffin, now in his fifty-seventh year, disappears from public life in Boston, and retires to his estate in Bristol. History dismisses him from her train of gentlemen-in-waiting, and relegates him to a place in merely parochial annals. His name appeared on the list of Bristol settlers in 1681, but his actual residence dates from 1688. He mentions the landing of his household stuff at his dwelling-house at "Boundfield," and the planting of an orchard there. He and his wife, with their eight servants (doubtless negro slaves) are enumerated in the list of inhabitants, and he heads the list of the church members, being the only one who bears the valued title of Mr. He was probably attracted to the township by the relation in which he stood to its minister, Rev. Samuel Lee, his father-in-law, the Oxford scholar who was styled "the Glory of both Englands." His local activities now begin, and he zealously serves the new settlement in all capacities, from the temporary office of constable up to that of deputy to the Assembly for four years. He was selectman and justice of the peace; was known as an eager mover in all local interests; and vainly endeavored to obtain for Bristol the confirmation of an early grant of freedom from import and excise. He was foremost in church matters, being a member of the committees for the settlement of the successive ministers, for providing the means of their support, and for finishing the meeting-house. Certain of the larger positions which he still filled, linked him to his former associations in Boston. By the fall of Andros in 1689 he was restored to a place in the General Court. He was the first judge of probate appointed for the newly formed county of Bristol, and he filled that office for ten years. He was made judge of the Court of Common Pleas; and he was a judge of the Superior Court of Massachusetts in 1701, being an associate with Judge Sewall. At the first popular election of a Governor's Council in 1693, under the new charter of William and Mary, he was chosen one of the ten who were preferred to ten others, and he was thus a member of that council upon which the executive power devolved, during the short interval between the death of Governor Stoughton and the arrival of Dudley in 1703. Upon Dudley's return to power, Saffin was rudely dismissed from public office, and never again held influential positions. After ten years of exile, Dudley's first act was to reject from the Council the five gentlemen who were members of the old Government which was restored in 1689, and by which he had been ignominiously imprisoned.

Hutchinson comments upon the insufficiency of Dudley's obstinate objection to these Councillors, who were all of good standing, Mr. Saffin being "one of the chief inhabitants of Bristol." It was but the second instance in which a Massachusetts Governor, under the charter, had challenged any name on the list of his assistants, and his course created much remark. He treated the House more cavalierly than did Phipps or Bellamont. Saffin sardonically deprecated Dudley's revenge in a rhymed address, which was apparently received by the magnate with that hearty disgust which the impracticable man of letters inspires in the arrogant officers of the State. Saffin warns his Excellency that his changes in Church and Commonwealth, if fully accomplished, would "Cause us to Cease to be Right Englishmen." Spurning Dudley's offensive description of him, he subscribes his epistle

> "From one, tho' aged, is not whimsey Pated,
> Or prone to dote, nor Superanuated."

In an indignant letter to a friend he cites a debate in the House of Lords, from which he draws authority for the spirit of his protest against Dudley's treatment of him. "I am not so stupid, nor insensible or Superanuated (as he was pleased most unworthyle to render me in the Council, when he put a negative on me and other Gentlemen, then legally chosen Members of her Majesty's Council) so as to incapacitate me of Enjoying the right of an Englishman's Birth, in point of honour, or other Interest."

Saffin despatched another caustic missive to Dudley in the following year, on hearing that his Excellency was in the month of January "going over Charles River upon the Ice, with a sley and four horses, with his wife and Daughters; the ice suddenly brake, and all the horses falling into the River, the two hindermost Horses were Drowned, and his Excellency and his hardly excepted but were Wonderfully preserved. Laus Deo." The congratulations on his escape are tempered with very plain admonitions, and pointed hints at his defection from the principles of the fathers. Should Dudley's plans prevail, "We must Return to Egypt once agen." The writer appeals to the revered memory of

> "Those Renouned Worthys, men of Name,
> Who first to settle to this Country came.
> But O consider what they preached and prayed,
> Who did denounce Great Woes to him who should,
> Rase that fair structure God by them did build."

These remonstrances are offered from one who boasts that "I doe Endeavor allways what I can approve my Self a Real Englishman," and the recent accident is candidly commended to the governor's expectant meditations,

> "It speaks to you in midst of all your Glory
> How fraile you are, how weak, how transitory."

Repeated references to his hostile relations with Dudley appear in his notes, which breathe a robust indignation. We take up his private life in Bristol after his quarrel with Governor Dudley had driven him into retirement. The retired official concentrated himself upon the local affairs to which Dudley's enmity had restricted him, and his unflagging energies found a channel in the interests of speculation in Bristol and Narragansett lands. He was seized with the same greed which possessed many of the early emigrants. The Englishman of middle class, transplanted to a country in which he might with fabulous ease develop into a landed proprietor, was dazzled by the ambitious vision; and not till a new generation grew up with a more moderate estimation of land, as an equivalent to power, did the keenness of this hereditary zeal disappear.

Judge Saffin held shares in the Taunton Iron Works, founded about 1656, and he was employed in the settlement of his father-in-law's large estate. His figure, which shows somewhat dim and distant in the Boston records, stands out clearly, and comes within touch, as studied in the Bristol annals. Here he found leisure to fill that note-book by which we know him most intimately, and in which by the changes in the script from firm and full to feeble and uncertain characters, we trace the writer's vicissitudes, through old age and decline. The artless revelations of this compilation furnish a study of Puritan manners, a map of the Puritan mind. It represents the literary industry and moral elevation of a man whose scholarly aspirations have helped to keep his pages free from more than an occasional hint of that coarseness which constantly recurs in the memoirs of his time, and forms one of the inevitable signs of likeness between the Old England and the New. The writer thus describes his work: "In this manuscript is promiscuously set down an epitomy of various readings of the author on divers subjects of Divinity, Law, History, Arts and Sciences; some of them poetical fancies of his own written in his youth (as well as later years) which he found scattered here and there in loose papers, and as a diversion at leisure put them as they came to hand into this mixed medley. Some of them Satiricall tho the most are rather Amorous or Encomiastich, which were most agreeable to his genius." The seventeenth century mind loved apothegms and moral narrations; and such passages, probably culled from the libraries of Saffin's learned friends, Mather and Lee, fill many of his pages. Among the items of fact is this curious entry: "There was a Morris-Dance of Ten men of the Welsh-side, which made 1000 years between them. The Fiddler, Philip Squire, and Bess Grimm, the Maid Marian, were above 100 years apiece." Saffin does not give his authority for this story, which was worthy of the melancholic extravagance of a Hawthorne. He quotes Bacon, Raleigh, Wotton, Sir Thomas More, Boyle, Bishop Usher, and Lord Falkland, makes legal citations and copies passages from Sermons, one by Rev. Mr. Wolsworth having been preached in 1632.

He indulges in some breathings against the Church of England, but he records the Arabella Letter, and even transcribes some "Maxims taken out Governor Pen's book," which look toward religious toleration. His early associations in Plymouth might temper a little the sterner Puritanism imbibed in Boston. The credulity of our ancestors was not wholly expended upon matters of religious superstition. The belief in witchcraft, for instance, was natural enough to a people who put faith in the repulsive receipts which were not confined to household medicine, but were the prescriptions of the most learned physicians of the age. Saffin collected many of these formulas, from among other authorities George Monk, the keeper of the famous Blue Anchor Tavern, Boston, Mrs. Eliot, wife of the Apostle to the Indians, and Rev. Samuel Lee, an Oxford scholar who was styled "the Glory of both Englands." A dissertation on "Climatericall years and Criticall Days" details the very hours when the several "Humours" most prevail. Notes on astrology are in keeping with his exact record of the hours of his children's births, evidently made with regard to the planetary influences. Two prophecies in verse, one of which "hath been in MS. in the Lord Powes his family for 60 years," furnish further hints of his taste for the marvellous. Some mercantile tales are found in his pages, but more space is allotted to an "Artificiall Divination of Numbers," and heraldry is a subject which is embellished with outlines of shields. Frequent extracts on questions of government, public speaking, and literary study illustrate his ambitions; while his personal prejudices are thinly veiled under moralizings and character-sketches, or are more broadly indicated by his repetitions of caustic sayings upon the traits of foreigners, and the follies of English travellers who are corrupted by foreign associations.

In the vein of historical comment he notes with

particularity the oppression of France under the absolute rule of "Lewis the 14th," and passes to the lack of encouragement in England for "that ingenious contrivance of the penny post" begun by "that worthy citizen, Mr. Dochmore," who was deprived of all benefit of his services by that "bigotted king James II." In a list of the kings of England, Saffin introduces characteristic touches. Charles I "Was beheaded in a Court of Justice by his subjects, against whom he had levied armies, and made war divers years." James II "endeavoured to bring in Papacy, and indeed slavery, for he kept an army of 30,000 men, but fearing to face the Prince of Orange, fled beyond sea." William and Mary "were crowned with all the solemnity, magnificence, pomp, and splendor of a willing nation." In "A Thankfull Memoriall," written during the reign of Anne, he repeats the same sentiments respecting "the Glorious Belgick Star," and other sovereigns, and relates that "by Divine Assistance I have seen seven Regencies before the present Queen." Under the colonial data he records "Prodigious Appearances in the World," as in anno Domini 1664. "This year a Blazing Star and Comett in New England appeared, in the 9th, 10th, 11th, and the beginning of the 12th month; in all lyklyhood it was visible to all the inhabitants of the Earth, for the blaze thereof did Beame to all the Quarters of the World; it was no fierie Meteor caused by exhalation, but was sent by God to Awaken the secure World." The awestruck observer subjoins some extracts from a sermon on the comet, by Rev. Daniel Danforth. Another "Prodigee," which, from the rude sketch appended, seems to have been an eclipse that was seen, and special notes taken of, by divers credible persons, in anno Domini 1681. Upon the view of this portent Saffin bursts into verse:

> "Behold the angrie frown of the Most High
> Gainst mortals is perspicuous in the skie
> The sable clouds encircling, Roll about,
> The unstring'd Bow, that Phaelous doth surmount,
> The dismal Darkness, moist with direful glare."

The poet warns his countrymen of

> "God's Dreadfull vengeances their overthrow,
> Which from the Almighty swiftly shall be sent,
> Unless they timely truly doe repent."

Another subject which fires this fervent versifier is "New England's Lamentation of her present State"—in the year 1708. Boston merchants complain of losses by shipwreck; the "Countrymen" of the "Rates"; the "Soldiers" are cheated; the "Courts" are meanly fitted; some of the judges are partial, and sundry of the lawyers sit and quaff in taverns and are no better than devouring "Catterpillars." These "Varlets" boast they get three hundred pounds a year, and three times more is spent upon them than had formerly served to maintain the government. The vagrant and vicious classes exhaust the public store, and the community becomes partially dependent upon supplies from other colonies. Extravagance in the citizens was never more glaring; but as the moralist sensibly decides, with regard to all these offenders,

> "No more of them, they 'd surely think it better
> To lay this by, and Read the next News Letter."

His most crushing rebuke falls upon "the Female Frame," who flaunt in luxury and idleness.

> "Come down proud Dames put on garments of Shame
> Sit in the dust Daughters of Babilon."

Truly this is a strain that never tires. But plain dealing with New England from another pen, possibly the sharp instrument wielded by Lechford, gives dire offence. From an epigram "On a Rogue that abused the people of N. E. in a printed Scurrillous pamphlet," we learn that with our sturdy satirist, "Indigent" and "Romantich" are epithets expressive of equal degrees of contempt. He has severer terms in store for "one Lyford, a pretended Minister," who proved himself "a hypocriticall wretch," to the scandal of the people of Plymouth. "And Oldham was another, an imprudent proud fellow, who also conspired with Lyford and others, seeking to Ruin this poor but hopefull Plantation, but they both came to untimely Ends. Especially Oldham, who was cutt off and Slayn by Indians, the Pequots or Peqods." The entries of a strictly autobiographical character are few, although a childish vanity is conspicuous among the traits of our compiler. But the egotism of the seventeenth century diarist was distinct from self-consciousness, in the modern sense. Saffin artlessly reveals the curious and grotesque phases of his mental personality in his voluminous verse, which occasionally affords quite a different sort of delight from that which was fondly anticipated by the poet. Some of his elegiac effusions attained the dignity of print, and all were much admired by the judicious friends, few of whom could have been omitted in life or in death from his poetical addresses. On glancing over his pages we find not only elegies and epitaphs inflicted upon the memories of scholars, divines, and statesmen, and clothed in such verse as the harsh Puritanic muse was pleased to bestow, but some productions appear which seem to be of a more lively character, until a closer observation proves them all to wear the same sad-colored livery. Acrostics, valentines, and madrigals are all taking their pleasure sadly, and scarcely differ in style from the elegies, or the lamentations over the evils of New England. Departed elders are embalmed in such tributes as that tendered to Wilson,

"A Lion
To Foes of this our little Zion,"

or to him of whom we read

"Here lyes the Darling of his time,
Mitchell, expired in his Prime.
Who five years short of fourty-seven
Was found full Ripe, and plucked for Heaven."

The death of John Hull, the respectable trader and goldsmith, is lamented by the pedantic poet, who invokes

"That saddest She
The ancients call the Muse Melpomene."

So lofty a dame will scarcely condescend to enlighten us concerning the Boston citizen's habits, and touches of local color rarely mingle with her sober designs. We only gather that

"In the Throng of Business Every Day,
Hee'd set apart some Select time to pray,"

and we glean one historical allusion from the farewell utterance put in the mouth of Hull:

> "I smile at sorrows past, and am secure
> From the wrath of men and Devils, to be sure
> Beyond the reach of Ran-Do, and all those
> That puff at me—N. Englands open foes."

Some explanation of the poverty of old writings in similar references may be noted in the partial suppression of the name of Randolph. Even in their private papers the early Colonists might sometimes be wary of expressing themselves freely on public disturbances. Our elegiac poet courts a lighter strain when he sings, "On presenting a rare book to Madam Hull," his "Vallintine,"

> "Heres Witts extraction, Morall and Divine
> Presented to you, by your Vallintine."

He writes acrostics to "Mrs. Winifred Griffin," and to other young ladies. Addressing "Mrs. Abigail Collins," he offers her a highly labored compliment, of a genealogical character:

> "Fairest Sweet Virgin, Natures Master-Piece
> Beauty's Exemplar; Cupid's Mother's Niece."

But there are deeper self revealings in this book than such as show the diarist in the aspect of a student, citizen, or friend. Love and grief have left their impress upon it, and still appeal to us from its faded pages, for to scan them is to measure the pulses of emotion as they came warm from the heart of the writer. In his home life he merits our regard as a man of honest and healthy sentiments, however obscured by the quaint or exaggerated style of his century. The glow of feeling pierces through the forms of pedantry, and lets in a welcome light upon an obscure period of our annals. It is gratifying to know that the Puritan Magistrate could be as fond and indulgent in his home as the merriest prelatist that ever ate mince-pies at Christmas, or danced at Merry Mount of a May Day. Saffin was the poet laureate of a household queen, and among his most cherished effusions he preserves a "Wedding Song," and a dialogue in verse, in which Exonius and Plimothemia (otherwise plain John and Martha) lament the griefs of separation. In a rhymed epistle to his Martha, written on his return voyage from Virginia, he rises to rhapsody:

> " Sayle, gentle Pinnace, Zepherus doth not faile
> With prosperous gales, Sayle, gentle Pinnace, Sayle."

His infant son is not forgotten by this homesick traveller:

> "Sweet Babe! how doe I mind thy pleasing Smiles
> And pretty toys thou usest otherwhiles.
> . . . .
> Methinks I hear thy Mother to thee prate,
> Like to Thyself, that thou mayest Imitate."

His signature recalls the style of Elizabethan melodrama.

> "Thine, or not his owne, J. S."

We learn that an illness contracted by Mrs. Saffin began with "a fall in a fainting fitt as she was goeing to meeting with her Mayd, Both on a Sabbath day."

This was probably the occasion on which a Mrs. Eddy was summoned from Plymouth, as appears by the records of that colony, which state that she was tried for Sabbath breaking, having walked to Boston when sent for, as her defence runs, by Mrs. Saffin who was nigh unto death, and did anxiously desire to see Mrs. Eddy. The Governor, though unable to recognize this plea, released the offender with a simple reprimand, instead of exacting the fine which he held justly due. It would be hard to discover a stronger instance of that lack of the finer moral perceptions which so often occasions the acts of rulers to exhibit the complete separation of the letter of the law from the spirit of the Gospel. John Saffin passed through his deepest experiences in the loss of his wife and children. His brief, stern record fails and pauses beneath the burden of one overwhelming sorrow, "And now alas; there lyes Interred in one Tombe att the higher end of the upper Burying-place in Boston My Dear Wife, Martha Saffin, and five of the eight sons she bore unto me." Two of the remaining sons were soon afterwards laid in the same tomb, and the last of the eight, dying in London, was buried in Stepney Churchyard, under the epitaph by his father that has become a classic in quaint funeral lore, having been copied by Addison into the "Spectator," commented on by Dr. Johnson, and referred to in Hutchinson's Colonial History. We learn that the subject of it had begun to be "much favored by his Prince, James II." Small-pox was the chief destroyer that thus swept away a family, the father alone recovering among those attacked by that disease. He characterizes his children with this touching tribute: "John, a faire, comely, and cowardly child, and sensible unto his last. . . . Joseph a brave witty and as beautiful a child as one shall see amongst a thousand. . . . My eldest tho second born son John, aged sixteen years, who was the Darling of his time for a sweet behaviour, and in the College was noted for his parts and learning above ye thirteen of his classe; But God took him also away by death to my amazing grief at ye loss of him and so many in so short a time." One of John's classmates, the Grindall Rawson afterwards known as a Puritan divine, sends to the mourning father some verses on his "much loved Friend."

There is a rude dignity of consolation in the close, which conveys a hope that the elegy

"May say to those who still survive
Though John and Martha die, yet God's alive."

The father dwells tenderly upon the descriptions of "Scimon, a faire-haired youth, had attained to a good degree of grammar, and almost a nonesuch for a natural veine of Limning, to ye admiration of all y^t saw him." This narrative of the last days of "My Sweet Son Scimon" reads like some kindred passage from the *Magnalia*, that Acta Sanctorum of the Puritan. This fair child of twelve years, a rare scion of English lineage and Puritan nurture, with his early talent flowing hardily in the chill atmosphere, was distinguished by the purity and sensibility which are always of most touching effect when associated with untimely suffering and death. His looks expressed his mind.

"Lovely in 's feature, his complexion fair,
Of comely stature; flaxen was his hair."

His banefull illness was borne with patience, and his death was crowned with triumph. His testimony of childlike faith was given to his doctor (who found the patient's mind clear and tranquil), and "with Soul Ravishing Expressions," to his minister, Mr. Willard, until speech failed him. "And so," relates his father, "he passed Triumphiantly to Heaven. He often said 'Mother, Brother John, come away, make haste,' adding that Mr. Thatcher [his minister who was dead] did look and wait for him, and that there was room enough for all in Heaven." They were soon to follow him, and the same hand that has recorded the children's deaths has traced many tributes to the memory of the mother; there remains an anagram on her name which is not without a rude pathos:

> "Martha Saffin
> In hart am Safe
> or
> Ah! firm and fast
> In hart am Safe;
> Ah firm & fast
> To my Beloved, to my last."

If the pedantic mourner's eulogies of the beauty and graces of his wife, and the talents of his sons, may sometimes suggest the question whether he does not, to use his own word, "hyperbolize," yet the exhaustless pathos of his afflictions touches keenly upon the springs of sympathy. Even after two hundred years the modest perfume of Martha Saffin's gentle household virtues comes upon us with the deep assurance that the obscure story of a life dedicated to duty and hallowed by tenderness stands higher in spiritual value than the teachings of many a pretentious page of history. Judge Saffin's last years were burdened with cares and disappointments, and deeply embittered by stern and lasting contentions with his neighbors and his family. The strongest lights upon his characteristics emanate from two papers of the Bristol period. One of these, a famous passage in the town annals, is his retraction, in which nothing is retracted. By the writer it is vigorously styled "the Portraiture of a pernicious Faction," and is perhaps the most notable specimen of that crude ore of rhetoric which fashioned many a missile for the confusion of such as dared to cross his inflexible will. An extract can but faintly indicate the pungency of its spirit. Having been enjoined by arbitrators between himself and sundry of his townsmen (among whom was Judge Byfield) to retract the statements made in a manuscript entitled "The Original of the Town of Bristol," "Now, in order thereunto, I do hereby own and declare unto all mankind, that if breach of promise to a person or people, in a matter of great concernment be so evil, if the chopping and changing of the town commons, to the great prejudice of the town; obstructing and stopping up several ways leading to men's lands (some of them that have been enjoyed above thirty years without molestation or disturbance) to be tolerable and not a nuisance strictly prohibited by the laws of our nation, then I am exceedingly to blame in charging with evil in so doing. If the granting of land upon a good consideration, and upon the same promising to give a deed for the confirmation thereof, but delaying it and after eight or nine years quiet possession by the granter these grantors give a deed of the same land unto others, if this I say be just and righteous dealing, then I am exceedingly to blame in charging with evil in so doing."

The other paper, which bears upon the experiences of his latter years, is a letter of pastoral rebuke from Cotton Mather, dated "Boston, d, 19, m. 5, 1710." Mr. Saffin, after long disagreement with his third wife, chiefly because of his unfriendly relations with her family, had separated from her, and was lingering out the last days of a morose and desolate old age in his Bristol retreat. That inevitable mingling of the grotesque with the tragic—which is characteristic of Saffin's utterances—appears in the spirit of his "Revised Elegie" of this period, on Martha. "Thus I alone," he grieves, with a fine obliviousness of his later domestic conditions—

> "thus I alone
> These five and twenty years am left to mone
> My unimpaired loss in Her, since gone."

Cotton Mather's letter shows that dread figure in an exceptionally pleasing light. Sound humanity and frank kindliness have prompted his act, though some sharp touches of remonstrance, and shrewd personal thrusts, show that the sketch is signed by the master's hand. Except for a shade of that pedantry inseparable from the New England Barton, it breathes a spirit almost modern, and is perhaps of all the utterances of the potent author, the most intelligible to the modern mind. Reading between the lines, we find Saffin's history in its allusions and warnings, and his epitaph in its hints of his better days and regrets over his decadence. He urges him in behalf of his wife to return to her, begging him to avoid all further "embroelment," and especially to refrain from any controversies with Madam on the subject of "Mr. George" (the brother-in-law), but to say directly to him whatever he has to say. "It is, you know, sir, better than I, the true spirit of a gentleman to make his conversation easy to every one." In his former conduct toward this gentle woman he had not forgotten the laws of complaisance. "Good sir, hold to them." Mather intimates that by the outcome of his disputatious spirit he had despoiled himself of his estate, and was no longer furnished with means "to carry on the wars." He ought to secure Madam's interest from any further "molestation," and she, for her part, would do all in her power to render his old age comfortable and honorable. All his friends look so anxiously to see him accept this offer that if he decline it he need hardly expect the offices of friendship from them. Meekness and repose of spirit dignify old age; other qualities, which are classed among its infirmities, are surely such as Mr. Saffin (of all men) is least ambitious to claim. Mather warns his aged friend of the approach of death, and solemnly summons him from the officious cares of his husbandry at Bristol, and from all worldliness, wrangling, and bitterness, to the duties of reconciliations and religious devotion. "Good sir, throw all embitterments into a grave before you go into your own."

These warnings, which Mather's contemporaries would receive as prophetic, found their natural fulfilment in the death of the infirm, aged, and unhappy man to whom they were addressed. He made his will, "being Weak of Body, but of perfect mind and memory," July 27, 1710, and two days later was no more, after a troubled life of seventy-eight years. Commentators on his history have refused to believe that he ever received this letter, since he bequeathed five pounds to Cotton Mather, yet makes no mention of his wife. But it may be that the pastoral reproaches hastened his decline. The alienation from Mather, his last friend, and his spiritual guide, broke his heart, but no earthly influence could quell his indomitable will. The passion of self-will had grown into moral disease so firmly fastened upon the man's nature, that death alone could release him from its tortures. He had the magnanimity to bear with his pastor's counsels, but not the meekness to adopt them, and the silence toward Mather which, from Saffin's standpoint, may be esteemed generous, becomes pitifully unnatural when it includes his wife. Dying childless, he divided his Narragansett estate of one thousand acres among seven relations, connections, and friends, and left one hundred pounds to Martha, daughter of Andrew Willett of Boston Neck. She was the niece and namesake of the wife of his youth. Fifty pounds were distributed among legatees, including Cotton Mather and the minister of the town. Five pounds were bequeathed to the poor of Bristol, to be spent in books for their children, at the discretion of his executors. If there is something touching in the futile fervor of Saffin's literary ambition, there is in his testamentary purpose to serve the cause of learning an honesty of homage which commands our hearty regard. Captain Andrew Willett of Boston Neck, his brother-in-law, was residuary legatee, and co-executor with Dr. Elisha Cooke of Boston, he who had ministered at the death-bed of Saffin's "Sweet Son Scimon." The testator directs that his body shall be buried in his tomb in Boston, and he commits his soul into the hands of God, hoping for pardon for all his sins, through the righteousness of Christ. To this prayer, who that has followed him through the sorrows and sufferings of his burdened life will not breathe a charitable Amen. John Saffin's studious pursuits seem to have been the most congenial to his temperament, and Scholars he esteemed in his sounding phrase as "celebriously Renowned." The Puritans paid devout homage to the funeral muse, and Saffin's elegiac offerings were doubtless acceptable, difficult as it is in this generation to conceive of them as received in the spirit in which they were offered. Probably the surviving friends and admirers were gratified by the epitaph on the Rev. John Wilson, which opens with an air of cheerful bustle:

> "Rejoice, blest spirits, sing a little higher,
> Here's one more added to your sacred quire,"

or by such graceful tributes as the one sacred to the memory of the relict of Governor Leverett, from which we learn that

> "She was a gentlewoman grave and sage,
> Yet juvenile and agille in her age,"

and which closes with this touching adjuration:

> "Let comfort rise;
> Forbear to weep, dear friends, muse wipe thine eyes."

But when the writer mingled poetry with politics, and served up petitions in verse, he was disrelished even by the childish statesmen of his time. A friend begs to know why he had thus addressed His Excellency, and is answered at length by the stubborn Saffin, who "relapses" into verse before closing. He naturally inspired intense disgust in Governor Dudley, and bitter indeed was the opposition of temperament between the unscrupulous man of affairs and the opinionated victim of his literary ambitions.

Considering the life of Saffin as a study of Puritanism, we find in him an example of the zeal for learning and the tenacity of political right and privilege with which that system has been identified. In other aspects he suggests the common limitations of the colonial character, rather than its most marked developments. Credulity, superstition, acrimony, obstinacy, and illiberality are prominent qualities of the unconscious recorder of his own deficiencies. Though he rose to high office, by means of his forcible though narrow abilities and effective if limited learning, he was marked by self-will rather than by genuine strength of character. He was a Puritan of the highly respectable type, neither manifesting the worst features of the persecuting spirit, nor rising to that degree of moral earnestness by which his most enlightened contemporaries were known. Cast in the Puritan mould by force of circumstances, his nature is yet of that Philistine development which recurs under all conditions. The fire that lighted the lamp of his earthly day was no coal from the altar, but too often burned luridly with the gusty flame of an unholy anger. Intellectually, his great defect was the lack of humor, which he shared with a generation almost destitute of that kindly quality. Must not a sense of the ludicrous, even, have been wanting in the "J. S." of his book, and in other diarists of his type? This deprivation affected the balance of their political as well as social structure. The ideal Puritan commonwealth was as palpably absurd in some of its features as was Jack Cade's, and because of the same flaw in the intellectual vision which marred the judgment of that uncompromising reformer. The absence of humor leaves all the outlines of character rugged and grotesque, and the unchecked cause of enthusiasm and fanaticism may be anticipated in minds closed to its humanizing influences. A sense of humor in the savage as in children appears in a rudimentary state, and may express itself in acts of brutality; but in its most refined form it is assuredly one of the last products of civilization. Possibly Milton needed not to number among the thronging powers that obeyed his will, this mundane sprite of the mind, this tricksy Robin Goodfellow of intellectual necromancy. Yet Milton stands almost isolated in his lack of that humble quality which in his peers often assumes a higher aspect, and commands homage lasting as literature, inextinguishable as the laughter of the Gods. And in the ways of common life, it is accepted as among American ideas that humor is necessary to the integrity of mental health and peace.

John Saffin's old age was unsoftened by the ideal atmosphere of that season which, in its chastened and tender calm, like a rare day in autumn, suggests the word of philosophy touched by the sentiment of humanity. He was a man of an honest temper, and in his solitary communings with his pen, he delights to deal in eulogy as unstinted as his satire is unsparing.

John Saffin, His Book

He mingled with local questions the same gall of bitterness which his Boston associates had found grievously unpalatable; yet sometimes acted from a truer sense of citizenship than that of his more guarded opponents. He grew morbid and vexed in spirit from the time of that heavy affliction in the loss of his entire family, which, as he has said, tended to his almost insupportable grief. Henceforth he developed that mind of discontent which found matter to brood over in the disappointment of his public life. His domestic hopes and his higher ambitions came alike to failure; and as he was gradually severed from his earlier associations he sank into the dregs of a sullen old age. Though he may hardly move us to pity as we contemplate him in the harshness of his desolation, a Lear who spurned the offices of his Cordelia; yet, as his body is borne to its burial, and as the tomb wherein wife and children had long been laid is open to receive him, we lose the thought of his grievous infirmities in the large sense of that awe with which we hail the passing of mortality. When Governor Andros, so fiercely hated by the provincials, followed the remains of his wife to the grave, the citizens of Boston, moved by a common impulse, did their reverence to the man which they had refused to the ruler. And though we may not deny that John Saffin was a man of bitter nature, and belonged to a stern generation, we are moved by a kindred sense of compassion for his departed spirit. Shall the charity granted to the individual be extended to the system that nurtured him? Time was when it pronounced all judgments, and heard no petitions. The most favored nation known to the dealings of history, the Puritan state, alone among despotisms, has found disinterested eulogists, even numbering among them the descendants of its victims. But the days of crude eulogy will never return. The old commentators extolled an Ehud, or a Jael, but their Puritan imitators no longer find apologists. The Golden Legend of New England, tested in the crucible of scientific research, yields up its dross. Even in the poetry of this generation, the Pilgrims, safe in the bosom of Dutch Calvinism, no longer fly from persecution. Realism in history employed by such practical inquirers as Dr. Coit, Judge Staples, Judge Potter, and broadened by the methods of a philosophical historian like Mr. William Weeden, compels the admission that the mass of the colonists emigrated chiefly to better their condition in life, their appetite for land, according to one authority, being very great. While among the leaders men of the highest purity of motive may be found, their counsels were unhappily not the prevailing ones (saving the honored name of Winthrop), and the Puritans of Massachusetts stand convicted before the tribunal of their own century, since their contemporaries, the Roman Catholics of Maryland, the Quakers of Pennsylvania, and the Baptists of Rhode Island, practised religious toleration, and had nearly developed the separate existence of Church and State. Alone among these spiritual forces, Puritanism, a spirit furnished with a body, remained exalted on the judgment seat, long after the vital energy had fled and but the dead hope remained to mock the rising emancipation of Massachusetts. If the counsels, customs, and traditions of our own state have now and again been tinged with the hues of a gloomy period, the worst evils of the time threatened us only as hovering shadows, having no substance of power, and soon to be dispersed by the reconciling word that restored to Christianity, as to a kingdom not of this world, the primitive conditions of peace and purity. Many anti-Puritan readings of history, and solemn arraignments of colonial bigotry and persecution, have formed a part of the teachings of this Society, speaking through some of its most honored members, who have shown that to all the spiritual wealth of the Puritan, Rhode Island is the rightful heir. But will it be asked, why search so unsparingly into the darkened counsels of the unhappy past? Why set in relief those passages of Puritan history that a generous forgetfulness would gladly cover? Because the voice of justice, the spirit of humanity, the honor of Massachusetts herself, demand that the dark chapters in her history, the cruel deeds wrought by her untitled hierarchy, shall never be condoned.

> "Still will ye ask why this taunt
> Of memories sacred from the scorner?
> And why with ruthless hand I plant
> A nettle on the graves of honor?"

The defence made by New England's loyal son and most honored poet may shelter all who humbly follow Whittier in his fearless judgment upon the works of Puritanism.

> "Not to reproach New England's dead
> This echo from the past I summon,
> Of manhood to the scaffold led,
> And suffering and heroic woman."

No—but to pay honor where honor is due; and not only to the martyrs of Puritan persecution, but to many witnesses of the last sufferings of their spiritual brethren, those Puritans commonly called Quakers, who gave sign, by ominous mutterings, or still more foreboding silence, that they were not consenting unto their deaths. The heart of the commonwealth was sound. If the subject of this paper, in some of his traits, inevitably suggests the sordid greed of the elders, the unselfish lives of his mother, wife, and son, so rich in spiritual beauty, represent the influences that redeem a people from the full weight of that reproach which their leaders must bear. Not from names which have been wrongfully canonized by an arrogant tradition, but from those which history will never know, comes the inheritance of that true spirituality which expresses itself in humble renunciation. What have we gained by all the advances of a civilization that separates us by so great a distance from the seventeenth century, if we are likely to lose that assurance to which the many inarticulate natures clung as an intuition, and the few illuminated minds held with the power of a revelation, that the sacred thirst after righteousness demands the sacrifice of man's nearer needs to his purer aspirations?

> "For through all life I see a Cross,
> Where sons of God yield up their breath;
> There is no gain, except by death,
> There is no vision but by Faith;
> Nor glory, but by bearing shame,
> Nor justice, but by taking blame,
> And that Eternal Passion saith,
> Be emptied of glory, and right, and name."

A SUNDAY IN OLD NARRAGANSETT

MIDSUMMER Sunday of 1754 shines bright and fair over the tranquil land, touching with serenest light the gentle slope so fitly chosen by the fathers as the sacred site of their house of prayer and praise. Here, deep in the enduring silence of these wooded hills, among these placid blue lakes and low-voiced streams, nature keeps an eternal Sabbath.

At the time we attempt to illustrate, the Narragansett Church (St. Paul's) has long been one of the most important in New England, and as such is well known at home, as the colonists still fondly style the mother country, perhaps with some dim, unacknowledged hope of a late return to her shores. "Let him go to Narragansett," wrote the Bishop of London, nearly fifty years before, in reference to the curate of King's Chapel, between whom and his rector some misunderstanding had arisen. "There he may have a hundred pounds per annum sterling, and what perquisites he may make upon the place, besides being his own master." But a self-willed missionary proves no less unpopular in Narragansett than in Boston, nor is it long before the bishop, in much perplexity of spirit, desires to be particularly informed "concerning the insolent riot which Mr. Bridge hath committed upon the church of Rhode Island." The congregation next sustained a severe loss in the death of one whose promised residence among them they had every reason to anticipate with feelings of hope and encouragement. This was the Reverend Dudley Bradstreet, grandson of the venerable Governor Bradstreet. "A native of the country," says the records of the Society for the Propagation of the Gospel, "and a proselyte of their way by education." In 1721 arrived in Narragansett the Reverend James MacSparran, of Scotch-Irish descent, and a graduate of Glasgow University; having been recently appointed to the rectorate of St. Paul's—possibly through the influence of his patron and friend, Sir Francis Nicholson, a colonial governor, and a founder of Trinity Church, Newport. He immediately, and with much zeal and diligence, entered upon the duties of his office, in which he has now continued more than thirty years.

Some hours ago, the parish clerk, who also acts as sexton, left the long, low, weather-stained cottage at the foot of the hill, to throw open the doors and windows of the church, and admit the delicious breeze freshly borne from the ocean, but here mingled with the warm odors floating in from the surrounding forest. Although it is too early for the usual time of morning prayer, a subdued murmur of many voices echoes through the church, and now rises upon the full strains of a closing hymn. Dr. MacSparran is catechizing a hundred or more of the slaves of his parishioners, with here and there an Indian among them. Even the "Independents" and "Quakers," between whom and the honest, but not too liberal doctor there is so much ill-concealed enmity, must own that he is doing a good work now—and against great opposition—for he has found it almost impossible to convince the wealthy planters of the colony, that it is not an irreligious act to bestow religious instruction upon negro slaves! Persuasive tracts for general distribution were forwarded by the Venerable Society; the Bishop of London addressed a pastoral letter "To the masters and mistresses of families in the English plantations abroad"; and even those sublime authorities, His Majesty's attorney-general and solicitor-general, were invoked to declare, in a learned opinion, that the rite of baptism was not incompatible with the condition of servitude. These remonstrances would have produced only a slight and temporary effect, had they not been enforced and recommended by the all-pervading energy, the genuine Christianity of the earnest incumbent of St. Paul's. His people yield to a firmer will than their own, but without perceiving that by admitting their slaves to the duties and privileges of responsible beings, they have virtually pronounced their emancipation. Some of them may have survived to share the general consternation that ensued, when, in the next generation, Thomas Hazard of South Kingstown, then in the zenith of his manhood and the fullness of his wonderful argumentative powers, began to illustrate, both by example and teaching, those broad principles of human freedom, from which, during the varied course of a long life, he never swerved, and the first promulgation of which has led to results of so vast magnitude throughout New England and the whole country.

The music ceases, the doctor's Sunday-school of larger children is dismissed, and the dusky crowd disperses about the sunny slope, already thickly set with gravestones, to await their masters' approach. Some of them will afterwards return to occupy the gallery until the close of the morning service. Many of these are old family servants, whose names and faces have long been familiar to the rector. Doubtless, his wife's maid, whom he has oddly christened Margaret African, is present. Here, too, are 'Mint and Dimmis, Rochelle (Madam Powell's woman), Luce and Bethany; while among the men are Peter and Plato, *Senegambia* (a kind of Æsop, whose sayings and stories are still current in Narragansett), with York, London, Dedford, Orson, and other such quaintnesses in names as perpetuate the thoughtless caprice or humorous fancy of the masters who conferred them. Perhaps we may also distinguish the gloomy features of the Indian woman whom the church records grandly style "Sarah, Queen Dowager." The Doctor is innocently fond of fine words, and describes Miantonomi (is it from a vague association with Dryden's play?) as "The Indian emperor." Her Majesty is accompanied by her daughter, crowned, previous to the Revolution, as Queen Esther — the last heir but one to the empire of the Narragansetts — as the Doctor would say.

At this season the church is well filled, — when the heat is not oppressive, — for, in the Doctor's somewhat petulant phrase, "Here, in *Nov-Anglia*, we are always either frying or freezing," — with the gentry of the surrounding country and their numerous guests. Many of those who most regularly attend the services, traverse distances of sixteen or twenty miles in going and returning. From Boston Neck and Point Judith, from Tower Hill and Little Rest, now Kingston Hill, and even from beyond Wickford, come the tall squires and stately dames, mounted on their famous Narragansett pacers, of Andalusian race; the gentlemen in wigs and cocked hats, the ladies gay in as much finery as can possibly be made consistent with the inevitable riding-

A Sunday in Old Narragansett

habit. It is a bright and varied picture which comes suddenly into view as the cavalcade winds through the green and shaded lanes, late so silent, but now blithely echoing to the swift hoof-beats and click of harness, mingling with the clear tones of cheerful and animated talk. For, in Rhode Island, Sunday was never regarded as a mournful occasion, and least of all by these simple, kindly people who count it no sin to enter upon the honest performance of their religious duties with right hearty English cheer and good will. Nor would it be very singular if some of them should even linger by the church door rather longer than is absolutely necessary for the mere exchange of cordial greetings. People are so isolated on those great plantations! and there are so few opportunities of coming together and discussing the latest European intelligence, as developed in last week's *Boston News-Letter* — or any other subject that may prove interesting. Less pardonable will it be if the gentlemen's conversation should be insensibly drawn, by force of irresistible attraction, in the direction of their recent field sports — the fox-hunt in Pettaquamscutt woods, or the pace races on Little Neck beach, for the prize of a silver tankard. Really, if any of the Doctor's worthy parishioners are betrayed into such errors of talk, it must be (as their wives judiciously decide) entirely the fault of their guests, these Virginian gentlemen, who to-day are attending church in such state, with a lofty and complacent air of taking the service and the parson into their sublime favor and protection. There was then much sympathy, and a frequent interchange of visits between Virginia and Narragansett. Probably the Doctor has already paid his respects to the imposing strangers, who may have condescended to impart to him several particulars concerning their governor, whom he mentioned in his "America Dissected," as "Mr. *Dinwoody*, my classmate at the college of Glasgow."

But the time of intercourse is brief, for the tolling bell summons this congregation of highly respectable miserable sinners to their large square pews, guarded by exclusive doors. Here are representatives of the old South County families — the *quality*, as they are called by their humbler neighbors. Here are those staunch churchmen, the Brentons, the Coles, the Gardiners, the Phillipses, the Updikes, with many others who sacredly cherished and strenuously upheld the traditions of home-rule in Church and State. Prominent among the parish officials are John Balfour (afterwards buried beneath his own pew), Charles Dickinson, and John Case, Esquires. The latter, although now past the sunnier region of middle life, is still active and even gay; warm hearted, public spirited; always a generous benefactor to the church and the poor. And Phillippa, his wife, or consort, in the stately phrase which was the fashion of that day, is she of serene and gracious presence, as befits her courtly name? We shall never know. "She was a lady of real piety and goodness." Thus far the inscription on her tombstone.

Madam Powell no longer occupies the pew so well known by her name, but it may perhaps be filled by her surviving sister, the widow of Colonel William Coddington, of Newport, and her daughter Content. They often visit Narragansett at this season, and Madam Coddington is godmother to most of the children of her niece, Mrs. James Helme, including Rowse, who passes his Sundays at home, but will be expected to-morrow by his legal instructor, Matthew Robinson, Esq., of Hopewell, as he calls his place near Little Rest Hill, and who has just entered the church-yard, deep in conversation with Colonel Lodowick Updike, the son of the colonial attorney-general.

Mrs. MacSparran is usually accompanied by one of her husband's classical students. Says the Doctor, in reference to "New Haven College," . . . "the president, Mr. Thomas Clap, was my scholar, when I first came into these parts, and on all occasions gratefully acknowledges his receiving the first rudiments of his learning from me." Seated in the "parsons pew," she is slowly undulating her large fan, with that air of languid and melancholy grace with which she still looks upon us from her portrait, painted by Smibert, when he and Bishop Berkeley were the guests of Dr. Mac-Sparran at the Glebe. She was a Narragansett beauty, "Handsome Hannah," the sister of Colonel John Gardiner, that worthy country gentleman, and "*so* distinguished," as good Parson Fayerweather exclaims, when alluding to her death. Another one of this lady's brothers, who became somewhat more widely known, out of Narragansett, than even Colonel John, was the Sylvester Gardiner, M.D., of Boston, who owed the advantages of an European education to the quick perceptions, valuable advice, and solicitous directions of his reverend brother-in-law.

From time to time, many glances are turned toward that attractive quarter of the church where Colonel Thomas Hazard of Boston Neck is surrounded by his family of fair daughters — Penelope, Sarah, Alice, and the rest. Not far from them are their cousins, Joseph Hazard, Esq., and his mother, Mrs. Esther, the widow of Governor Robert Hazard, and well known through all the country side by the appellation of "Queen Esther" in recognition of her great energy of character and commanding presence.

Esquire Willett is not quite punctual this morning, rather later, in fact, than a churchwarden has any right to be, and his usual serene dignity is just touched with a slight consciousness of his unwonted dereliction in this respect. Yet the good squire need not reproach himself very severely. He ordered his horse in good season for an early ride to his beloved plantation of young oaks, and, once engrossed by his woodland favorites, became heedless of the passage of time, until at last, roused to a sense of his neglect, he has hastened to arrive just at the moment when service begins.

The squire's delight in trees is not shared by his neighbors, the residents of North Kingstown. He is greatly esteemed and respected by them, no doubt; at town meeting it is customary for them to say: "We can't commence business till the squire comes"; but in this matter of tree-planting he is held to be decidedly eccentric. To so many of our first settlers the idea instantly and involuntarily associated with the sight of a tree was that of a "murdhering Indian Salvage" in lurking behind it. Their immediate descendants liked smooth fields, with a clear outlook from their doors, and retained an unreasonable dread of affording any covert to a stealthy foe. Memories of the Great Swamp

Fight, and the burning of the Bull Block-house, were still thrilling in the minds of the older people, who often repeated by their firesides the story of the terrible manner in which Hezekiah Willett, the squire's uncle, came to his death in the time of Philip's War.

But now the reading-desk is filled by the portly form of Dr. MacSparran, radiant in all the glories of crisp surplice and full flowing wig. With impressive solemnity of voice and aspect he conducts the service; while, at each measured pause, the deep rich tones of the congregation raise the rhythmical response, or the music of chant and hymn wanders far out upon the hush of summer noon, to be echoed by the birds from distance to distance, in a thousand varying harmonies. The Doctor is an effective and, so to speak, florid reader; his sermons are always hearable (why is there no such word?) and sometimes are finished, elaborate performances, abounding in classical quotation or allusion. He is an enthusiastic admirer of his great countryman, Dr. Swift, and recently sent to Dublin for the print of him which this morning hangs in his study at the Glebe. To us who know him by tradition, he seems a quaint original, a character of delightfully racy individuality, an egotist, but a not unamiable one. By his contemporaries he was justly viewed in a more serious light, as an able divine, a persevering and resolute missionary, devotedly pursuing his adventurous journeys through the toilsome wilderness intervening between Providence and New London. "Last winter," as he wrote in 1752, "I rode thirty miles upon one continued glaze of ice upon the land, to assist a neighboring clergyman, who was sick. 'T is fine traveling," he cheerfully continues, "for one that can sometimes 'light and run, to bring the blood into his feet, and increase the checked circulation." A faithful, unquestioning soldier of his revered Church, in her service,

> "A frame of adamant, a soul of fire,
> No dangers fright him and no labors tire."

And what manner of people are these to whom he has so long ministered in sacred things? Is it not enough to reply that they are the immediate descendants of English country squires and exhibit in a marked degree both the virtues and the errors of the parent stock? The blood of the anxious Puritan, of the restless versatile Huguenot, is an alien element here. Not so scholarly, perhaps, as our Massachusetts provincials, of whom the Doctor acutely observes: "They have one college at New Cambridge, and many petty ill-taught grammar schools; yet, under these disadvantages, are a more polite, regular people, than some of their neighbors." Among these worthy squires even a false quantity would fail to produce any very startling effect, supposing, indeed, that it were possible for such to occur in the somewhat painfully familiar classical fragments with which their good rector delights to embellish his discourses. Most of them, it is to be feared, parted as willingly from the classics as from their tutors. Certainly not so orthodox as their brethren of Connecticut, among whom the alliterative temptation to call them a "godless generation" sometimes proves too strong to be resisted; yet, with all their faults, how kind-hearted and hospitable, how generous, frank, and honorable they were! Honest, straightforward in all their words and deeds, they loved their friends and hated their enemies without reserve; yet found life so enjoyable, that we may well believe the love to have far exceeded the hatred. The country life of the eighteenth century, how simple a thing it was! like hearing sweet, old melodies, that vary from the gay to the pathetic, played again and again in some twilight room, until the quiet listeners pass into a last profound and grateful slumber. If the future historian, who, from the sublime heights of the twentieth century shall review the calm tenor of their artless lives, may call them a race of children, how much better will be our own fate in that day, and in what age of the world have not men justly regarded their ancestors as their children? In the words of one who has carefully studied the traditions of which he writes: "Like the old English country gentlemen from whom they descended, they were a fox-hunting, horse-racing, feasting generation"; yet, it is also true of their inner lives, that they were instinctively guided by the lofty rules of reverence toward God and justice toward man.

Although a High Churchman and a Tory, the Doctor bears true allegiance to the Protestant succession, and prays with especial fervor and unction "for our most religious and gracious king, George . . . and for all the royal family"—while the hearty responses of the people indicate their untroubled loyalty. If any voice is silent, it must be that of the Scotchman, Gilbert Stuart, who has now been a resident of Narragansett for perhaps six years. He is understood to cherish Jacobite principles and sympathies, and by some of his neighbors may be shrewdly suspected of knowing more of the recent rebellion of '45 than a good subject should. Certain it is, that when his second son, who was destined to achieve so splendid and enduring a fame, was born and christened at Narragansett, he bestowed upon him the name of Gilbert *Charles* Stuart, in faithful memory of the young prince so lately exiled from his ancestral home and kingdom.

To-day the Doctor preaches with more than usual force and spirit. The prospect of a European visit affords him fresh encouragement, and inspires him with a new interest in life. Two years have already passed since he wrote: "As the shadows lengthen, as the sun grows low, so, as years increase, my longings after Europe increase also. My toils are inexpressible, and age renders them still more intolerable." With a natural desire to meet once more the old associations of home, he has dwelt with a fond pleasure upon the anticipations of his visit. "I know," he remarks, with his usual *naïveté*, in a letter to his relatives, the Reverend Paul and "Cousin Tom" Limrick, "that you would be pleased with the person and accomplishments of my consort, but how you would fancy a full-bodied, fat fellow, like old Archibald of the Hass, I can't tell till I try. God grant we may once see one another!"

The immediate occasion of his journey is the unfavorable conclusion of his lawsuit of thirty years standing with Dr. Joseph Torrey, the Congregational pastor at Narragansett, respecting the title to the tract of three hundred acres reserved by the seven purchasers of Pettaquamscutt for the use of an *orthodox* minister, and, to the lasting honor of English jurisprudence, determined in favor of "the dissenting teacher," who is of the same faith as the original holders of the land. Dr. Torrey's experience in Narragansett was in many respects, peculiar. He came there to practice medicine; soon after obtained Congregational ordination, and, until his death, *sixty* years after, continued faithful in the duties of his two-fold cure; enjoying an equal degree of acceptance and success, as pastor and physician.

The indomitable will of the rector of St. Paul's remains unaffected by this adverse and unexpected decision; he even hopes to derive some final advantage from it. It is said, indeed, that during his stay in London, the American bishopric was offered him, but, well knowing how much bitter prejudice and jealous suspicion was always aroused among the colonists by the very name of that office, he chose to decline the preferment, in those sensible and manly words for which his memory deserves to be held in perpetual honor: "*That he would rather dwell in the hearts of his parishioners, than to wear all the bishop's gowns in the world!*"

Other reasons, too, may have induced him to set but little value on the rewards of earthly ambition. He was fast approaching the close of all his cares and labors—and he was alone. To-day, as he alludes in solemn and touching words to his intended journey, and asks the prayers of his people for himself and his companion, that they may be preserved from the perils of the great deep, and by the blessing of Heaven may be restored in safety to their home and friends, a responsive thrill of tearful sympathy is felt by all the congregation. How profound would be their awe, how keen their emotion, could they foresee how short a time shall pass before the daughter of Narragansett is committed to her early grave within the shadow of Westminster Abbey, while their broken-spirited rector must return to them alone, and gather resolution to write in the church records: "Dr. MacSparran having returned from his sorrowful voyage he made to England, where his wife died and lies buried in Broadway Chapel burying-yard, in Westminster." Does the grief of the afflicted husband find some solace in the statement that "the hearse was drawn by six horses, and there were two mourning coaches for the two mourners and the bearers," and that these last were "all but one New England men"? "She was the most pious of women, the best of wives in the world, and died, as she deserved to be, much lamented." A few months more, and his own gloomy prediction that he should fall in a foreign land is fulfilled, and his sorrowing people lay him to rest beneath the altar of his beloved church, where now rises the massive cross of polished granite that, in simple words, fitly commemorates his labors and sacrifices.

But to-day these scenes and events still belong to the future, and the unconscious throng that listened with eager interest to the thrilling aspirations of the sermon, and knelt in reverential hush to receive the sacred benediction, now rapidly dispersing, leaves the churchyard to keep its breathless trance of quiet undisturbed until the dawning of another Sunday morning.

And while the last flutter of life and motion is lost in the forest shadows; while the faint sound echoed from the tread of a distant multitude eddies for a moment in the air, and then is still, suddenly the ghostly

A Sunday in Old Narragansett

light of a buried century fades like a departing dream. Church and priest and people are swept away as by a rising flood. The sound of prayer and psalm recedes into eternal silence. Nothing remains but the ceaseless sighing of the wind in the tall grasses drooping over the ancient gravestones. The heart goes out in fervent pity for these desolate neglected wrecks, scarred, seamed, shattered by the mighty waves of time's viewless ocean. No flowers are ever laid upon these graves. For many years no mourner has leaned tenderly over them. Long ago they passed into the darker shade, the second death, of oblivion. Can the lost memories be found again? Shall life indeed arise from death?

High above the encircling grove mounts up the sweet unconscious song of a bird. It gathers volume and meaning; to the sensitive ear it is fraught with the saddest music of memory and pensive regrets. In a pure and lofty harmony it dwells upon the blameless thoughts, the warm affections, the undying aspirations, which once gathered here, and, borne on the rushing, deepening tide of melody, comes the vision of an eternal future. There is a sure message of promise for this sacred spot, sacred, as any spot of earth must be, where humanity has wrought, suffered, loved, and passed peacefully away, in the bright tranquillity of hope—the hope of immortality.

THE NARRAGANSETT GLEBE

THE stranger in Narragansett who explores the secluded valley of the Pettaquamscutt, following the stream through all its beautiful windings to its headwaters, is attracted by the sheltered situation and home-like aspect of a spacious old gambrel-roofed house, standing below MacSparran Hill. For many years the home of Dr. James MacSparran, one of the earliest Anglican missionaries to the Colony of Rhode Island, it has been known for more than a century as The Glebe House.

In the records of St. Paul's Church may be found occasional brief references to the Glebe, beginning with the date of its purchase by the gentlemen of that parish, from the heirs of their late rector. These inherited under the conditions of his will, drawn up previous to his last European journey, during which his wife, who accompanied him, died in London. By this instrument the Doctor, after giving Mrs. MacSparran a life interest in his real estate, provides that it shall eventually become the residence of the first missionary bishop of the English Church, whose jurisdiction shall include the Narragansett country, reserving an appropriate spot commanding a varied and extensive view, as the site of a new church and burial ground. But should no bishop arrive within seven years after the death of Mrs. MacSparran, the house and farms should pass to the Doctor's nephew and namesake, and to his wife's brother, Dr. Sylvester Gardiner, of Boston, the devisees, who, in 1758, sold the estate which was henceforth to be held "as a glebe and parsonage for advance-

The Narragansett Glebe

ment and behoovement of the present and all succeeding ministers of St. Paul's Church in Narragansett, for time immemorial." The principal purchasers, as afterwards enumerated by an incumbent of the parish, were: "John Case, Francis Willett, Thomas Browne, Matthew Robinson, Lodowick Updike, Esquires, and Captain John Browne, of Newport; and Colonel Thomas Hazard, of Boston Neck." The sum of the purchase money was three hundred pounds sterling, "of which Dr. Gardiner, to his honor be it here recorded, gave out of his share or amount of one hundred and fifty pounds sterling, *one hundred dollars;* to help forward the purchase, or rather to lessen the cost thereof to the parish of St. Paul's. As to the three first named purchasers, viz: Case, Willett and Thomas Browne, Esquires, each of them gave most liberally and generously; and their names are again recorded to their honor, for they signalized themselves in the distinct purchases of said farms, and their donations did not amount to less than Two Hundred and Thirty Dollars each."

The wardens of the parish, earnestly desiring the presence of an Episcopal missionary in Narragansett, proceed to inform the Society for the Propagation of the Gospel of the successful accomplishment of this affair. "And that we might render the living of St. Paul's worthy the acceptance of gentlemen of character and reputation, whenever in the providence of God it becomes vacant, we shall do everything further that is required of, or may be expected from us. Entreating the Venerable Society to accept this dutiful address, and thanking that honorable and august body in a proper and becoming manner for all favors, we beg leave with the greatest deference, duty and regard, to subscribe ourselves your most obedient, devoted, humble servants, John Case, John Gardiner, *Wardens*."

To this letter the reverend secretary of the society replies favorably, and soon engages in a correspondence with Mr. Samuel Fayerweather, rector of Wineyaw, South Carolina, finally giving him due notice of his appointment to "the church of Narragansett in New England," with a salary of fifty pounds per annum, the highest then allowed by the society's rules to any missionary. "And the church of Narragansett hath provided what they call a good house and glebe, and obliged themselves by a writing to pay twenty pounds per annum to the rector of their church."

An official communication to the secretary, dispatched by Mr. Fayerweather, soon after his establishment in Narragansett, states that, unhappily, he has his dwelling in the midst of certain persons who take many occasions of expressing great bitterness against the Church of England. Thus situated he finds it best to be mild and gentle, peaceable and forbearing. He also writes that his parish church is well filled in the warm and moderate seasons, but in winter the congregations are small, on account of the extreme cold. He has been urged in imitation of his predecessors, to officiate in his own house in severe weather, but has refused to comply till he had obtained the requisite leave.

The reply, which breathes the spirit of the best days of the English church, assures Mr. Fayerweather that the society heartily approves and commends his mild and courteous manner toward the dissenter, which

The Narragansett Glebe

is such as the society most sincerely desires may be adopted by all its missionaries. In regard to the Sunday services, if his church cannot be made warm and comfortable, and his house is large enough for the reception of all who are willing to attend, the poor, as well as those of better rank, he may have permission to officiate there when necessary.

So late as 1820 it was customary for the rectors of St. Paul's to hold occasional services at the Glebe, but since 1842 it has no longer been retained as church property. The succeeding years have not materially altered its aspect. The chance visitor still walks the flaggings and mounts the terraces by the rude, irregular flights of stone steps, which have so often echoed to the firm and energetic tread of Dr. MacSparran. Still in its old place by the gate stands the long disused mounting-block — curious reminder of the manners of the time when the cavalier habits, naturally adopted by the early settlers of a wild, untrodden country, threw a tinge of romance over the quiet lives of our sober sires, so that the wayward imagination persistently invests each grave clerk, each prosaic squire, with the spirit of adventure, daring, and chivalry — in fine, with all the fancied attributes of a young Lochinvar! Silently, season after season, the lilac hedge lets fall its fragrant blossoms on the turf; but the less hardy shrubs and flowers that once adorned the Glebe garden have slowly withered and died. The wide-spreading orchards of delicious peaches, plums, and pears that clustered on the sunny and sheltered slope of the hill have long since disappeared. Only the apple trees remain among the descendants of the original scions imported by Dr.

MacSparran from English nurseries, and are yet bright in bloom and jewelled with fruit from year to year.

The interior of the house presents those rough hewn timbers, those massive beams crossing the low ceilings, with the solid paneling, and the elaborate and inaccessible mantelpieces, which are all of so familiar occurrence in the simple homes of New England colonists. Passing through these wide rooms and noticing the breadth of the cavernous fireplaces, or looking up to meet the frown of the grim black rafters supporting the garret roof, we are aware of a closer companionship, not only with the human interests of a vanished century, but even with the remote life of the primitive forest—the life that once endued this long withered trunk, this petrified form, with the changeful grace of motion, and the varied harmony of coloring.

But leaving the thin air of shadowy memories like these, to enquire of the nearer associations thronging this ancient house, we find that it has not yet lost all traces of the strong individuality of its first occupant. Despite some modern alterations, a reverent tradition still restores the ample outline of the principal room, with its sloping floor, and the large and numerous windows by which it received light on three sides. This was the household chapel, where a small congregation frequently assembled for social services, during the severest winters of the eighteenth century. The guest chamber above, of the same spacious proportions, was familiar to Smibert, the artist, to the good Dean Berkeley, to Bishop Seabury, Parker, Bass, and other dignitaries of the early church. We fancy their cordial reception at the Glebe, and note with them the honest pride of the hospitable Doctor in his new-built house and thriving farm, or listen for the soft gliding rustle that announces the stately and graceful form of Handsome Hannah—"the beautiful American"—as she was styled by the London world. The years roll away like shrivelled wintry leaves from the buried grass of spring, and the household of that long-past time lives and moves again for us.

It is a fair Sunday morning in May. The early mists have vanished from the blue surface of the Pettaquamscutt, and Willett's Point, crowned with its tapering firs and pines, rises sharp and clear from the water. Bright drops of dew are still clinging to the orchard blooms, or hidden among the clustering lilacs, while nestled in the sunniest garden-nook, the first hardy spring flowers are dreaming of their English home.

Within, the reverend Doctor has just left his desk, closing it upon the goodly tome of church records, and the smaller manuscript volume in which the passing events of his daily life are minutely noted. With the restless and fiery activity that characterizes him, he rapidly paces the length of the great room serving at once as chapel, study, and parlor, but pauses by the open casement, where the sun shines warm and the wandering perfume of the lilac hovers for an instant in the air. Does stern Time himself forget to speed the lingering moments of this serene morning? Has he not sought and found a lasting repose in this enchanted spot? Suddenly the sweet spell of silence is broken, as the slow-voiced English clock, "like something starting from a sleep," gives solemn warning of the hour, and the Doctor, roused from his brief and unwonted reverie, hastily crosses the hall and throws open the staircase door, to remind "Mrs. MacSparran," in tones that bear a slightly authoritative ring, that it is full time for their departure. So presently the worthy couple mount and sedately ride away. Our best wishes attend them, our glances follow them in their distant course, until they finally disappear from sight around the sudden, sharp curve by which the highway divides the lofty hill still called by their name.

The mingled lights and shadows of many seasons pass swiftly over the Glebe, and it stands revealed in the level glow of a fast sinking sun. The red beacon fires of autumn are kindling from wooded hill to hill, and fallen leaves from the scarlet oaks are driven across the garden paths by fitful gusts of wind, like blazing brands whirled from the grand conflagration. Now the wide hall door swings heavily open and the master of the house comes down the walk to mount his Narragansett pacer, that has long been patiently standing at the gate, and lifts his fine head in joyful recognition of his rider, whose cheerful, genial, smiling face can be none other than that of our good old friend, Parson Fayerweather. We may readily divine his destination, by a glance at the freshly written inscription on the fly-leaf of the book he treasures carefully: "Presented to the worthy ESQUIRE WILLETT; by his obliged and affectionate friend Samuel Fayerweather; to whom this volume was given, by HIS LORDSHIP, THE BISHOP OF LONDON, through the hands of HIS EXCELLENCY, GOVERNOR BERNARD, in 1763." Although the Parson evidently regards this distinguished volume, so graced by courtly associations, with great veneration, our re-

The Narragansett Glebe

publican eyes are more critical, and we observe that it is simply a miscellaneous collection of discourses, and is of quite ordinary, not to say plain, appearance. It is much to be feared that His Lordship, of London, when searching his library for some appropriate token of esteem, to be forwarded to a remote colonial clergyman, was attracted rather toward the obscure closet which held the hopeless assemblage of forlorn, unmated volumes, than by the towering shelf, where

> "In close compact array,
> The Elzevirs their classic wealth display."

But the little gift will be graciously accepted by so good a subject and so staunch a Churchman as Esquire Willett, the Parson's nearest neighbor and most valued friend. Both host and guest will sit late by the glowing fireplace this chilly October evening, for the present threatening aspect of public affairs involves many omens which command their anxious interest and attention. Loyal sentiments are exchanged; loyal resolutions grow firmer for the hour of friendly intercourse; and the confidential visit only closes when the mellow harvest moon rises over the glittering waters of the Bay. In that sober light the Parson slowly pursues his meditative way homeward, and soon all is quietness at the Glebe. As the moon gradually declines from the zenith, and at last sinks below the rounded outline of the western hill, the ancient house, now encompassed by the deeper hush of darkness, seems a vision far withdrawn from daily life, and passes into the ghostly realm of dreams and fancies.

Peace and blessing to the house of dear and sacred

memories! the olden home of learning, virtue, and religion! Honor to these venerable walls, forever hallowed by the spirit of domestic tranquillity and happiness! the centre whence radiated the cheerful influences of strong-hearted endeavor, warm sympathy, and soothing ministration. May the elements deal gently, reverently, with the cherished structure that in its silent eloquence recalls the earnest faith, the simple worship of our ancestors. Long may its serene presence remain untouched by time, uniting us by the ties of strong association with all the holiest aspirations of our unforgotten past.

THE WILL OF
JAMES MacSPARRAN, CLERK

THIS antique document, containing several charitable and ecclesiastical bequests, possesses an especial meaning and value, in relation to the annals of Narragansett. It is not without a deeper and more enduring claim upon human interest, in its earnestness of benevolent motive, its profound simplicity and sincerity of tone. There is a thoughtful charm in tracing the changeful course of its unconscious self-revelations of mind and character. No mere legal summary, but the genuine record of the wishes of the testator,—expressed in his own language, written by his own hand,—it is deeply imbued with the definite tints derived from his peculiar habits of thought and feeling; bearing the original impress of his complex individuality. Composed with not a little of that fatal fluency which so frequently animates the over facile clerical pen, the entire paper, however curious and valuable in the estimation of antiquarians, might be regarded as presenting too unlimited a demand upon the attention of the general reader; but a few extracts from its principal items will, it is believed, appeal to the common interest and sympathy.

There is something eminently characteristic of the writer of this instrument in the careful precision and particularity of statement comprised in the opening paragraph, although its sentences, sequent to the solemn invocation of the Trinity, usually found in ancient wills, are merely occupied with the inevitable formalities respecting the *status* of the testator, and his positive possession of what our ancestors called "a sound disposing mind." It is followed by a reverent acknowledgment of dependence upon the Creator, and of devout and humble gratitude to Him for all the blessings of life; this simple statement being very fully amplified, in accordance with the prevailing customs of a time when it was judged essential or at least fitting, that the preambles of wills and other formal papers should afford a complete "body of divinity."

"First, I think myself now and at all times obliged to return my thanks to Almighty God, through whose mercy I have been baptized into the Christian faith, and by a gracious turn of Providence have been advanced to the honor of Priesthood in the Church of England, which I reverence as most agreeable in its doctrines and constitutions to the purest ages of the gospel; beseeching God to protect it, to heal its unhappy divisions, to repair the breaches of its discipline, and to defend it from those many enemies who labor for its subversion. And I passionately pray to God that that part of it under my care may be supplied with a successor to me, more successful than I have been, in edifying and enlarging that glorious Church in this place."

There are occasional unstudied effects of contrasted light and shade in the Doctor's quaint but not undignified style; a certain terse and startling vigor of expression, such as vividly recalls the days of the old English divines of massive minds and winged words. Who can follow the frank and manly utterances of the succeeding act of confession without a ready recognition of its impressively real and earnest humility?

Dr. MacSparran's Will

"I implore the pardon of God for all my open and secret sins, and everything in me that has been less agreeable to the purity of that religion I have professed, and the true dignity of the sacred office I have sustained; to accept my weak endeavors to serve Him and His church, which I have, in many instances, labored, with great pains and at an expense exceeding my ability and increase. As I freely forgive all men and wish them well, both here and hereafter, so I beg the like charity of them; especially I beg the Lord to forgive any imprudency that may have attended my prosecution in law, of what I then thought, and still do, the just right of the church whereof I have the care. Finally, I most humbly bequeath my soul to God, my Maker, beseeching His most gracious acceptance of it, through the merits of my most compassionate Redeemer, Jesus Christ, who I trust will not reject me from His merciful presence. In this hope and confidence I render up my soul to God through Christ, and give my body to the earth, in full assurance of its resurrection and reunion to my soul at the last day. But in the meantime my body to be buried with a decent Christian burial, at the discretion of my executrix hereafter named."

As to the testator's "merciful share of worldly goods," the somewhat complicated provisions of the instrument may be thus briefly sketched; rejecting its legal *formulæ*, but retaining as nearly as possible its original phraseology:

To his dearly beloved wife, Mrs. Hannah MacSparran, the testator bequeaths all his personal estate; she paying into the hands of the wardens of St. Paul's for the time being, £20: the annual interest thereof to be used for the relief of the poor of the parish. And the wardens shall be obliged to give a discharge for the sum, and an engagement to convert the same to the aforesaid use, and no other. Also he wills that she give £10 to each of his friends, Captains Philip Wilkinson and Joseph Harrison, of Newport, merchants, to buy each of them a mourning ring.

To his wife he devises all his books and manuscripts, desiring her to sell them to the best advantage, except two volumes in folio of Dr. Whitby on the New Testament, one volume folio of Bishop Burnet on the Thirty-Nine Articles, one volume folio of Bishop Pearson on the Creed, three volumes octavo of Bragon on the Parables, and the Book of Homilies; which eight books he wishes her to place in the custody of his successor, as being the only remains of the Narragansett Library, the greater portion of which was embezzled at Marblehead in Mr. Massom's time. In a word, he leaves to his wife his entire personal estate, with all such as he may die possessed of, particularly his service of plate, and all his negro servants, assuredly as if each one were designated by name.

Also to his dearly beloved wife he devises, in fee-simple, those lands bought by him of Samuel Gardiner and of Samuel Watson, Anno Domini 1743. And to his wife he gives all the remainder of his land (being such as were bought by him of Dr. Sylvester Gardiner, of Boston, and of William Gardiner), with dwelling-house and appurtenances, during the term of her natural life, whether she contracts another marriage, or remains sole.

Dr. MacSparran's Will

After the demise of his wife these farms shall be converted into a manor for the use and residence of such Bishop of the Reformed Religion (as the same is now received and established in England), and to his successors forever in that high and holy office, as shall be regularly sent and set over that part of His Majesty's plantations where the seat or farm lies. But this donation he makes with these two provisos: I. That at least the first three bishops in direct succession shall have been born and educated in Great Britain or Ireland (which condition is not required by him out of any national spirit, but because he imagines that Episcopacy cannot be so well preserved in its purity and true dignity in any other manner at the first).

II. That the Bishop be sent within seven years after the decease of Mrs. MacSparran. And lest the Town Council who (by an unadvised law of this Colony) are empowered to that purpose, in respect to estates given to pious uses, should intermeddle with the estate, he gives the rents and profits accruing from it, during this term of seven years, to Dr. Sylvester Gardiner and to Captain Philip Wilkinson—a moiety to each, for their trouble in keeping things in repair. Should no such Bishop be appointed to preside over these American and non-American churches, then he wills that these rents and profits shall determine, and the estate shall pass unto Dr. Sylvester Gardiner and unto James MacSparran, eldest son of the testator's only brother, Archibald MacSparran, of New Castle in Delaware (lately deceased), to be equally divided between them, as an indefeasible inheritance, in fee-simple forever.

For as much as the testator and his wife are meditating a voyage to England, and should it please God in His sovereign will so to order it that they should die at sea, or never return, and no new disposition be made by either, then he directs his executors to make sale of all his goods and chattels, half the proceeds to belong to Dr. Sylvester Gardiner and half to Captain Philip Wilkinson.

Further, he gives a convenient spot of ground as a site for a church and burial yard, whenever claimed for that purpose, meaning that portion of the northwest corner of his farm, comprising a space fifteen rods east and west, and thirteen rods from north to south, and bounded northerly by land of Samuel Wilson, and westerly by the great road of the country.

Should there be any defect or impropriety of expression in this instrument, it is the testator's desire, because it is his true intent, that the same may be construed in favor of his dear wife, Hannah MacSparran, for he means and repeats that he hereby bequeaths to her all his personal estate, goods, and chattels, absolutely, except one silver tankard, which he requests her to give, when she can spare it, to William Gardiner, eldest son of her brother, Dr. Sylvester Gardiner.

Having been as particular as possible to prevent all future cavils, it only remains to name the executors of this instrument. The testator therefore appoints his wife, Hannah MacSparran, his brother-in-law, Dr. Sylvester Gardiner, of Boston, and his true friend, Captain Philip Wilkinson, of Newport, merchant, the executrix and executors of this his last will and testament, and the Honorable, the Society for the Propagation of the Gospel in Foreign Parts, as trustees to his prop-

Dr. MacSparran's Will

erty, so far as shall concern the donation made to a bishop. That they may be duly apprized thereof, he directs an authentic copy of this will, as soon as it shall have passed its probate, to be transmitted to that venerable corporation by his executors. As for his debts, which he thanks God are small, they are to be justly and punctually paid. Revoking all other wills, he confirms this alone, according to its true intent and meaning.

Signed. Dated May the 23d, Anno Domini 1753, and in the twenty sixth year of the reign of our Sovereign Lord, George the Second, of Great Britain, France and Ireland, King, Defender of the Faith, &c.

Subscribers: John Brown, John Gardiner, Peter Mumford.

Proved and recorded by the Town Council of South Kingstown, in the county of Kings, Dec. 13th, 1757.

The English birth of the writer of this paper is evident in every unconscious turn of phrase, in the one familiar measure to which all his thoughts are moving through the deep, worn channels of early prejudices and prepossessions. It is as palpable a reality as his very looks and tones, which we know so well from his portrait and from the finer and livelier limning of tradition. A true Briton, in his instinctive distrust of any scholarship or churchmanship other than such as was indigenous to his native island, and in his hearty insular contempt and misliking for the ways of colonial courts and their magistrates; yet, with a generous inconsistency, always keenly interested in public affairs, seeking admittance to the privileges of a free man at a very early period of his residence in Rhode Island. Adhering with sedulous care to the minutest customs of his own country, he does not forget to bequeath mourning rings to his pall-bearers and executors, while in his scrupulous fulfillment of the usual expectation prevalent at that time, that no clergyman, however small his estate, should neglect to make some provision, or leave some remembrance, for the poor of his parish. He illustrates the common course of the many good priests of his church and nation, who, dwelling contentedly in the peaceful quiet of their rural homes, were affluent in all the essential comforts of life, and were not denied the luxury of administering a judicious and kindly charity. His act cannot fail to recall a certain remarkable and perfectly literal realization of the poet's conception, familiar to every attentive reader of Wordsworth, and readily found by any one who will take the trouble to consult the detailed account of the Reverend Robert Walker (justly called *wonderful* Walker), given in the Third Appendix to the "Excursion."

The Doctor's generosity (or justice?) is evinced in his ample and unconditional bequest to his wife, which indicates a depth of unselfish feeling seldom manifested in the ordinary testamentary dispositions of his time. There is a singular delicacy in his request that she should give a particular piece of plate, whenever she could best spare it, to her own nephew, the son of her brother, Dr. Gardiner. Mrs. MacSparran, although many years younger than her husband, did not live to inherit under the provisions of this will, dying in London in the summer of 1755.

Among the manuscripts which were to have been placed in her care, the Doctor's early history of Narragansett was doubtless included. This valuable record, now unfortunately lost, would have afforded an inestimable assistance in the special study of our colonial annals.

Anticipating all the prejudices, dismay, and alarm, certain to be evoked in the New England mind by the mention of an established bishopric, the testator makes careful preparation for the safety of his gift of a house and farms for the future residence of a missionary bishop. How anxiously he strives against the possibility of "all cavils"! How ingeniously he provides for all contingencies,—save the inevitable! The idea of an impending revolution that should completely sever all civil and ecclesiastical relations then subsisting between the colonies and the mother country had never intruded upon the mental vision of the believer in divine right in State, and apostolic succession in Church; the acute and attentive witness, for nearly half a century, to the weakness and disunion, the mutual jealousies and prejudices of these struggling dependencies of the Crown. What a significant lesson on the vanity of that seemingly most real and solemn act, the last arrangement of all worldly affairs, the final announcement of personal wishes. How curious and lamentable a record would that be which dealt with the secret history of wills remaining unfulfilled, either from unforeseen changes in the movement of events, or from unfaithfulness on the part of the executors. Monarch and subject are alike powerless in death, and the desires of the one scarce command more respect than those of the other. The reception accorded by George the Second, "our most religious and gracious King," under whose auspicious reign this humble instrument was executed, to the august will of his royal father, was secretly noted by the diarist of his time. From their guarded phrases later writers have elicited the ignominious story how, the paper having been duly read in council, the best of monarchs quietly took it from the unresisting hands of its servile executors then present, and coolly transferred it to the royal note-book — a grave from which it never arose. George the First, Elector and King; James MacSparran, Clerk; the sovereign, and one among the indiscriminated millions of his vassals are instantly and irrevocably equalized by the accident of death, and their helpless ghosts vainly strive to retain a feeble hold upon the mighty sphere of human influence and activities whence they have been so suddenly reft, and which sweeps on, uncaring. Verily, this also is vanity. Still, through all earthly vicissitudes rises that deep undertone of despairing mockery, echoing from the primal ages of humanity. The Eastern text is fitly chosen; its universal shadow encompasses all time, all space, within its gloomy dominion. But does the habit of *simply* moralizing upon the errors and littleness of the race tend to promote individual improvement in the practice of moral precepts? Did the preacher himself gain in wisdom and in favor by the sombre course of thought? Is the wholesome bitter of truth flavored with a stolen sweetness when its application chiefly concerns *others*, not *ourselves?*

The final disposition of the MacSparran estate was in full harmony with the owner's well-known preferences and sympathies. Purchased from his heirs by the representatives of the parish, and, for a goodly num-

Dr. MacSparran's Will

ber of years, retained and occupied as the glebe of St. Paul's Church, it long remained the enduring centre of associations the most sacred, the most endearing, to many true and kindly hearts.

The "convenient spot of ground" on the summit of MacSparran Hill, intended as the site of a new church and burial enclosure, was never required for those purposes, and to this day continues as serene in its lonely loveliness as when the departed master of the ancient house that still sleeps beneath its shadow sought its wide terraces at sunset, for a student's quiet walk, and looked abroad over the far-receding expanse of ocean view with the sore longings of an exile from the dear familiar presence of home and friends. "The great road of the country"[1] is no longer a busy highway, the resort of commerce and travel. Silent and deserted, it winds above the brow of the hill and loses itself in the blue distance among the softly rounded outlines of waving meadows and wooded slopes. Its faint, remote, thrilling echoes waken only at the infrequent approach of some more thoughtful observer, some gentler wayfarer, who comes to yield such rational homage as the modern pilgrim may.

---

[1] The old Pequot Trail of the Indians became the "great road of the country" and declined from the days of its activity when Washington marched over it, and Franklin travelled from Boston to New York upon it, to the quiet Miss Carpenter describes in the last quarter of the nineteenth century. It now echoes to the roar and rush of countless motor cars, bringing many people close to the places she describes.

PARSON FAYERWEATHER

SUCH was the half familiar, half affectionate *sobriquet* by which the successor of Dr. MacSparran was universally known among his parishioners of the Narragansett Church, during the fourteen years of his rectorate.

Samuel Fayerweather was a son of Thomas Fayerweather, a resident of Boston, and presumably one of the straitest sect of the Puritans, to judge from the literature he read with admiration and religiously transmitted to his family. Of these books a copy of the *Magnalia* bears the marks of most frequent use. Doubtless the severely good old man often turned its pages more in reverie than in reflection, while proudly anticipating the time when Samuel should fulfil the promise of his name, and become as eminent in the sacred vocation for which he was early destined as any of the ancient worthies commemorated by the quaint Herodotus of New England history. But the son's ultimate course in life was far removed from the parental hopes and counsels. Graduating at Harvard College, he entered the Congregational ministry, and in 1754 was pastor of the Second Church at Newport, Rhode Island. Two years later he is in London, seeking Episcopal ordination, while the charge of his vacant parish has just been accepted by Dr. Stiles. Receiving an appointment to a missionary station in South Carolina, he continued to officiate there until the climate proved injurious to his health.

At this time the wardens of St. Paul's, Narragansett, were anxiously striving to secure some worthy successor to Dr. MacSparran, "in whose light we rejoiced many years."

"And the Venerable Society took compassion on us, sending us a missionary to break the bread of life to our souls, . . . one whom we had once and again heard preach in our parish church. . . . Mr. Samuel Fayerweather, *a native of the land in which we live*, . . . to whom, after we heard of his appointment to our mission, we wrote a respectful letter, inviting him amongst us, which miscarried. And to whom the society also wrote, which packet was for a long time intercepted, and we not hearing from him, kept us destitute of the stated exercises of public worship—from the death of Dr. MacSparran, [December 1, 1757,] to [August 24, 1760,] when the Reverend Mr. Fayerweather laid before his congregation two letters from the society, one to himself, the other to the parish to which he came—in the HOLY ORDERS OF THE CHURCH OF ENGLAND."

To this letter the wardens return an appropriate reply, speaking in high terms of their new incumbent, "the amiableness of whose views is visible and clear, . . . whom . . . we have comfort in, . . . whose valuable gifts and accomplishments will be greatly acceptable to us."

The MacSparran estate was immediately purchased of the Doctor's devisees, to be held as a Glebe for the perpetual benefit of the rectors of St. Paul's.

Parson Fayerweather, now comfortably established in Narragansett, became at once very popular with all classes, and probably soon obtained the friendly appellation by which he is still known to us. His people could not have been long in finding their new rector to be as remarkable for innocent eccentricity and genial simplicity of character as was Parson Adams, whose entertaining history must by that time have found its way even to "the Narragansett country in New England," as native Britons were then accustomed to say, with a generous breadth of expression and that noble disregard for the intricacies of American geography of which they have not yet entirely divested themselves. But whatever his occasional familiarities, even peculiarities, of manner may have been, they would certainly appear much more striking to us than to his contemporaries, who perhaps found it quite natural for him to tell them, when blaming their frivolous excuses for staying away from church, "None of your reasons is more common than the plea of *foul weather*, but come here whenever you will, and you'll always find Fayerweather." While not unlike Dr. MacSparran in keen relish for the harmless pleasures of this life, and in general scarcely inferior to him as a preacher, in choice of matter, and impressiveness of manner, he was also his true successor in the spirit of earnest Christianity, and was known as the faithful and affectionate guardian and friend of all his people. Of eminently social and companionable disposition, he is remembered as having been, in his latter years, a frequent visitor at the house of "King Richard" Greene, then one of the magnates of Old Warwick. He must have been an ever welcome guest at the colonial tea-tables, for he was as eager an enthusiast for the merits of that pleasing beverage as the saintly Cowper, or the revered Dr. Johnson. Indeed, tradition has been so invidious as to record that on one of these occasions the tiny teacup of the period was *thirteen times* re-filled for him! So trifling a circumstance should have passed unnoticed in an age when the great moralist habitually partook of unlimited quantities of his favorite drink until four o'clock in the morning. In his person he was tall and handsome, with brilliant complexion, full black eyes, and clear-cut features. Such were the smiling lineaments preserved by the immortal art of Copley, in the portrait painted in London, when the youthful scholar had just received his degree of A.M. from the University of Oxford, and which represents him in all the grace of his flowing academic robes.

The even course of his secluded life is best told by the self-revealing of the curiously unconscious phraseology which merges the formality of a church record in the lively interest of a personal narrative.

"Feb. 27, 1763 (an exceeding cold day), Mr. F. journeyed to Newport," to meet his betrothed, whom he somewhat resignedly and funereally described as "Surviving Relict of the Reverend Peter Bours, of Marblehead." They were married in Trinity Church by "the Rev. Marmaduke Browne, and Mr. F. preached on the occasion, to a large auditory, from these words: 'Do all to the glory of God.'" This lady was a daughter of Colonel Thomas Hazard, of Boston Neck, in South Kingstown.

The Parson's journeys, after his settlement in Narragansett, though frequent, were not extensive. His missionary work called him to all parts of the Colony, but he seldom passed its southern boundary, and Portsmouth, New Hampshire, appears to have been his extreme northern limit. He always attended the annual convention of Episcopal clergy in Boston, often preaching before them at King's Chapel, and once, at least, "in the presence of His Excellency Governor Bernard." A certain mysteriously worded (but remarkably transparent) paragraph shows him to have delivered a discourse in Boston, June 24, 1772, "before an ancient and truly honorable society, . . . the most numerous, brilliant and splendid assembly, . . . the grand officers, adorned with robes and jewels to illustrate the splendor and magnificence of the day, and do honor to John the Baptist."

As a pastor he was especially assiduous in visiting and relieving "all who were distressed in mind, body or estate."

"Jan. 9, 1767. Mr. F. performed the funeral service for the consort of the Reverend Mr. Browne, in Trinity church, Newport. — An exceedingly large concourse of people attended, but no sermon, as both the lady herself and her husband too, had an utter aversion to pomp and show on these occasions and utterly against all parading."

"April 16, 1769. Mr. F. visited old Mrs. Willett, who was taken ill with an apoplexy, and prayed with her, soon after which she died, on the 18th. She was buried, and a funeral sermon preached by Mr. F. at Esquire's house."

"Feb. 15, 1771. Dr. Robert Hazard was buried and a funeral sermon preached, and on Sunday, 24th, preached at the house of mourning of the late Dr. Hazard, on mortality — a large congregation present. The Honorable James Honeyman was present, who came from Little Rest, where the court had been sitting the whole week."

Parson Fayerweather

Many similar notices could be taken from the records. The following scattered extracts possess particular interest:

"April 16, 1772. Mr. F. officiated at the marriage of one of the descendants of old Colonel Whalley, who came from Great Britain, being one of the regicides of King Charles I., of ever blessed memory, who sat in the mock court before which that excellent Prince, that blessed martyr, was arraigned, tried and condemned, and who was called proverbially (in the day of it) one of King Charles' judges."

"July 18. Sat out from Boston . . . and at Taunton administered the sacred rite of baptism to a male child of Mr. James Hill, . . . and grandchild of the Reverend Dr. Sewall, an independent teacher in Boston, whose zeal was always remarkably distinguished against the Church of England, . . . her forms and ceremonies, . . . in special the rite of baptism. The sponsors were the child's natural parents and aunt, and the name of the little infantile was James, after its father's name."

"Sept. 10, 1773. Mr. F. preached in Portsmouth Church, which he found to be a small but a gay and shining congregation in . . . dress and appearance."

The circumstances detailed in the next year's entries are highly significant:

"Sept. 14, 1774. Mr. F. met the Reverend Convention of the Episcopal Clergy in Boston. General Gage present, and dined with the clergy at Dr. Caner's. 18. Mr. F. preached in King's Chapel for the King's Chaplain, the Reverend Mr. Frontbeck, before General Gage and his officers, . . . and a very numerous and polite assembly, from these words: *Be kindly affectioned one to another with brotherly love.*"

Sunday, November 6, 1774, is the date of Mr. Fayerweather's last contribution to the parish record. Dark days of trouble and anxiety were fast succeeding to the long sunny season of Colonial tranquillity. Narragansett was divided in opinion, but patriotic sentiment was in the ascendant and the services at St. Paul's ceased. The church was used as a barrack for various companies of Continental soldiery. The rector occasionally read prayers, by request, at the houses of those among the gentry who sympathized with the royal cause. It is easy to imagine those scenes. Perhaps the loyal parson is summoned to Exeter, then the stronghold of Tory refugees from Newport and Narragansett. The Squire, his lady and family, and the little circle of earnest adherents to the Crown, who make up the congregation, are all present, while the most faithful of the gray-headed slaves are trusted to guard the doors against the sudden surprise of Republican indignation. We may hear the grave voice of the clergyman offering the ancient petitions of his Church, and praying with almost defiant fervor for the King, that he may be victorious over all his enemies: or note the more sacred and softened emotion that steals into the good man's mood as, in broken and trembing tones, he ejaculates: "From battle and murder, from all sedition, privy conspiracy and rebellion, *Good Lord, deliver us!*" We, whose hearts through four terrible years of strife thrilled to the sound of the self-same words—shall we not be slow to blame the clinging affection, the reverential loyalty of pious age for its long-cherished sym-

Parson Fayerweather

bols of all that is sublime in human faith and devotion? Since our civil contest we have gained a personal knowledge of the slight and arbitrary causes that determine the balance of opinion in so many honest minds. Have we not also insensibly learned to look in a gentler spirit upon the trials of our earlier national life? Let us hope that the Continental troops did not invade that simple sanctuary.

Happier destinies have replaced the sad fates of those old days. There are nobler rulers of men than poor Farmer George, whose misfortune it was to inherit a throne. Shall we not strengthen their hands by infusing all our duties with the spirit of loyalty, though the word, in its restricted sense, may perish with the fading traditions of an outworn past?

Parson Fayerweather did not live to see the close of the war, dying in the summer of 1781. He was buried beneath the communion table of the parish, beside the remains of his predecessor. Their names are united in the inscription upon the monument which now marks the site of the ancient church. They survived all family ties; and each of them, in death, belonged solely to the people who followed him to the grave with heartfelt mourning, as for a departed father and friend.

He appointed Matthew Robinson, Esquire, of Little Rest, executor of his will, from which this interesting article is extracted:

"I give all my library to King's College, New York, and ten pounds sterling and my large picture of myself. And my desire is that the Corporation may suffer said picture to be hung up in the library of said College forever. Also my silver framed square picture of myself to my sister, Hannah Winthrop, of Cambridge. My wife's picture of herself to her niece, the wife of John Channing. My oval picture of myself framed with silver, to my nephew, John Winthrop, of Boston, merchant."

Not one of these bequests was ever executed. Mr. Robinson was then greatly oppressed, not only by the infirmities of advanced age, but by the pecuniary embarrassments in which a member of the family had involved him. Dying insolvent not long after, Mr. Fayerweather's effects were publicly sold with those of his late executor. Nearly all of the books are lost, and but one or two of the portraits can be found.

It was a characteristic and touching desire of the lonely scholar, whose sequestered life as the priest of a rural parish had isolated him from the great centre of intelligence, that the painted semblance of his youth should find a congenial home among the quiet alcoves of classic lore. It was fitting that he should thus "forever" look down in calm scholastic peace and dignity upon the restless and changeful course of the life he once shared—with its ambitions and disappointments; its radiant hopes that dissolve in mists; its beckoning visions that vanish into heartless vacancy. Should not the dying wishes of one whose mild and gentle ministrations had soothed the last hours of so many of his fellow-creatures have been met by a faithful and grateful acknowledgment?

But there are higher honors than even those of the intellectual life, and better memorials than such as are inscribed upon marble. The praise of the good and kindly pastor is still fresh in the places which once

Parson Fayerweather

knew him so well, and his name is a familiar word on the lips of those whose fathers never looked upon his living face. Our suffering humanity can claim no title more noble, more sacred, than his, for his mission was that of a consoler in adversity, and he was not unworthy of the high office. Lighter and inferior traits of character might mingle with the genuine qualities of his nature, and might deceive those who sought for conspicuous professions of sanctity, or affectations of ascetic gloom. But these were the mere externals of the man. They fell from him in the dread presence of the higher realities. With the sick and suffering and afflicted, in the time of tribulation, in the hour of death, he was the simple, sincere Christian, the tender-hearted, sympathetic friend, whose words of affectionate consolation are not forgotten by the people among whom he once lived and labored; for the wealth of a generous nature is never poured out in vain, and the graces of the heart are immortal. Their grateful memory is revered by man, is treasured by the Recording Angel, is acknowledged and rewarded by the Most High.

PARSON FAYERWEATHER'S WILL

THE testator, Samuel Fayerweather, clerk, of South Kingstown, county of Kings, State of Rhode Island, being advanced in years, and laboring under bodily diseases, and thereby warned the more earnestly to consider the great uncertainty of life, and to settle his temporal affairs before it be too late, enjoying a sound state of mind though suffering under an ill state of body, makes and ordains this, his last will and testament. His soul he commits into the hands of his Heavenly Father, and his body to be decently buried; and he hopes for a glorious resurrection at the last day, through the merits of his blessed Saviour.

As to his worldly affairs, he ordains his body to be buried in a decent and Christian-like way, and his just debts to be paid by his executor as soon as may be after his decease.

His library he bequeaths to the Corporation of King's College, in the city of New York, in America; and ten pounds sterling, to be paid by his executor out of the salary of the parish, when he shall have received it; and his large portrait of himself; and his desire is that said Corporation may suffer said picture to be hung up in the library-room of said College forever.

To the poor of the parish whereof he is minister, he bequeaths sixty Spanish milled dollars, to be distributed among them by the executor of this instrument, as he shall find objects of charity.

To his sister Hannah Winthrop, of Cambridge, in the Massachusetts Bay, New England, he leaves his negro girl called Phillis; also ten pounds sterling; his silver-framed square portrait of himself; one silver cream-pot; a red-stone ring set in gold; a silver toilet case; and a piece of blue silk, to be to her own use.

To his sister Anne Mason, wife of Thaddeus Mason, Esq., of Cambridge, in the Province aforesaid, he devises his negro boy called Caesar; his gold watch; and all his household plate; to be to her use and that of her children, as she shall think proper to distribute it among them.

His late dear wife's portrait he gives to her niece, the wife of Mr. John Channing.

His silver-framed oval portrait of himself he gives to his nephew, John Winthrop, of Boston, merchant.

He leaves to the Rev. Mr. Bass, minister of the Church of England, at Newburyport, in the Massachusetts Bay, a suit of black Padusoy, also a "Guineybag," sent him by Parson Quague from the coast of "Guiney."

To the Rev. Mather Byles, senior, of Boston, he bequeaths his silver watch and a black coat; also fifteen pounds sterling.

The Rev. John Graves, of Providence, receives the testator's black horse, with his sulky, or chair for one man, and the harness belonging to it; besides some specified articles of wearing apparel, and fifteen pounds sterling.

His negro man called George, he gives to his friend Matthew Robinson, and to him and his heirs, forever, all his undivided lands, situate in the town of Topsham, in the State of Massachusetts Bay; with those lands lying in common with his sister's lands, or those of their grantees; being in the whole a large tract that belonged to our late honored father, Thomas Fayerweather, of Boston, merchant; and it is to be noted that said lands lie near to lands of Dr. Noyes.

The residue of his estate, real and personal, he devises to his sister Mason, and her three daughters, to be by her distributed to them. And he nominates his friend Matthew Robinson to be sole executor of this his last will and testament, revoking all others whatever. In witness whereof he sets his hand and seal, at South Kingstown, in the year of our Lord, 1781.

Proved and recorded, September 13, 1781.

To those who can read between the lines, there is a distinct shade of regret in the thought that these carefully planned bequests were not to be executed. The Parson's legacy to his friend Matthew Robinson (a well-known lawyer of Colonial Rhode Island) did not redeem him from insolvency. After the death of Mr. Robinson, in 1795, at "Hopewell," his Kingstown estate, Mr. Fayerweather's effects were sold with those of his executor, at auction. Thus the Parson's books were scattered, and his portraits were sent out on a wandering career. One has found a home in the Redwood Library, Newport. Another (the same which he intended for King's College) is in the possession of a Rhode Island family. It is by Copley, and represents him in his academical robes.

It is creditable to the Parson that he devotes a share of his small store of Spanish dollars to a charitable bequest "for the poor of the parish." Rich relatives and well-to-do brother clergymen are to receive their legacies out of his arrears of salary, when these shall have been paid, a doubtful contingency, in the depressed

Parson Fayerweather's Will

financial condition of the parish during the Revolutionary period. It is much to be feared that his clerical friends never received anything more than the homely tokens of remembrance which are bestowed with the unquestioning freedom marking the manners of those simple times. The Rev. John Graves, who receives the most valuable bequest, was, like the testator, one of the royalist clergy, and had resigned his parochial charge early in July, 1776. The Rev. Mather Byles, though a Congregational minister, was a favorite intimate of the Parson's, owing to his Tory principles, and the wit with which he seasoned his quaint discourse. The Narragansett rector, too, was guilty of a taste for punning, and was somewhat given to a choice of odd texts, which were in no way related to the decorous manner of his sermons. Mr. Bass, the third legatee, afterwards Bishop Bass, sacrificed his loyal sentiments in conformity to the preferences of his parish.

A sworn inventory of the testator's personal estate, taken September 29, 1781, comprises some curious entries. They really afford a sort of Dutch picture of the manners of the time. Beginning with the "parlour," we find "a large black walnut table, left by the Rev. Dr. MacSparran," with other tables, from mahogany to maple. Two looking-glasses, one gilt-framed, are valued at £3 12s. A green screen, lined with blue, and six prints, also adorn the Parson's parlor. The humbler companions of these splendors are "six black leather-bottomed chairs, mahogany frames," and two "elbow chairs," one "half-mooned," the other "oaken,"—let us hope, not also "broken," like Dr. Swift's, as he sets forth in his rhymed inventory of a parson's goods and chattels.

In the "northeast bedroom, below stairs," we note, in addition to the solid wealth of the feather-beds, the finer elegances of a "Windsor chair" (held at £4 6s.), a mahogany case of drawers, and a desk, concerning which the appraisers candidly add that it is "very old." These, with sundry tables of pine and maple, a "small Dutch looking-glass," and the somewhat singular ornaments of "two pieces of old painting, one of a pair of pistols, the other of a fiddle," make up the furniture of a room which we may suppose to have been commonly occupied by the Parson.

In the "great chamber," or guest-room, the bedding, including "fine quilted cover-lids," is appraised at £13 10s. A "high case of drawers" is elegantly "phinered." Some "needle-worked chairs" are estimated at £11 14s., but, alas! the work is "moth-eaten." An inventory is as merciless as a photograph. One almost fancies a quiver of apprehension among the staid respectabilities of the Parson's belongings, as the dread appraiser appears, bearing the measure and the note-book that are to crush the pretensions of many a dignified piece of furniture that has stoutly held its own, in spite of age and infirmities. A "maple couch, with a red damask settee and squab," is still able to pass muster. We hear nothing against the character of the dressing-table, or the frame for a *twigh light* (French of the period) having a "patch-work silk cover." But the two looking-glasses are broken, and of an old writing-case we are told, with the unimaginative coldness of an appraiser, that it is "without implements." A stand and screen, both of mahogany, with eleven "Mezetinto prints," also minister to the comfort and luxury of the Parson's guests. This room boasts a square of carpet and a rug, and is brightened by a red silk quilted "cover-lid." One who sleeps here is indeed magnificently lodged. But the inventory maker has somewhere found "two yards of chexed flannel, very poor," and will insist on inserting this item in his ruthless list, where it appears opposite the sum of three shillings. He also insults the venerable age of a chest and trunk by reducing them to some quite pitiful denomination.

Among the articles of "closet furniture" are pewter plates, platters, and "basons," a good supply of glass and "queensware," earthen pipkins, stone ware, copper kettles, and "dimmy Johns." The Parson is provided with brass candlesticks and brass "chaffing-dishes." In his character of host, he can offer his guests their choice of "flowered wine-glasses, ale, and cyder glasses." They are served from decanters, and their servants are doubtless regaled from the honest earthenware mugs of which the closet affords good store. Fruit-dishes and cream-pots help out the household repasts, tin bake pans and paste pans are in diligent use, and the whole array is presided over by an emblematic "Corna Copia." Some fine table-linen, and more homespun, is carefully laid by, with sundry yards of blue silk, and blue worsted damask. The Parson's especial personal belongings include, among the articles of his wardrobe, one "morning-gownd," in which we may imagine him examining the "wig-case," or possibly the "lead tobacco-box," or the "saddle-bags," the "battle-dores," the "glass lanthorn," the "writing-desk," or even the three cases of bottles, which, with other miscellaneous property, the legal Asmodeus attributes to him.

South County Studies

The "store-room, northwest chamber," contains a quantity of uninteresting old rubbish, which indeed seems to have become stranded all over the house, during the Parson's absence at Esquire Robinson's, leaving household matters to the unrestrained tastes of Caesar, Phillis, George, and the rest.

The "great chamber closet" shows seven good Geneva jugs, with "phials" by way of antidote, a store of spermaceti candles, a side-saddle, and a spinning-wheel.

In the "kitchen chamber" appears an assemblage of articles best described as "assorted, various," in the phrase of the character whom Dickens sketches as the presiding spirit at a similar revel of insane old movables. Here the candle-box confronts the watering-pot, the "cullender" balances the coffee-mill, steel-yards are making acquaintance with a Windsor chair, driven into banishment, while the "tobacco-tongs" and the "iron dogs" are meeting with all the fervor of old friends.

The "old kitchen" presents much the same aspect. "Hand irons," with "tongs and *slice*," are fraternizing with "trammels, skillets and bellows."

In the "south room," farming utensils are gracefully grouped with kitchen furniture. China and tea-canisters are found in close proximity to saddles, whips, ploughs, "iron bars," with "cyder mills, presses and tubs"; also "walking-canes," and a stray "pair of backgammon tables, having two boxes and a set of dies."

"At Mr. Robinson's house," to which the Parson has conveyed his special belongings, we count up "a pair of green spectacles and a reading-glass." Slippers and

Parson Fayerweather's Will

a "double-reined bridle" are coupled by the chaotic-minded appraiser. "One blue broadcloth cloak" would be a very goodly garment were it not sadly moth-eaten. But we hear of a fine red and blue damask morning-gown and other articles of luxury, as linen and even silk handkerchiefs, a toilette box, a pocket book, silver buckles, sundry yards of lawn and of gold thread (valued at £18 6s.), suits of broadcloth and of velvet, rings, seals, and *fiddles*. His plate weighs eighty ounces, "including the pillow-case," as our appraiser cautiously adds, and is worth £24. The Parson has brought with him plenty of household furnishings of which his host and executor takes account. " Counterpins and Holland napkins" are set down with the shagreen case of silver-handled knives and forks, the tin and glass canisters containing a store of the green tea which the Parson loved, also one mahogany teapot, "contents unknown," as the writer of the list solemnly observes.

The whole amount of the Parson's inventoried property stands at £241 7s. 8½d., and the list has been copied into the town records by James Helme, Clerk of the Council.

In the densely literal mood which assails the weary compiler from much manuscript record of a concrete character, even a hero would assume an air of prosaic reality. Our poor Parson can hardly preserve an atmosphere of ideality, after the relentless dealings of his legal adversaries. The painstaking fancy, put under antiquarian instructions, insists on placing him among his inventoried surroundings, and laboriously presents him in the somewhat remarkable apparel of his daily wear, as we learn it from the grotesque exactness of the authorized list. The red and blue damask dressing-gown and the cloak of deep blue broadcloth must be near connections of the long cape, of cardinal red, in which the benevolent Dr. Hopkins, of Newport, was wont to ride about that town, suggesting, as some critic remarks, an animated vision of the lively Friar Tuck, rather than a sober Puritan divine. Nor did the harmless vanities of the world appeal in vain to our pastoral lover of little luxuries.

Yet, if he did not live with the severe simplicity of George Herbert's country parson, he was scarcely less faithful in relieving the sick and poor than that ideal personage. "The amiableness of his character," recognized by his friends and neighbors, led him to find pleasure in the quiet duties of a rural parish. This sympathetic quality of his nature makes the picture of his lonely age the more touching. There is a sad lapse from the fortunes of the young student, passing a bright season in London, receiving the degree of A.M. from Oxford University, and preserving the memory of that flattering honor in his portrait by the famous artist of his time, to the griefs and calamities that pursued the declining years of the old Parson. Losing popularity and influence, while sacrificing his chief means of support in his devotion to the cause of Church and King, he sought a home with a friend — of similar views — whose last days were even more gloomy than his own. His host, having enjoyed great prosperity until the coming of old age, was, through the misconduct of a member of his family, involved in unwonted embarrassments, and subjected to much suffering. Still, one fancies that the two old friends must have had some hours of unbroken comfort together, and that the naturally gay and cheerful temperament of the Parson often proved a cordial to the saddened spirits of his companion, exclusive of those higher consolations to which he doubtless directed him. It is often the *unconscious* ministration to the wants of others that is truest and deepest, and the fitness of the kindly rector of old St. Paul's for such an office may be read even in the precise formulas of the legal instrument which so curiously reveals the quaint but not unpleasing traits of his simple character.

THE WILLETT FAMILY IN RHODE ISLAND

THE ancient burial-place of the Willetts is at the head of a small cove which makes in from Narragansett Bay, nearly two miles above Barrington, Rhode Island. It is described, in an old note-book, as "a little hille in Swanzey, being on thiere owne lande." Here also were buried, according to the writer, "John Brown, Esquire, Father-in-law to Captain Thomas Willett,"— and "My Grandmother Brown, who Departed this life 1673, in ye good olde Age of about Ninety-Six years." The almost illegible inscription on one of the leaning and moss-grown stones shows that it marks the last resting-place — not, as the *Providence Journal* once stated, of Colonel Marinus Willett,— but of *Thomas Willett*, his ancestor and predecessor in office.

Perhaps the earliest notice of the first mayor of New York is to be found in Prince's "Chronological History of New England," and the readers of that curious old annalist will remember the terms in which Willett is described as a young man of energy and ability. Little is known of his ancestry, although it is believed that it might easily be traced. The following notice of his father, the Reverend Andrew Willett, is taken from an "Encyclopedia of Religious Knowledge":

"Andrew Willett, D.D., a learned and laborious divine [is this the modern version of *pious and paineful?*] of the English Church in the reign of Elizabeth. He engaged himself most sedulously, in addition to his professional labors, in digesting the Fathers, Councils, Ecclesiastical Histories, the Civil and Canon

The Willett Family

Law, and other matters. His *Synopsis Papisme* is his most celebrated work. His character as a minister was pleasant and gentle; rather drawing by persuasion than driving by fear. He was killed by a fall from his horse, in his fifty-ninth year, Dec. 4th, 1621."

Thomas Willett, who was one of the last of the Leyden Company, came to New England in 1629. He was then in his twentieth year. Many Rhode Islanders are familiar with the story of his public life, as it is briefly told in the late Wilkins Updike's valuable "History of the Narragansett Church." The notice seems to be partly condensed from Dr. Stiles's "Regicide Judges":

"He was conversant in the fur and Indian trade of the whole coast of Kennebec to Hudson's river, became very opulent, and settled on a plantation in Swanzey, now Barrington, where remains his grave, six miles below Providence. Being an intelligent and respectable person, he went as a counsellor on board of beloved Colonel Nicholls's fleet, at the reduction of Manhadoes, 1664, and was by him appointed Mayor of the new-conquered city. He owned houses in New York and Albany. The Dutch resuming the government, he afterwards returned to his settlement, and died in Barrington." On the stones of his grave there is this inscription:

(*Head Stone*)	(*Foot Stone*)
1674	
HERE LYETH THE BODY	WHO WAS THE FIRST
OF THE WORTHY	MAYOR OF NEW YORK,
THOMAS WILLETT, ESQ.,	AND TWICE DID SUSTAIN
WHO DIED AUGUST 4TH, IN	THAT PLACE
THE 64TH YEAR OF HIS AGE	
ANNO	

He had married, in 1636, Mary, daughter of John Brown, Esq., of Plymouth, and she is buried with him.

The following "epitaph on my worshipful father-in-law" was written by John Saffin, of Boston, who married, in 1658, Martha, the second of Thomas Willett's thirteen children:

> "Here lies Grave Willett, whose good name
> Did Mount upon the wings of Fame;
> Who into Place did not intrude,
> (A Star of the first Magnitude,)
> But's prudence, pietie and zeale
> For God, in Church and Commonweall,
> His reall worth, and Generous Spirit,
> Which constantly he did Inherit,
> His hospitality and love,
> And courteous carriage, like a Dove,
> Did so Excell, that all might See
> He had attain'd to the First Three.
> Now he's hence gone to his long home,
> And taken from the Ill to come—
> Liv'd here Desir'd; lamented Dy'd;
> Is with his Saviour, Glorified."

The will of "Capt. Thomas Willett" is a very long document, drawn up with minute particularity. It contains legacies to the "overseers" of the instrument, and to the churches of the neighboring towns. Some old servants are also remembered. He then devises his extensive estates in New Plymouth, Swanzey, and Rehoboth to his sons, James, Hezekiah, Andrew, and Samuel, and his Narragansett lands to his grandchildren; but Thomas, son of John and Martha Saffin, is to inherit a double portion. As early as July 4, 1659, certain lands in ancient Namcook, afterwards part of

The Willett Family

the "King's Province," but generally known as Boston Neck, and situated near the present Narragansett Ferry, had been purchased of three sachems by Willett and others. This small part of the Willett property, reserved by its owner as a suitable portion for his grandchildren, is still held by his descendants, while all the other estates have long since been divided and alienated. A singular provision of the will was, that if any one of his *sons* (the daughters were all married but one) should marry without the consent of a majority of the five executors, he would by that act forfeit all claims to his inheritance.

James, the eldest son, like the rest, probably consented to accept a wife from the grave and discreet committee who were charged to look after the family interests in that respect, for he married Eliza, daughter of Lieutenant Peter Hunt, of Rehoboth, and continued to live on the paternal estate. Hezekiah married his cousin, Anna Brown, daughter of John Brown, 2d, also of Rehoboth, and was killed in King Philip's War, 1676. Samuel was sheriff of Queen's County, Long Island. His son Edward died in 1794, at the great age of ninety-three. One of his thirteen children was Colonel Marinus Willett, a Revolutionary officer, who afterwards became mayor of New York. He is also remembered as a correspondent of Aaron Burr, and by his portrait in the City Hall. He died in 1830, aged ninety years. His name is still represented by his descendants in New York City.

Of the Willett sisters, Sarah was married to an Eliot, and Mary to Samuel Hooker, of Farmington, Connecticut. Dr. Stiles says that another married one of the family of the Reverend John Wilson, of Boston—the "Holy Wilson" of Cotton Mather's eulogies. Hester or Esther Willett (the name appears under the latter form in her father's will) was the wife of the Reverend Josiah Flint, of Dorchester, now a part of Boston. He preached before the Ancient and Honorable Artillery Company, of Boston, in 1677. Their daughter, Dorothy, married Edmund Quincy, the ancestor of Josiah Quincy, the Revolutionary patriot, and of his son, who was president of Harvard College. This lady's daughter was the "Damsel Dorothy, Dorothy Q.," whom we all remember in one of the most spirited and graceful of Dr. Holmes's recent poems. She married Edward Jackson. Their son Jonathan was father of the celebrated Dr. James Jackson, and their daughter Mary married Judge Oliver Wendell of Boston, whose daughter Sarah was wife of the Reverend Abiel Holmes, D.D., author of "American Annals," and mother both of Dr. Oliver Wendell Holmes and of Mary Jackson Holmes, who married the late Usher Parsons, M.D., of Providence.

Martha Willett, who is said to have been remarkable both for beauty and amiability, became the wife of "John Saffin, eldest sonne of Simon Saffin, merchant, of Exeter, England, and Grace his wife." He was Speaker of the Assembly of Massachusetts in 1686, lived in Boston and Bristol, and has left a curious manuscript book (dated 1665), half diary, half a collection of "Sundry Readings Epitomized," the whole interspersed with verse, chiefly elegiac, of which the specimens already given will perhaps suffice, although some of his effusions attained the dignity of print, and all were

The Willett Family

much admired by judicious friends, few of whom could have been omitted from his poetical addresses. He was indeed a most persistent rhymer, and even wrote lines to his mother-in-law, after her death. A versified letter to Governor Joseph Dudley was prompted by "the newes that his Excellency was on the —— of January, 1704, going over Charles River upon the Ice, with his Wife and Daughters, in a Sley drawn by four Horses, when the Ice suddenly brake, and all the Horses falling into the River, the two hindermost were Drowned, and his Excellency and his, hardly escaped, but were Wonderfully preserved, *Laus Deo!*"

In glancing over these pages we find not only elegies and epitaphs inflicted upon the memories of scholars, divines, and statesmen, all in such verse as the harsh Puritanical muse of the New England of that day was pleased to inspire, but some productions which at first sight appear to be of a more lively character, until a closer observation proves them all to wear the same sad-colored Puritan livery. Acrostics, valentines, madrigals, all are taking their pleasure sadly, and scarcely differ in style from the "Elegies," or the "Lamentations upon the Dolefull State of our Newe Englande."

More interesting, and not less quaint, are the occasional glimpses of his personal history, recorded with a fidelity and simplicity worthy of his contemporary Pepys. The following is the first record in his journal:

"*Memorium.* That in the Beginning of November, 1665 I was joyned to the First Church in Boston: GOD in Mercy make me faithful to His Covenant."

He relates his marriage to Martha Willett by "Mr.

Wm. Collier, one of the Magistrates." He was afterwards the survivor, by many years, of her, and of their eight sons, who are interred, with their mother, in a tomb in "the upper Burying Place of the Towne of Boston." The deaths of "my thrice Dearly Beloved Consort," of "my Sweet Son Scimon," and of four other sons, are attributed to that "Deadly Disease of the Small Pox." Even so slight notice as the manuscript affords of this child, who died in his twelfth year, is yet enough to show his nature to have been distinguished by that purity and sensibility, always so touching and interesting when associated with the memory of early suffering and death. Such illustrations of the power of religious teaching could have been of no infrequent occurrence in New England, where, for the first time in modern history, the appeal of spiritual truth was directed to spiritual perceptions only, and a whole people lived in the sense of constant communion with the Invisible and the Eternal. His conversations with his minister, and with his physician (who seems to have thought his mind, although in an exalted state, quite calm and free from any disturbing influence), perfectly simple and childlike as they are, plainly express the depth and fervor of his religious feeling. "And so," writes his father, "he passed tryumphantly to Heaven. He often said, 'Mother, Brother John, come away, make haste'; adding, that Mr. Thatcher did looke and waite for him, and that there was Room enough for all in Heaven." They soon followed him, and their deaths are recorded by the same hand. It is not difficult to read between the lines in this brief, stern story of the sudden and fearful calamity which swept away so many hopes and affections with these young lives — closing, as it does, with the heart-broken utterance, referring to his eldest son: "But GOD tooke him alsoe away by Death with ye same Disease of ye Small Pox, to my amazing grief at ye loss of him, and so many in so short a time." This was John, who, at sixteen, had already entered upon his college course, with the fairest prospects of future success, perhaps eminence. A classmate, Grindall Rawson, who was afterwards an eccentric Puritan divine, sends to the mourning father an "Elegie upon the death of his much-esteemed Friend." There is a rude dignity of consolation in the concluding lines, which express a hope that the elegy:

> "May say to those who still survive,
> Though John and Martha die, yet God's alive."

Judge Saffin was subsequently married by the "Worshipfull Joseph Dudley, Esquire," to Mistress Elizabeth Lidgett, and after her death in 1687, to Rebecca Lee, daughter of the Reverend Samuel Lee, whose misfortunes as a prisoner of war are so well known. Her son-in-law records his death in a foreign land, "to the great and irreparable loss of the whole family, and a university of learning," and, it is needless to say, devotes some closely written pages to a rhymed memorial of his virtues. It is followed by an address to "Richard, Earle of Bellamont, Governor of His Majesty's Province of the Massachusetts Bay" (and whom, of course, "Heaven hath *sent* To be a star in this, our Firma*ment*"), upon his assumption of that office. It contains an allusion to the writer's recent losses in Rhode Island. These are explained by the curt language of the public record of that colony for 1679: "John Saffin tried for adhering to another jurisdiction, sentenced to forfeit all his estates and pay a fine" — at all of which John Saffin was naturally indignant, and, in these lines, expressing himself in the usual fraternal style adopted by the Colonists of the Bay when referring to those of the Plantations, he brands them as

"False, perfidious, vile Rhode Islanders!"

But we may contemplate this stubborn upholder of his fancied rights against his real interests — who might well say of himself, in his own artless verse,

"I doe endeavor alle I can
To show myself a true-born Englishmanne,"

in a more pleasing aspect, by recalling his filial devotion, so apparent in the following words, which certainly are no less touching for their precision and quaintness:

"A copie of a patheticall, pious, Instructive Letter, written by my owne deare and Hon'd Mother, Mrs. Grace Saffin, alias Ellsworth, her owne hand-writing, w'ch, being worne allmost in pieces, I for its singular worth, here Revived it.

Dated London, the first of March, 1654.
Deare Sonne:
Three Letters I Rec'd. by Mr. Winslow, hereby I perceive you are goeing a Voyage for Virginia; I cannot but admire at God's Love and Mercy, both to me and mine, that He doth look upon us in all Estates and conditions wheresoever we are, Either far or near; O my

The Willett Family

Soul, bless the Lord, that heard our Prayer, and hath not left us to the will of them that would have Trodden us Down, and cryed there is no help for us [this was in ye Civil War, between ye King and Parliament. J. S.] But the Lord was in the Mount when men rose up against us... And I may say againe, with Jacob, The Lord hath blessed me and mine.... Your loveing Mother,

Grace Ellsworth."

Judge Saffin died in Bristol, in 1710, aged seventy-eight, having, as he says, seen the Commonwealth and the reigns of five English Sovereigns. The home which he built on the Boston Neck estate in 1692 — the terrible witchcraft year — was only occupied by him for three years, afterwards passing, together with the land, into the ownership of his brother-in-law, Andrew Willett, who has been previously mentioned as a son of Thomas Willett. He made his home in a wild region. The Indians, it is true, must have been nearly subdued by this time, but tradition speaks of the foxes and wolves that disturbed the early settlers, much later than this. The original tract, like most of those selected by Boston purchasers, consisted of six hundred and sixty acres, but the newcomer, doubtless glad enough to secure a neighbor in the unsettled country where his house as yet stood alone, sold three hundred acres to Rowland Robinson. The remainder is still in the possession of his lineal descendants. He had been for some years a merchant in Boston, where he married Anne Coddington. He brought with him to Boston Neck, an iron-bound, oaken chest, about three feet square and containing four metal bottles. It came from Leyden among other effects belonging to Thomas Willett, and had been the property of his father. This rather curious relic of ancient times and customs remained standing in the old house until 1857, when it was forwarded to the Rhode Island Historical Society. Andrew Willett's grave was the first to be made in the family burying-place on the farm. His children were: Francis, Thomas, Mary, Anne, and Martha. The latter married Simon Pease, a well-known merchant of Newport. Thomas died young. Anne married, in 1707, Joseph Carpenter, eldest son of Joseph Carpenter of Glen Cove, Long Island. She lived but a few years. The widower afterwards married her sister Mary. Francis, the eldest, married Mary Taylor (whose niece of the same name was afterwards the wife of John Gardiner, son of William, the first of the Narragansett family), and inherited the whole estate on the death of his father, which is thus recorded in the son's finished and elegant handwriting: "My Hon'd Father, Captain Andrew Willett, Departed this Life on ye 6th of April, Anno Domini, 1712, in ye 57th yeare of his age." An interesting account of "Francis Willett, Esquire," is furnished by his friend, Dr. Ezra Stiles:

"This is the gentleman with whom I was intimately acquainted. He was educated a merchant, but did not pursue commerce. He had a good genius and was a man of much reading and information, and, settling on the paternal estate, he lived the life of a private gentleman. He was hospitable and generous, of excellent moral, and highly respected and estimable character. The fine tract of Boston Neck was owned by the

The Willett Family

Sewalls, and other gentlemen of Boston. This, with his father's former residence in Boston, and transacting business for these Boston land-owners, and for Harvard College, brought him into an acquaintance with the first characters of Boston. They visited him through life, and often gave him great public information. Once a year these gentlemen visited their estates, and at his father's house. After his father's death, in 1712, the management and superintendence of these estates, and of the College estates, together with the extensive family acquaintance, fell into the care of Colonel Francis Willett, whose aunts had married into ministers' families — Wilson, in Massachusetts, and Hooker, in Connecticut. The Willett farm was a tract extending from Narragansett Bay northward, perhaps one mile and a half in length on the bay, and about one mile or more east and west from the bay across to an oblong pond called Petaquamscott, and was the original seat of the great Sachem Miantinomi. [A large boulder on the farm is still known as Miantinomi's Rock.] At the north end of this pond, and on the Willett farm, the celebrated Colonel Whale or Whalley, styled one of King Charles's regicide-judges, resided, and before his death removed to West Greenwich, and died there."

Dr. Stiles collected, among the Willetts and others, several particulars relating to this somewhat extraordinary man, all of which may be found in his "Judges." The Doctor's conclusion was that Theophilus Whale, formerly a resident of Narragansett, had been an officer in the Parliament wars, and through the Protectorate. His grave is in Greenwich, on land belonging to a descendant, and can be seen from the highway, there called the "Ten Rod Road." It is a very long one, lying north and south, with stones, but no inscription. "He was a large, tall man, six feet high when a centenarian, and then walked upright; not fat, but thin and lathy; was one hundred and three when he died."

The scholar and antiquarian who sought so diligently for some shadowy memories of this strange being is now himself a shadow, haunting the traditions of the place. Mrs. Stowe's novel shows him in the most unfavorable light; but, whatever his speculative opinions may have been, his learning was certainly extensive and varied, and it is not too much to say of him, that his faithful search among the memorials of our Colonial time was one of the greatest services that could be rendered to New England and to the whole country. It is said that in one of his visits to Boston Neck, toward the close of the eighteenth century (Colonel Willett, his early friend, had passed away, but he continued his intimacy with the family), the conversation happening to turn upon the powerful current of the Mississippi, and its imperfect navigation by flatboats, the Doctor expressed to the lady of the house his belief that the great river of the northwestern territory would yet be traversed by ships propelled only by *steam*—"the same familiar force, madam, which you may observe at any time lifting the cover of your tea-kettle." Remembering that Mr. Parton, in a recent paper, mentions Dr. Stiles among Jefferson's regular correspondents, it would seem that one of his letters might have furnished the foundation for this opinion. The idea of the use of steam as a motive power in navigation, although destined to be rejected some years later by the First Consul and his advisers, must have already assumed greater proportions in the calm thought of the quiet scholar than among many less "visionary" persons.

A few more particulars of Colonel Willett's life may be added here. He was several times a Representative in the Colonial Assembly, and for a long time kept, in his own house, the records of a large tract of country, now divided into three townships. He was one of the principal contributors toward the purchase of the Glebe estate, intended as an endowment for the rectors of old St. Paul's. This church represented the parish of which he was vestryman for many years. The church, the oldest, except Trinity in Newport, ever used for the Episcopal form of worship in Rhode Island, has since been removed to Wickford, Rhode Island, where it is still occasionally occupied for commemorative services. He had a truly English love of trees, and, besides his orchards, planted hundreds of sycamores and hickories in groves, or set them, like hedges, by his boundary walls. A row of Lombardy poplars before the house was destroyed by the great gale of 1815, but a really magnificent plantation of oaks survived to a much later date. Some of them had attained a century's growth. His successor, who shared his taste in this particular, was the first to plant the horse-chestnut tree in the Narragansett country. One of these trees, which has seen more than a hundred years, is still alive.

Francis Willett was, until quite lately, remembered by a grandniece, who described him as tall and dignified, but very old, and supporting himself by a cane. Far too old to change with the changing times, he died a loyal subject of King George, early in 1776, aged eighty-three years. As he left no children, the Willett name died with him, but his vacant place in the homestead was filled by his nephew,[1] whom he had educated as a son.

Some plate marked with the initials of "Francis and Mary Willett," some china, and the tall English clock which appears in the inventory of his grandfather's estate have escaped the Revolutionary confusion, and are still in use among his remote kinsfolk. A few books, too, the scattered fragments of his rather large library, display on the fly-leaf his name, "Fra: Willett," as he occasionally signed it, or sometimes the inscription denotes that the book comes from Parson Fayerweather, who is liberal in compliments to his "worthy, esteemed, respected friend and parishioner."

The simple virtues of an honest country gentleman are not commonly supposed to outlast the ink of his obituary by very many years; yet one sometimes meets with a pleasing exception to the general rule which leads each generation to efface, with ruthless haste, the memory of its predecessor from the worn palimpsest of Time, to trace thereon its own immortal record. In a recent conversation between two middle-aged gentlemen, in which Francis Willett's name was casually introduced, the listener, who had heard him spoken of by one as "Uncle" and by the other as "Esquire" Willett, would have believed that they must at least have known him in their childhood, whereas the tall blue slate-stone, whose cherubic effigy is graciously veiled from sight by the clinging mosses, has been his

---

[1] This nephew was Francis Carpenter, great-grandfather of Esther Bernon Carpenter, who spent her earliest years in this house.

The Willett Family

only representative to them. A memory, a sentiment, seems to linger in the still air of secluded places, undisturbed by the changeful and stormy currents which prevail elsewhere. May it not be said that a blessing dwells with this tranquil presence? In our restless times, in our rapid alternations from anxiety to frivolity, the grateful memory of the past comes to us with a cool freshness, and we may certainly be the better for thinking over the simple, natural lives of people who might perhaps be unworldly and unambitious, but who were thoroughly high-minded, intelligent, honorable, and sincere.

THE WORLDLY GOODS OF A PURITAN
FROM THE WILLETT PAPERS

THE inventories of our forefathers' worldly goods, made out with the conscientious and painstaking diligence customary in the Colonial times of leisurely simplicity, afford a sort of photographic record of the every-day life of a Puritan household. Whoever has unearthed one of these creased and yellowed old documents will readily recall the interest with which he explored its dusty pages for suggestive items, as he followed the worthy appraisers in their tortuous progress through all the nooks and corners of the house, while engaged in the minute examination which duty obliged them to make of its contents after the departure of its master for a far country. In the faded chirography of the paper now before us, the inventory of the estate of Captain Andrew Willett, a Boston merchant in middle life, but at the time of his death a substantial householder of Boston Neck, Kingstown, Rhode Island, and a son to the worshipful Thomas Willett, first mayor of New York City, we may find enumerated among the goods and chattels sundry inanimate acquaintances of long standing, familiarized to us by their associations with the pages of old English novels, or even with the lines of Shakespeare, the amber of whose verse has preserved many stray sticks and straws floated down to us from eddies in the current of time.

The date of our paper is 1712, and the house described is the homestead built by John Saffin,[1] son-in-

[1] On the hill in Saunderstown, known as the Carpenter Place.

Worldly Goods of a Puritan

law of Thomas Willett, in 1692, and which stood until 1872.

"In the Haull," as our recorder hath it, we find imprimis:

1 napkin press of wallnut	£3	—s.
1 oake table ovoll	2	—
2 ditto square	—	10

One of these last-named tables, "turned all over with knobs and rings," but having only the usual complement of legs, was of the variety mysteriously known as "hundred-legged" (our rude forefathers had not learned to say *centipede*). To continue our brief selections from the list:

7 leather chairs	£3	—s.
6 do wooden bottoms	—	12
3 do flag bottoms	—	9
2 joynt Stooles	—	1
2 Turkey work carpets	2	—
1 looking glass	1	—
1 paire bellows	—	1
1 do hand irons	2	—
Shovell and tongs	—	12
4 brushes and prospective Glass	—	7
1 case of knives and forks	—	10
1 silver tankard, 2 porringers, 2 cups and 9 Spoons	26	—
20 glass bottles of severall sorts	5	—
1 clock	3	—

The valuation is most punctiliously made; and we learn, for instance, from this accurate paper that the above-named "joynt Stooles" are estimated at absolutely no hundreds and no tens of pounds, but are simply to be rated at one shilling. The eight-day clock is still in use, and has not yet faltered in its stern duty of ticking away frail mortal lives. It has told the hours of birth, bridal, and burial for five generations of its owners, and it stood for more than one hundred and fifty years in the same homestead where this inventory was prepared.

"In the roome adjoining below stairs" (the sleeping-room lately occupied by the deceased) are found:

1 feather bed, curtins, vallons, pillows, bolster and blankets, coverlid and bedstead	£10	—s.
1 trunnell bedstead and feather bed, blanket and rugg	5	—
3 larg chests	1	10
2 portmantell and 2 pillions	—	10
2 wast belts	2	—
2 sworde silver hilts	5	—
2 pr. of pistolls	4	—
1 silver buchell and wast girdle	8	—
2 pr. of old curtains	2	—
1 pr. money scales and weights	—	9
1 pr. brass scales and 1 brass compass	—	12
Bookes of several sorts, history and other, 94	15	—

This library, of nearly a hundred volumes, was a large collection to be owned by our Narragansett captain and yeoman, at a period but little later than that of which Macaulay writes: "An esquire then passed for a great scholar among his neighbors if 'Hudibras,' and 'Baker's Chronicle,' 'Tarlton's Jests,' and 'The Seven Champions of Christendom,' lay in his hall window, among the fishing rods and fowling pieces." The hand that had girded on the "wast belt" and grasped the "sworde" and "pistoll" of the list, had also known the finer uses of the "bookes of history" which were studied here in this little corner of an obscure province at the close of that century which our authority calls "the least intelligent in the later English annals."

One significant word, the name of Puritan, will indicate the contrast between the British and the colonial esquires, and show us why we find the latter furnished not only "Like a servant of the Lord, with his Bible and his sword," but not devoid of interest in those branches of learning to which, as our own Palfrey has shown, the genuine Puritan was no stranger. One of these volumes was the ponderous "Du Bartas," of 1621, and another, a "Practicall Catechism," of 600 closely printed octavo pages of Puritan theology, bears on the title-page the autograph of "Tho: Willett," the father of Andrew, whose estate is the subject of our inventory. Both were doubtless zealous readers of so precious a manual, and it is still, if not "daily conned," at least regarded with the respect due to its weight of learning and its association with the departed worthies.

We will now inspect the goodly plenishings of the "Haull Chamber" or "spare room." Here are £28 worth of bedding, and an equal valuation is set upon the stores of "Linning," "Holland," and "Diaper." We also note such choice luxuries as the following:

6 Turkey worke chairs	£6	—s.
6 chairs covered with serge	3	—
1 ouall table	1	—
1 chest of drawers	2	10
1 looking glass	—	15
1 case with pewter bottles	—	10

South County Studies

This last-named relic of old-time customs, an iron-bound, oaken chest, about three feet square and containing four bottles, was brought by Thomas Willett from Leyden in 1629. It had belonged to his father, and, as tradition says, had been carried by him in sundry campaigns under the English flag. It is now in the possession of the Rhode Island Historical Society.

1 pr. larg brass andirons	£4	–s.
1 pr. small brass doggs	–	6
1 chimbley iron back	–	12

From a hasty glance at the humble "kitchin chamber" we bring away a list of bedding at £10, while the bedstead and its "curtains and vailins of Camblet," are valued at £1. "Two pair andirons," with a "wrought quilt coverlid," and "two old flag-bottom chairs," are worth no more than £5 19s. "In the long room" the "oats, barley and wheat," with the "two old chests and two boxes" which contain them, are estimated at £3 4s. "In the garrat," the "twenty pounds feathers and three old flock beds with bedding" are set down in the sum of £3.

"In the kitchen" are found:

36 pewter dishes	£12	5s.
1 copper pott	1	4
Brass kettles of severall sorts	6	18
1 large iron kettle and 2 small ditto	1	5
3 iron potts	–	6
1 pr large andirons	1	–
1 iron back	1	–

This chimney back bore in rude figures an early date of the seventeenth century.

Worldly Goods of a Puritan

3 trammells	£1	—s.
2 frying pans	—	15
3 spits	—	18
2 gridirons	—	3
1 iron fender	—	3
3 pr pot hookes and 2 chafindish	—	10
1 ladle and flesh fork and 2 smoothing boxes and heaters	—	10
2 gunns	3	—
3 brass candlesticks and 3 iron ones	1	2
2 pr sheep shares and 1 hammer	—	6
2 skillet frames	—	2
2 spinning wheels wooden and 2 linning do	—	14
1 iron driping pan	—	12

Brass and iron seem to have been among the precious metals of the period. When they were so highly valued it was not strange that in the stories which a certain old Guinea negro used to tell in this kitchen he always described the household utensils of the king, his father, as made of gold-iron.

1 brass pestell, & mortar, and 3 axes	14s.
2 sawes, 1 drawing knife, 2 augers, 1 goug and chisell	12
1 pr of old wheell boxes	10
2 sithes, 1 carpenter's addze	6
3 old sithes & 3 forke	15

"To more in the house" is the next entry under which appear such miscellaneous matters as:

3 chaines	£1	4s.
Iron for 2 horse garrds	—	6
2 saddles	1	—
1 pillion	10	—
2 brides	2	—
1 cart & ox bow, & irons and yoakes	3	6
1 iron bar, 3 hoes	—	16

23 old milk keelers	£2	3s.
1 churne & a cheese Tub	—	12
8 cheese fatts	—	10
Old barr'ls & tubs	—	5

"In the Crib" the appraisers find:

Corne, about 40 bush'ls	£4	—s.
2 oxen	10	—
6 cows	44	—
2 three-year old heffers	5	—
2 steers, three-year olds	2	6
1 bull	4	—
6 yearlings	7	10
180 sheep	63	—
2 horses	7	—
13 hogs, young & old	3	14

With a singular sense of the fitness of things, the appraisers here insert the item:

To his wearing apparell of all sorts	£30	—s.
Silver-headed cane	15	—
3 silver salts	1	—

After this casual interruption, the list of stock is thus resumed:

1 negro man	£30	—s.
1 negro woman	25	—
1 pr. of brass scales	—	6
1 cart rope	—	2
Country bills	22	—
A warming pan	—	10
6 milk and water pales	—	6
1 currell and whisell	—	15
3 sickells	—	4
1 copper wattering pot	10	—
1 grindstone	—	10

Worldly Goods of a Puritan

The whole amount of the inventoried property of Captain Andrew Willett is but £515 15s., according to the valuation of the appraisers, "Cha: Dickinson," a vestryman, in 1718, of St. Paul's, Narragansett, and "Nath'l Coddington," a relative of Andrew Willett's widow.

The formula signed by "Sam'l ffones, Town Clerke," runs as follows: "Major Nath'l Coddington and Mr. Charles Dickinson, the above subscribers, did both personally appear before the Town Counsel of Kingstown the 22nd day of Aprill 1712 and Did Declare upon oath the above and within written Inventory, upon two Sheets of paper was a True Inventory of what was presented to their View to the best of their Understanding."

A great part of the old Kingstown records having been destroyed by fire, there is probably no copy extant of this faithful inventory. After the searching examination which we have made of the personal effects of the deceased, we feel that we cannot accuse him (even according to the primitive standards of his time) of devotion to the vainglory of the world, nor deny him whatever merit there may be in the moderate use of comforts and the renunciation of luxuries. Such insight as the legal record affords concerning his character and surroundings leads us from this particular inquiry to more general speculations, and that mild form of moralizing into which the reader of much musty manuscript naturally falls, prompts us to muse upon the mental and spiritual legacies which are occasionally left by those whose worldly goods would not fill even so long a list as stands in the name of our Puritanic yeoman.

THE HELMES OF SOUTH KINGSTOWN

THE Helme family homestead, dating from a century and a half ago, and built after the usual fashion of esquire's houses at that period, is still standing, on Tower Hill, in South Kingstown, Rhode Island. On the opposite side of the ancient highway is a large burial-ground, the former site of the Congregational Church, of which Dr. Joseph Torrey, of Newport, was pastor, from the organization of the parish, 1732, until his death, some sixty years later, and here are buried many of the Helmes, with others of the first settlers of Narragansett.

> "Go where the ancient pathway guides,
>   See where our sires laid down
> Their smiling babes, their cherished brides,
>   The patriarchs of the town;
> Hast thou a tear for buried love?
>   A sigh for transient power?
> All that a century left above,
>   Go, read it in an hour!"

Tower Hill was named, and to some extent settled, so early as the days of Roger Williams, who mentions, as a familiar landmark, the craggy ledge on the summit of the Hill, called by him Pettaquamscutt Rock, although now known by the less distinctive, if more agreeable, name of Narragansett Rock. Although it is claimed for Tower Hill — and no doubt justly — that it was once the home of hospitality, ease, and elegance, few vestiges of its former estate now remain, and the occasional visitor cares less for the faded splendors of a century ago, than for the immortal beauty of the landscape, to which Nature has granted the fairest features of both coast and inland scenery — the rich green fields and slopes, the wall of purple forest, dark against the western horizon, the gracefully winding stream, the glimpse of New England's most beautiful seaport looking far and unreal through the fast-gathering mists, and beyond all, the broad freedom of ocean-view. Still the traditions of the spot will always possess a certain interest, especially for those who belong to the Narragansett country. Here, for instance, is the old house once occupied by the descendants of Jireh Bull, and built on the original site of the block-house, held during Philip's War by a garrison of fifteen persons, including women and children, and where Captain Church's men expected to pass the night before the battle, known to Narragansett tradition as the Great Swamp Fight; but arrived to find only the smoking ruins of the building, and to learn that only two of the garrison had escaped torture and death at the hands of their savage foes. What wonder that they all fought with so desperate a courage on the morning that succeeded such a night?

Tower Hill was the ancient seat of the County Court, since transferred to Kingston Village. Here stood court-house, jail, church, and school-house. The school was supported by the Sewall Fund. The building in which the boys of 1773 conned their tasks, constructed with an ingenious defiance of all the sanitary regulations which modern science has taught us to regard as indispensable, still survives;[1] too insignificant to suffer

---

[1] This old school-house was blown down in October, 1923; the Helme and Bull houses long preceded it.

from the envy of time. Here, also, was the old-time tavern, with its swinging sign, classically lettered "*Pro Bono Publico*," underneath which the cheerful stage-coach drew up, with much rustic ceremony, once a week, while the village idlers gathered to hear the latest intelligence from New London or Newport. The broad, natural plain at the foot of the hill, used by the Colonial militia as a training-ground, was also the place of execution for capital offenders. Here once stood the gibbet on which Carter, the execrated murderer of Jackson, after protesting his innocence in a speech, the hardened assertions of which thrilled the spectators with horror, suffered the last rigors of English law, which sought to avenge the crime by denying a burial to the lifeless remains of the criminal. Strange picture of Colonial times! Strange union of the purity and sacredness of domestic life with the senseless barbarities of an uncivilized age and nation!

In the graveyard mentioned above, the stones, of the shape so aptly described as "high-shouldered" by a New England poet, display the rude likenesses of cherubs, or, in those of later date, of weeping willows, with borders of carving intended to be ornamental—the inscriptions, plain and concise—mere names and dates, hallowed by a text of Scripture, thus marking the transition period from the simple unconscious quaintness of our earlier times to the greater complexity of taste which now prevails. Hence, no epitaph can be found in the least suggestive of that one on a respected citizen of primitive Boston, so manifestly inspired by "the unlettered Muse," who, after solemnly pacing through several long-drawn lines, replete with

The Helmes of South Kingstown

the usual pious commonplaces, with a suddenness quite startling in funereal literature, turns a sharp corner by hoping, in well-meant but slightly unsteady rhyme, that, in a future state of existence,

> "We ever may be happy
> With virtuous William Paddy."

Little, indeed, can be learned from the monuments, almost as silent as the buried tenants of the graves beneath. What does this sunken stone, on which the brief line of record is nearly effaced by the storms of more than a hundred winters, tell us of the changeful life of the "Madam Hester Powell," to whose memory it was erected?—a native of Rochelle, but, exiled from that Huguenot stronghold in early womanhood, accompanying her mother, the wife of Gabriel Bernon, in her dangerous flight to Holland, then marrying a Protestant gentleman of Welsh family, emigrating with him to the town of Newport, in the hospitable Rhode Island Colony, and, after his death, coming to spend her few remaining years near the quiet country home of her children. The reticent stone gives no hint of all the strange chances which brought a daughter of ancient Rochelle, "proud city of the waters," to find a last resting-place on the remote Narragansett shore.

The Helmes were probably of Puritan ancestry, in the direct line. A *Gawen* [Gawain?] Helme was one of the "Massachusetts Company." The family history is so interwoven with that of the Bernons, that it will be necessary to refer briefly to the latter. Gabriel Bernon, a Huguenot exile, and ancestor of several Rhode Island families, as the Dorrs, Allens, Dyers, Hoppins,

Crawfords, Whipples, and others, was of an honorable family in Rochelle, France, where he held the office of hereditary registrar. The name of Bernon appears in Froissart's Chronicles. Benjamin Faneuil, the father of Peter Faneuil, the Boston merchant, was a relative of Gabriel Bernon, and came with him to America. The latter, after suffering two years' imprisonment for his Protestant opinions, escaped to Holland just before the revocation of the Edict of Nantes, sailed from there for England, remained some years in London, came thence to Boston, lived in Newport, and for ten years in Narragansett; but fixed his permanent residence in Providence, where he was instrumental in the establishment of St. John's Church. His first wife was Hester or Ester LeRoy, daughter of François LeRoy, of Rochelle; his second was Mary, daughter of William Harris, who landed with Roger Williams, at What Cheer Rock. This lady accompanied him to England, where both were presented at the court of Queen Anne. He died in 1736, aged ninety-two years. "He was decently buried, under the Episcopal Church at Providence [St. John's, where a mural tablet to his memory has recently been erected], and a great concourse of people attended his funeral, to whom the Rev. Mr. Brown preached an agreeable eloquent sermon, from Psalm xxxix: iv."

Hester, a daughter of the first wife, married Adam ap Howell, or Powell. Her widowhood was passed in Narragansett, where she died in 1746. Her grave on Tower Hill has been already described. "Madam Powell's pew" could still be identified in the old Narragansett Church, prior to its removal to Wickford, in 1800.

The Helmes of South Kingstown

Her husband's name is connected with a curious anecdote, which so vividly recalls the time of the witchcraft delusion, that it is here quoted from a letter of his great-grandson, the late Willett Carpenter, of North Kingstown:

"My mother was wont to relate the following story as an instance of her grandfather's shrewdness. He was a Newport merchant, and made frequent journeys to Boston and Salem, attended by his negro servant, Peter, who, whilst at one of these places, went into the Court-house, where some of the witches were on trial. On his return to the house where his master lodged, he was taken apparently with convulsion fits, falling down in great agony, and the people of the house called him bewitched, but Mr. Powell, who had expressed much indignation at the scenes he had lately witnessed, declared with much energy that nobody should be hanged for Peter, for he would himself undertake his cure. Accordingly, having observed him some time attentively, he applied his horsewhip to Peter (but for the first and only time), with such effect that he gladly returned to his duty."

It is also *storied*, as the quaint old diarists say, that one of the Helme family once visited Salem Court House when the "witches" and their accusers were confronted with one another. He had scarcely entered when one of the sufferers, a young woman, was attacked with convulsions, which, of course, elicited much sympathy from the spectators. When, on her recovery, she was asked the name of the sorcerer whose spells had been the cause of her suffering, she promptly replied that it was the stranger who had just come in!

South County Studies

But while the officers of the law, animated by the indignation of the whole assembly, were sternly seeking the offender, whose recent entrance had been overlooked, all attention being centred on the afflicted girls, Mr. Helme lost no time in escaping from the court house and the town, no doubt glad enough to regain the land of Roger Williams and liberty.

This story is suggestive of the examination, in Salem Meeting House, of honest Captain Alden (son of the first John Alden, of Plymouth). His sword was taken from him because it was said that he afflicted his accusers with it. "He was bid to look upon the afflicted, at which they would presently fall down. Then Alden asked [Judge] Gedney why his looking upon *him* did not cause *him* to fall down also, but Gedney could give no reason."

The only children of Adam and Hester Powell were Ester and Elizabeth, both of whom were educated in Boston. The latter married, in 1733, the Reverend Samuel Seabury, a graduate of Harvard College, who had been preparing for the Congregational ministry, but was induced by the arguments of the Reverend Dr. MacSparran, rector of St. Paul's, Narragansett, to take orders in the English Church, was appointed by the Venerable Society first missionary to New London, and was afterwards rector of Hempstead, Long Island. At the time of his marriage to Miss Powell he was a widower with one son, the Samuel Seabury who was, in 1784, consecrated as the first Bishop in America.

Ester Powell married, in 1738, James Helme, Esq., of Tower Hill, eldest of the twelve sons of Rowse Helme, the first of the name in Narragansett. She died while

The Helmes of South Kingstown

still comparatively young—in her forty-sixth year,—leaving a family of seven sons and one daughter, and was sincerely mourned by her husband, who remained constant to her memory all his life.

His election by the General Assembly as Chief Justice of the Supreme Court of the colony took place in 1767, and he was reëlected through all the changes of the times as Chief or Associate Justice of the same until 1775. He died two years later, and is buried on Tower Hill. His political sympathies may be divined from the tenor of the following letter, addressed to Martin Howard, Jr., a Newport lawyer and politician, who had been, in 1765, appointed by the Crown stampmaster for the colony, jointly with Augustus Johnson and Dr. Moffatt. Their houses were immediately attacked and much injured by a mob. The unpopular trio fled, but Mr. Howard received a more lucrative appointment. Some time afterwards, when visiting his Newport friends, he observed to Secretary Ward, "Henry, you may rely upon it, I shall have no quarrel with the Sons of Liberty in Newport, for they made me Chief Justice of North Carolina, with a thousand pounds sterling a year."

S. Kingstown, Dec. 30th, 1766.

My Dear Sir:

By my good friend Dr. Moffatt I rec'd your favour of Aug. 10th, as also your most acceptable Present; so extremely welcome, so exactly useful, that you have really given Sight to the Blind, and I beg to return my most hearty thanks.

Your appointment to the Chief Seat of Justice in

North Carolina, and your safe arrival, gave me the most sensible Pleasure, especially as I am told the Post will be worth £1000 or £1200 sterl'g a year. I heartily congratulate you thereon. Your favourable Reception by the King's Ministers, and the Honours you have received, as they give your Friends the greatest Pleasure, so they are the most mortifying circumstances to your Enemies. . . .

The Dr. only called upon me one night, Nov. 14th, and that we spent with company. The next morning went to Newport, from thence to Boston, from whence he returned to Providence, preferred a petition (for they would not receive a memorial) to the General Assembly, for compensation for the damages of August, 1765, returned to Newport, and I have not heard from him since, though at parting he promised to write me by the post. So that I have had no opportunity to hear the particulars of your European adventure. I impatiently await his return, when I hope to have his company some days. . . .

I have many things to tell you of the politics of this distracted little colony, but will defer them till we meet.

Mr. John Cooke certainly deserves the returns of a most sincere friendship, which he has manifested for you on all occasions. I love him for this and a thousand other things, where he has proved himself an honest, hearty, candid, *clever fellow*.

My Neighbour, Esq Case, who is as Gay as ever, presents to *your favour* his most sincere congratulations, and wishes God bless you, and that you may live forever.

Last night and to-day we had a violent Snow Storm.

The Helmes of South Kingstown

I have a Bank before my window that measures [*word torn out*] Feet deep, and is increasing.

I salute you with the greatest esteem and am
Your most obliged and obedient servant,
JAMES HELME.

The following extract will show the manner in which Judge Helme's character was regarded by his contemporaries. It is from a letter (dated 1767) to a Boston friend, written by "George Rome, Esquire, a gentleman of estate from Old England," as Parson Fayerweather affectionately describes him, and who passed his winters in Newport, and his summers at "Bachelor's Hall," Narragansett. The letter, containing many charges against the Colonial governments, caused so much indignation that he was, in 1775, confined in the common gaol of South Kingstown. After his release, still apprehending danger, he fled on board of the Rose, British man-of-war, then lying in Narragansett Bay. All his estates were immediately confiscated. Thus it will appear that he could never have been inclined to partiality towards *any* Colonist:

"The iniquitous courses of their courts of justice in this colony deter men of wisdom and virtue from serving the public; or, if they do so, their wisdom and virtue, unless patronized at home, are turned against them with such malignity that it is more safe to be *infamous* than renowned. The principal exception I have met with here is James Helme, Esquire, who was chosen Chief Justice by the General Assembly at its last session. He accepted his appointment, distinguishes himself by capacity and application, and seems to be neither ashamed to administer impartial justice to all, even to the native and residing creditors of the mother country. I have known him to grant them temporary relief by writs of error, when he and they were overruled by the partiality of the court, and in vain—though with great candour and force—plead with the rest of the bench, that for the honour of the colony and their own reputation they ought never to pay less regard to the decrees of his majesty in council because the property was determined in Great Britain than to their own. I have also heard him, with *resolution and firmness*, when he discovered the court to be immediately partial, order his name to be enrolled as dissenting from the verdict. For such honesty and candour I am persuaded he will be deposed at next election, unless they should be still in hopes of making a convert of him.

"I wish it was in my power to prevent every American from suffering for the cause of integrity and their mother country; *he*, in a special manner, should not only be protected and supported, but appear among the first promotions. Is there no gentleman of public spirit at home that would be pleased to be an instrument of elevating a man of his principles and propriety? or is it become fashionable for vice to be countenanced with impunity, and every trace of virtue passed over unnoticed? God forbid!"

It may be possible for us, at this distance of time, to forgive Judge Helme's political error, especially in view of the fact that at least two of his seven sons became good patriots. But his daughter would always say that, while admiring the character of General Washington, and hoping that her children might realize all that they expected from the new government, the old still claimed *her* affections, and she could never forget the principles of loyalty so often inculcated by her honored father.

Judge Helme's domestic character will be best illustrated by some notes from his correspondence.

His sister-in-law, Mrs. Samuel Seabury, writes from Hempstead, Long Island, under date of July 15, 1764, announcing the death of her husband:

As to my own deplorable state, my dear husband left me and his family the 19th of June, [last year] to go to England, from whence he returned the 7th of June, a sick, and, I may say, a dying man, for he lived one painful week, and then resigned his soul in the arms of his dear Saviour.

Dear sir, I am both a widow and a stranger. My husband did not lay up treasures on earth, though, I have reason to think, he did in Heaven, where no rust doth corrupt, and my whole trust is in Him who hath said He is the Father of the fatherless, and the widow's God.

Sir, as there is in your hands a legacy left me by my mother, I should be glad to hear of you what I am to expect from it, for I shall be in want of it by next May.

Commending you and your children to God Almighty, and begging your prayers for me and mine, I am, sir,

    Your affectionate sister and humble servant,
                    ELIZABETH SEABURY.

To Mr. JAMES HELME.

The answer conveys to Mrs. Seabury the sad intelligence of the death of her sister, Mrs. Helme, "the dearest of women, the tenderest of mothers, and the sincerest Christian." Judge Helme continues:

After taking a final and affectionate farewell of the whole family, in full assurance of a blessed immortality, she breathed her pious soul into the arms of her Redeemer.

Her last admonition, "Live so that I may meet you in Heaven," still sounds in my ears.

Oh, my dear sister, to return your own words, "your own heart will better suggest to you what I feel than any words I can make use of." Imagine to yourself the best, the dearest, the tenderest wife torn from the bleeding side of the man who loved her above all earthly good. Imagine to yourself a man destitute and forlorn, to whom the whole world is a blank and a wilderness; imagine the concern of a parent for eight motherless children, the youngest of whom is but two and a half years old, and then tell me, my dear sister, if my case is not truly wretched.

Your legacy, like all other estates in this Colony that lay in money, is greatly depreciated in value. However, I shall do you all the justice in my power, by making good the deficiency, and, although I have not made an exact calculation, believe it will amount to about £1,550, which, at £7 per dollar, the now legal and current price, may be in value about two hundred and twenty dollars, which I shall endeavor to have in readiness by the time you mention, or when (or before) I hope to see you here, and if I can collect any considerable sum to the value of one hundred dollars, more or less, before that time, should be glad if you would give proper orders to whom I may pay it.

May the God of all grace protect, comfort, and support you and yours, is the sincere prayer of, my dear Sister,

Your affectionate brother,
And humble servant,
JAMES HELME.

To Mrs. ELIZABETH SEABURY.

Mrs. Seabury writes in reply to this letter:

Hempstead, Nov. 26th, 1764.

MY DEAR BROTHER:

I received yours of the 23d of July, charged with the affecting account of the death of my dear and only sister; in regard to which, and my own troubles, I beg to say with Job, "The Lord gave and the Lord hath taken away; blessed be the name of the Lord."

I have been much hurried with business, having, with the assistance of some gentlemen of this parish, raised a dwelling-house and got it under cover, but do not purpose doing any more to it this winter, as I see no prospect of being obliged to quit the parsonage.

That God Almighty may assist, comfort and direct you in all your difficulties, is the earnest prayer of your affectionate sister and humble servant,

ELIZABETH SEABURY.

To JAMES HELME, *Esq.*

The date of the next letter is lost.

My Dear Sister:

Agreeable to your desire, I send you, by my nephew, Nathaniel Seabury, £500, old tenor in gold and silver, as the value for your legacy. I have made good the depreciation of the money, and allowed interest to you for the whole time; though I have been obliged to receive it at the depreciated value, and often had a great part of the money lying by me, for months together, for want of a proper person to let it to; at other times have been at the trouble and expense of lawsuits, and in such cases with us, we are always obliged to levy six months after judgment, for the money, without a farthing of interest being allowed; and I cannot help thinking that, upon the whole, I have not received so much value for the legacy. I hope, in this affair, I have approved myself to your acceptance; if not, let me know, and if any mistake has been made it shall be rectified; although, I believe there is none.

Your near relation to that person who was the comfort of my life and the joy of my heart, and that sisterly kindness with which you have treated me, will always make you and yours very near and dear to me. My children all make their most profound compliments of duty to their dear aunt, and love to their cousins.

With my sincere love to all my dear nephews and nieces, I am, my dear sister, your affectionate brother,
JAMES HELME.

Mrs. ELIZABETH SEABURY.

The strict integrity, and something more — the *nobility* of character to which this correspondence testifies, needs no word of comment, especially to the people of

The Helmes of South Kingstown

Narragansett, where "honest as a Helme" might well become a proverb.

The biography of Rowse J. Helme, second son of Judge Helme, being included in Mr. Updike's "History of the Rhode Island Bar," it need only be said here that he obtained his classical education from a private tutor; was instructed in the principles of law by the learned and accomplished Matthew Robinson, Esq., of Kingston; commenced the practice of his profession in that village, engaged in politics, was a member of the State Council of War during the Revolution, and also of the General Assembly, for many years. "His opinion concerning the paper money laws, in the case of 'Trevett *vs.* Weeden,' did him great credit. He was an able debater, a man of ready wit, a sound lawyer and a skilful draftsman; fond of society and of convivial habits. He died 1789, and is interred with his ancestors at Tower Hill."

Another son was, in early life, a school-master, and his *ferule* of solid "walnut-tree" wood, bearing date 1760, was long preserved in the family. Subsequently, when a dealer in flour, he was wronged in some business transaction (probably relating to army supplies) by the infamous Arnold, who is well known to have been no less treacherous in private than in public life. They met again some years later, after Helme had entered the Continental army. He was one of the ill-fated garrison of Fort Griswold, near Groton, Connecticut, which was captured by a detachment of soldiers under the command of Arnold, when he was threatening New London, and as one of the few survivors of the attack on the fort, was brought into camp, and passed before the triumphant General, as he sat on horseback at the head of his troops. Arnold (so runs the family tradition) suddenly and tauntingly called out, "Young man, I have seen you before. Your name is Helme." The insulting tone, the memory of past injuries, the sense of defeat, all roused the indignation of the late weary and spiritless soldier, but he conquered himself, and, with seeming calmness, replied to the traitor: "Sir, you are quite right. My name is Helme, and I hope never to disgrace it!"

Two of Judge Helme's sons, James, the eldest, and Samuel, lived at Kingston. The former built and resided in the large, rambling structure since occupied by several families. His unaffected amiability of character gained insensibly upon the esteem and confidence of all who knew him. Although one of the few Kingston men who persevered in their political opposition to the late Elisha R. Potter, yet when Mr. Helme died, at an advanced age, Mr. Potter, that man of iron mould, as all his friends have agreed to call him, was observed to show a natural and honorable emotion at the funeral of his old neighbor and contemporary.

Mr. Helme's son, Bernon, was for several years the respected Clerk of the Court of Common Pleas, Providence. His brother Nathaniel, who was intended for the law, died young. His daughter, Mary, died about thirty years ago. Her cousin, Powell, son of Samuel Helme, of Kingston, died there in 1859, leaving a wife and four children. The present James Helme, of Woonsocket, is a great-grandson of Judge James Helme, of Tower Hill.

Ester, the only daughter of the latter, a lady of excellent sense, cultivated mind, and amiable disposition, married in 1768, Francis Carpenter, son of Joseph Carpenter, of Long Island, and nephew and heir to Francis Willett, Esq., of Boston Neck. Their eldest daughter, Ester, died unmarried. Their eldest son, Willett Carpenter, was born at the Helme Place, Tower Hill, in 1772. One of the earliest recollections of his boyhood was of climbing through a trap-door to the roof of the house, in order to witness the final departure of the hated British fleet from American waters. The hill was crowded with people, all looking seaward, and all silent with breathless emotion. In 1801, he married Elizabeth, only daughter of Joseph Case, of North Kingstown, and sister to Dr. Benjamin Waite Case, of Newport. He died at the age of eighty-two,—"the very last of the old Narragansetts," as the late Wilkins Updike fittingly described him. His children were five sons, one of whom was the Reverend James Helme Carpenter, of Wakefield, Rhode Island.

Among the most interesting of the family relics may be enumerated a small edition of the Psalms, in the version of Marot, so often sung by the Huguenots. It was used by Gabriel Bernon during his imprisonment at Rochelle. A gold rattle, carefully preserved by his children in affectionate memory of their early home, has been transmitted from one eldest daughter (of the name of Ester) to another, for more than two hundred years. Some paintings, and several pieces of very elaborate embroidery, are the work of Ester (Powell) Helme, wife of Judge Helme; the needle still attached to an unfinished design, as she left it in the long-past days of her girlhood. There are also silver cans, porringers, drinking-cups, and, perhaps, most curious of all, the apostle-spoons, formerly presented by the "gossips" at a christening.

What do we most desire to know concerning our ancestors, when we have summoned them, for a brief space, from the shadowy past? Shall we ask if they were masters of broad lands and spacious houses? How little do we care to learn this, except as it makes their remote personality more real to us. Shall we inquire if they were lovers of literature, or shared in the speculative thought of their day? Even such questions as these are silenced by the dread presence of death. But when, rising to the highest aspiration of our natures, now become the highest fulfilment of theirs, we seek to know if they were of pure and honorable life, kind and gentle in thought, word, and deed, we approach their own degree of spiritual intuition, and our communion with the sleeping yet breathing memories of the past has not been in vain, since it has taught us the relative values of the temporal and the eternal. The true life, then, is that of the virtues and the affections. How often we had heard it, how little we had understood, even while thinking that we believed it? Now many apparently trivial things are eloquent with a new and deeper meaning. A few words in fading ink on yellow and crumbling paper, as we read them, a husband's tenderness, a wife's devotion, the blended love and duty of their children, live again for us, and the sacred star of home shines brightly through all the mists of time.

THE OLD FRIENDS' MEETING HOUSE IN NARRAGANSETT

"The Quaker of the olden time! —
How calm and firm and true,
Unspotted by its wrong and crime
He walked the dark earth through!"

Whittier

I

THE ancient highway of South Kingstown, originally an Indian trail, and known to the first settlers as the "Pequot Path," was long familiar, in later days, to all passengers by stage-coach who travelled between Philadelphia and Boston. A mile to the eastward of the present village of Wakefield, it traverses the bleak summit of a lonely, wind-swept hill. Here, on the left, the arid ground is faintly ridged with neglected graves that are marked by slanting and crumbling stones, or are deep-sunken beneath those broad prostrate slabs of massive weight and rough-hewn surface, that form the saddest, most eloquent memorials of the bitter sorrows and struggles of our earlier time, and which may still be found in some of the historic burial-places of New England,

"Where the sad Pilgrim watched to scare the wolf away."

This deserted spot was once the site of the first Friends' Meeting House in Kingstown (not then divided into North and South), and probably in the whole Narragansett country. Dating from the closing years of the seventeenth century, it was constantly occupied by the Society, for First Day and business meetings, until its removal in 1860, when a more central situation was chosen for the erection of a new building. It had been a gloomy, storm-beaten structure, eloquent with a certain rugged impressiveness of aspect, partly derived, it might be, from the stubborn strength of its foundations, and the giant endurance of its solid, firm-set timbers, but rather due to the solemn force of the manifold associations rightfully belonging to its length of days in the land. Who that regarded its gray and venerable form, mounted like an ancient sentinel on the brow of the hill, could forget the long years through which it had been hallowed by the true consecration of a silent and spiritual worship? Who did not, at that view, summon from the past the shadowy procession of those faithful followers of the Divine Humility who had so often gathered here, seeking, in single-hearted earnestness, to be taught of that *inner light* which they counted the one supreme possession of every human soul?

Would we survey the rude house of worship and its simple assemblage with the eyes of contemporaries, we must inquire of the observant Madam Knight, a heroine who made the tour of Narragansett in 1704, on horseback and alone, resting at such inns as the country then afforded. Half a century later, Mr. Postmaster Franklin—who is on his way to Boston, having come this morning from Matoonuc Tavern with the intention of staying over night at Tower Hill, with some family of the resident gentry—may have looked out from the heavily laden coach as it slowly climbed the hill, and scanned with keen, attentive eyes the composed faces of the Friends, just coming from Fourth

The Old Friends' Meeting House

Day meeting. A shrewd, thrifty people, the Quakers; Mr. Franklin thinks well of them; believes their influence will promote colonial intelligence and prosperity here in Rhode Island, as long since in Pennsylvania. Or may we even hope that the dim atmosphere of tradition will brighten into some vivid, if transient, gleam of reality, revealing to us the genuine form and presence of another traveller, whom the troubled chances of Revolutionary days have called from his quiet country home to the foremost post of danger and responsibility? We see the narrow road crowded with the mounted figures of a military party; and one, the leader among them, presses forward, up the winding ascent of the hill. Although the stranger cannot have numbered many years, the resistless power of his commanding mien, the enkindled majesty of his look, inspire a universal reverence that is almost awe. It is but a hasty and preoccupied glance that he throws upon the landscape, as he gains the summit and meets the fresh ocean breeze. His thoughts are burdened with the anxious destinies of an imperilled nation; his eyes are watchfully seeking the white sails of the friendly fleet of Rochambeau, riding secure at anchor where late the British naval force kept an armed and hostile vigilance over the capital of the insurgent colony — the historic town of Newport. When, in the closing hours of the day, the stranger enters its ancient streets, he will be met by the eager acclamation of its people, who recognize in him their trusted Commander-in-Chief, their beloved Washington!

The interior of the building which we have seen to be so familiar an object for many years to the travellers by the old post-road was planned in strict conformity with that rigid plainness of design so strongly enjoined by "Friends' rules." No dim religious light was that which the noontide sun poured through the wide, shadeless windows; and the only incense pervading the atmosphere was the pleasant aromatic odor diffused from the goodly logs of pine and hemlock redly glowing in the vast fireplaces. A broad gallery of ponderous construction extended across the south end of the room, which was also supplied with the usual sliding partition, contrived for the purpose of effecting a temporary division of the monthly business gatherings, in which the men and women of the Society held separate conferences, and forwarded distinct reports to the New England Yearly Meeting at Newport. The "high seats," for the preachers and elders, and the narrow entry, with its two doors leading to the inner apartment, completed the chief arrangements. How often have a meek Quaker maiden and her betrothed paused by those dreaded portals, which they must nevertheless presently enter, and, in the set phrase of their people, "lay their intentions" before each silent, expectant assembly. The solemnity of betrothals and marriage-vows among the Friends, the inviolate sacredness of their family ties, the dove-like purity and plainness of the dress adopted by their women, the grave simplicity of comfort enjoyed by their households,— these afford no remote suggestion of the poetry of the ideal German home; and indeed it is evident that our poets and novelists find no more simple, sweet, and idyllic element of American life and character than such as may be evolved from the Quaker records and traditions.

The Old Friends' Meeting House

Obscure and secluded as this quiet spot may be, it is not without its inspiring memories and associations; it has been visited by some of the mightiest of the sect. Here, according to tradition, George Fox has often addressed large congregations of his followers — doubtless at a period but little later than that during which Roger Williams was holding weekly exhortations to the Indians who assembled at Richard Smith's Blockhouse — the first civilized habitation erected in the Narragansett wilderness. "Grand old Roger Williams," says Mr. Curtis, who describes with admiration the brave solitary voyage of the aged man down the Seekonk, thence to the Bay, thence to his destination at Newport, where he ably fulfilled his appointment to meet the great advocate of Quaker doctrines, for a close and searching discussion of the various points of difference between them. Well may we imagine the adherents of Fox, in Narragansett and elsewhere, as eagerly awaiting the result of an interview so characteristic of the seventeenth century keenness for controversial debate, but now held chiefly memorable as the historic encounter of two minds distinguished by intense original power of speculative thought. Roger Williams, — George Fox, — James MacSparran, — these were the spiritual fathers of ancient Narragansett. Without the mention of the third and comparatively unknown name, we should not have indicated all the *principal* influences formative of theological opinion at that period; the Congregational faith, so potent in other regions of New England, being naturally the last to gain ascendancy in Rhode Island. Widely diverse in many points of character as were these three religious teachers of our earliest time, opposite as might be the various articles of belief formally accepted by each, they were yet unconsciously one in their aims and labors, one in whole-hearted energy of effort to awaken the higher natures of the people among whom they engaged in their sincere and self-forgetful ministrations. It was their office to summon the care-worn fathers of a State to thoughtful consideration of nobler and more spiritual interests than such as were involved in the stern anxieties, the toilsome, unceasing struggle, by which the wild, ungenial territory was to be subdued and made a goodly inheritance. Then it was that America was taught of the true apostles, of devoted men, of prophetic souls, who were as voices crying in her wilderness, calling her people from their engrossing pursuit of the transitory interests of time, and leading them to final rest and hope in the unwavering contemplation of the bright vision of eternity. Were not those days of her adversity more blessed than these of her careless prosperity?

It is admitted that, in Rhode Island, polemical controversy never attained that degree of bitterness by which it was marked in many other quarters of New England. The numerous sects that made this Colony their home lived together, upon the whole, in mutual toleration and content. Dr. MacSparran refers to the power and consideration long enjoyed by the Quakers of the Colony. The Rev. Marmaduke Browne, rector of Trinity Church, Newport, describes "the good harmony here subsisting between Churchmen and Dissenters, in particular the Quakers." Still, since human nature is always the same, we cannot doubt that the average Episcopalian of that day looked upon the disciples of "mad George Fox" with all that shrinking wonder and disapproval which proceeds rather from imperfect sympathy than from voluntary harshness of judgment. "The man of thirty-nine beliefs counts the man of one belief a pauper." Nor is it quite improbable that many a worthy "member of society," prominent among the chiefs of the old slaveholding Quaker aristocracy of Rhode Island — whose ships were perhaps even then slowly making their homeward way from African ports, laden with human merchandise — might have been heard to dwell, with a most edifying emphasis, upon the sinful follies of the world's people, in especial that giddy generation who walked after the unspiritual teachings of the hireling priest James MacSparran, perverting the sincere word with the vanities of mere human learning. Meanwhile, the humble follower of Roger Williams austerely rejected the erroneous doctrines of both, and in his wayside talks, or during the pauses of work in the field, was wont to exhort his neighbors and friends to continue diligent in the somewhat limited round of belief and duty honestly accepted by him as the undoubted, immutable legacy, bequeathed by the Father of the Colony to his children in the faith.

Amid this armed neutrality of opinions, this harmless clashing of spiritual weapons, all that was truest and worthiest in the nurture, discipline, and worship of the Society of Friends obtained a firm and lasting hold upon the heart and the intelligence of a thoughtful people. The benefits of "a guarded education" became more and more apparent in the pure and noble lives of its best exemplars, those sacred teachers whose testimony, inspired by steadfast faith, was delivered with a zeal that welcomed the severest tests. Their holy tasks, pursued in the "stillness and the quietness," were attended by those chastening and strengthening influences that afford composure and resignation in the darkest hours of sorrow and trial.

Imagination, with one magic touch, restores the simple outline of the primitive structure so long frequented by the Friends in Narragansett, presenting to the mental vision the grave, calm-featured elders and matrons assembled in that profound silence that seems the fullest and fittest means of communion with an invisible world. Not without a thrill of awe comes the sudden remembrance that among these quiet worshippers there is not one who does not recognize, as one of the ever recurring events of daily life, a constant allegiance to the "familiar divine sign" of Socrates, which Professor Jowett's wonderful translation has of late made so intimate a reality to the mere English reader. In obedience to the inward prompting of a similar impulse, one of the number kneels to offer prayer. "Our friend appeared in supplication" is the sad, meek, humble phrase that compresses, within the limits of a single word, the history of a persecuted people. Or, like one commissioned to declare the truth, he rises to address the listening Friends in such words as it shall be given him to utter, and which will be fully accepted by the devout assemblage as a genuine message from the sphere of a Higher Intelligence. With hands firmly grasping the railing before him, or slowly moved, from time to time, in the carefully repressed access of emotion, with fixed, far-seeing eyes, with high-pitched voice rising into a shrill, unmodulated chant, the speaker proceeds, followed by the rapt and reverential attention of his hearers. Is this, then, eloquence? It is more; it is conviction! Here the loftier virtues were nurtured in sternness and in gloom. Here, amid loneliness and obscurity, the rugged strength of a people was matured. Here the young were taught the grand lesson, the central truth of revelation, that RIGHTEOUSNESS exalteth a nation. These were religionists far too deeply in earnest, too sincere in seeking the fullest realization of the holy life possible on earth, to admit that most undermining, soul-ensnaring disparagement of "mere morality," which some sects have been so thoughtlessly ready to adopt, and which has wrecked so many lives of fairest promise that rose in the glow of ecstacy and went down in the darkness of despair. They were Christians of even unassuming character, upright and moral, no less than devotional, calm and hopeful rather than enthusiastic. It was the power of their honest teachings, their consistent example, that wrought upon the lives of those men of sterling worth, whose deeds of integrity and humanity are written in our brightest annals. In the deep repose of that holy silence were unfolded those gentle natures, those mild and lovely spirits, the Quaker wives and mothers of our land, whose tender benevolence, unconfined by the limits of their own households, has flowed on, in ever brightening, ever broadening streams to soothe and bless the afflicted, the degraded of the race, with loving help and sympathy and consolation.

II

Many eventful years have passed since these ancient walls were hallowed by the rise of a special mission of peace and good-will to man. It was here that the principles of universal freedom were first announced to the people of this Colony, by a preacher of the Society of Friends in Narragansett. The circumstances attending his adoption of such sentiments have already been related by one of his descendants; but they cannot lose their interest while the purest moral courage and the generous influence of a lofty example shall continue to command the willing tribute of human gratitude and reverence.

Toward the middle of the eighteenth century, Thomas Hazard, of South Kingstown (a "birthright member" of the Society), was about to identify himself with it more closely by marrying a daughter of William Robinson, the Quaker governor. His father, wishing to provide him with a separate establishment, sent him on a journey to North Stonington, Connecticut, in order that he might make some of the large purchases that would be required for his new estate; also recommending him to obtain the advice of an old business acquaintance residing there, a deacon of the Presbyterian Church. It was late on a Saturday afternoon when the young man arrived, and, unwilling to offend the well-known prejudices of old Connecticut concerning the due observance of the Puritan Sabbath, he made no attempt, at that hour, to enter upon the transaction of any business, merely securing lodgings at the village inn. But the deacon, happening to meet the son of his friend,

The Old Friends' Meeting House

insisted that he should accompany him home. The invitation was accepted, and, soon after sundown, "holy time" having begun, the good deacon turned the conversation upon religious, or rather polemical subjects, then so frequently the chosen course of thought pursued by a New England evening fireside. The merits of several sects having been reviewed, the Friends were at length mentioned by the Rhode Island guest. "Quakers!" exclaimed his interlocutor. "They are not a Christian people!" As the young representative of the Society was lately from Yale College, where his natural taste and ability had disposed him to pursue with especial interest the close investigation and analysis of metaphysical and logical subtilties, he believed himself able to silence any of the objections commonly urged against the doctrines of his people, and would willingly have led his host into those thorny and tortuous paths of controversy. But, greatly to his surprise, the deacon, waiving all argument, merely replied with the settled calmness of long-matured conviction: "They hold their fellowmen in slavery." To so unexpected a diversion, the eager advocate of Friends' doctrines could make no reply, or rather, did himself honor by attempting none. As the sudden shadow of doubt rapidly darkened into greater and graver proportions, he silently committed the question to the solemn keeping of his conscience, and availed himself of the first opportunity to change the subject of conversation. Nothing could more clearly indicate the higher order of minds to which he belonged.

After concluding the business which had called him to the village, he departed for home. How seriously meditative, how anxiously thoughtful a journey must not that have been! Many doubts and questions arose in the course of that long ride, to be firmly answered or swiftly dispelled by the energy of an awakened conscience. As the son of the largest landed proprietor, and consequently one of the largest slaveholders in New England, his duty was no less difficult and painful than imperatively urgent. Nor could he recall, without some natural degree of apprehension, his father's proverbial force of will. How would *he* receive so unexpected a decision as that now gradually forming in the mind of his son? What would be the course of the Society, so sincerely honored by its young disciple, at the avowal of sentiments so strongly at variance with the practices then followed by its members, as by all their contemporaries, without scruple or hint of blame? At that time the Quaker merchants and farmers were even prominent among the slaveholders of the country, and there was one point of morals upon which "a guarded education" was guarded indeed! Temptation came then to him, as to all of us in some supreme moment of our lives. How subtle a whisper it sent into the ready ear of inclination, bidding the brave young inquirer after truth abandon all thought of so fruitless a struggle, and acquiesce in the tried wisdom and virtue of the elders. It was surely best to leave all these grave questions of duty to them. But the passing of a moment, and the feeble counsels of a false humility had died into silence, and everlasting Right had conquered. We know that his thoughtful consideration had been directed, more than once before, to the injurious conditions of life involved by the custom of enforced servitude. Perhaps the sad scenes witnessed by him in the past swept in sudden review before him, and indignant sympathy completed the work of judicious and conscientious reflection. As in the last glow of sunset light he enters the broad avenue leading to his ancient home, he rises before us a figure of moral grandeur, prepared to meet all opposition with the calmness of a mind that is firmly stayed on the rock of principle.

His intention to employ free labor only on his estate was, in due time, communicated to his father. Then the anticipated storm broke forth. The paternal resentment was, for a time, intense and indeed portended to be lasting. Threats of disinheritance were repeatedly uttered, threats which the son never doubted would be fully executed, and for some years a degree of estrangement existed between the two; but it is pleasant to record that this injustice finally yielded to the feelings of nature; and the sincerity of the reconciliation was practically evinced in that the elder Mr. Hazard not only left all his slaves free by his will, but also made his son Thomas co-equal heir with his other children.

Meanwhile, regardless of all discouragements in the course of duty, the youthful philanthropist immediately began the serious work of his life. Becoming a preacher among the Friends, he constantly presented and forcibly urged his convictions, first before the Society of South Kingstown, and subsequently as a travelling Friend in various parts of New England and New York. A similarity of views and interests was the foundation of the close friendship which he formed with one who was then engaged in the same humane pursuit—the noble John Woolman, who is known to have visited Narragansett, where he doubtless preached in the old meeting-house. Giving his life unreservedly to the cause of his helpless and suffering fellow-creatures, he, during forty years, persevered in his self-imposed mission, and at last had the happiness to arrive at the desired result of his labors. He brought before the General Assembly a plan for the gradual abolition of slavery in the Colony, which he lived to see adopted as law by the revolutionized State; while, previous to his death, in 1798, at the age of eighty years, his views had been generally received throughout New England and the Middle States.

Perhaps we cannot contemplate this truly noble man, this worthy leader of a people, at a more impressive moment than on those occasions when he rose to address his friends in the obscure place of worship on the bleak Narragansett hillside. Tradition delights to describe those scenes; to recall the earnestness, the inspiration of the speaker; his tall, majestic form erect, his eyes kindling with the grandeur of the theme, as, in the strong and vigorous words of a natural eloquence, he presented to his hearers the fair, the glorious ideal of liberty, or softening into pity for the wrongs and sufferings of the unhappy race to whose release the best years of his life were solemnly dedicated. In him the weak, the afflicted, the oppressed, might find the true impersonation of a Greatheart—the noble genius of protecting strength and guidance. A consistent Friend—yet in the unconscious dignity of his look and bearing, a king of men—there was a degree of impressiveness approaching the sublime in the thought that all this power of personal presence, this supremacy of intellect, had, from earliest youth, been wholly devoted to the highest and purest purposes that can engage the human will.

And now the chief office of the old meeting-house on the hill would seem to have closed with the mission of its apostle, who came bearing the lofty decrees of freedom, arousing all hearts and all consciences to a stern contest between the lower instincts of self-interest and the holy commands of an exalted religion. Many and varied were the associations united with its past, from the seasons when its worshipping congregation had heard in sad, humble resignation, the recitals of afflicted Friends but lately liberated from severe imprisonment in the persecuting town of Boston, to the later time when Thomas Hazard had boldly borne testimony against the grievous sin of the age. How dim in the fading past lay those days of probation and struggle! The quiet, faithful people, who met from week to week and from year to year in that humble building, had meekly accepted the thrilling words of exhortation uttered by their earnest guides; they had followed the divine leadings; and now, secure in the respect and regard of their fellowmen, they were worthy to receive the affectionate message of friendly sympathy and good-will, borne to them across the sea from thousands of sober English homes, by the gentle Gurney. He came as if to bring peace and rest after the stormy hours of a spiritual conflict—as if to bless the sacred tasks here begun in the fear of God, and in the love of liberty—purposes the ultimate results of which are yet to be traced in the far future of humanity. Many who then listened to him in the meeting-house, or knew him as a guest in their homes, show a ready interest and pleasure in relating their reminiscences of him. They love to recall the manifestations of his serene and saintly life and sunny temperament; or to describe his noble features, his full, sonorous voice,—in a word, to revive the gracious impressions communicated by the mild harmonies of a generous and genial nature. It is whispered that some of the older and plainer Friends looked askance at his rich velvet cloak, worn with an easy grace quite foreign to the accepted traditions of the Society—but none could doubt the genuine goodness of the heart beneath it. Responsive to each appeal of the afflicted and the disconsolate, cheerful in his kindly visitings at the houses of the Friends, gentle and winning in his intercourse with children, he was an honored and regretted guest in Narragansett, where his memory still lingers in unfading bloom, a winter flower set in the brown slope of the bare and rugged hillside.

Still the Friends continued to gather at the old place of meeting, coming in sunshine and in storm, through all the varying seasons, ever seeking and finding, as the tranquil years glided by, the strength and hope and courage infused into the soul from the calm repose of consentient silence and meditation. Then, as their numbers declined, and the younger members of the Society left the homesteads of their people for the distant west, or perhaps, while never forgetting the benign influences of their early training, chose rather to mingle with the spheres of other religious sects, the few remaining worshippers judged it best to depart from the long-hallowed spot, sacred to them by the presence of

The Old Friends' Meeting House

countless associations. The austere teachings of their faith forbade them to attach any sentiment of reverence to the ancient structure, the spiritual home of many generations, but none the less will those of us who own a less rigid creed continue to hope that at least its memory is still dear to their hearts.

What though, as kindly Charles Lamb lamented, "the goodly sect is dwindling, dwindling"? What though the youth of the Society are to-day turning to other thoughts and following in other ways than those their fathers knew? Inevitable changes, such as these, do not lessen the power of the pure teachings early implanted in their minds. They may change the fashion of their dress, the custom of their speech; they may cease to be known to the world as "Quakers," but by whatever name they are called, they will still be Friends at heart. They cannot, if they would, do away with the enduring impulses derived from an heroic ancestry. When the inspired peasant of Leicestershire bore a stern testimony against sins enthroned in high places, when the martyrs of New England were made strong through faith to pass the trial of the scourge, of the prison, of slavery, even of death, they left a lasting witness in the memory of their deeds, to be recognized and revered by a wiser generation than that which was drawn on by the fanatic ardor of ecclesiastical power, to visit with the cruel baptism of persecution the gentlest race that ever suffered beneath the multiplied severities of a two-fold tyranny. If the externals of a system perish, it is because these were immaterial to its true life and growth. The outward form of Quakerism may change, may vanish, but its highest thoughts, its broadest principles, are of another sphere than that which comprises the arbitrary regulations or customs of a sect, and have become a part of the universal heritage of mankind. Thus has it come to pass that the meek-spirited have possessed the earth. Individuals, races, systems, creeds,—these rise, fulfil their mission, and pass away, summoned by inexorable fate. But humanity remains. Into that mighty ocean roll all the rivers of thought. Is their collective volume lost, because forever blended with the greater mass? Rather let us trust that, in the spiritual, as in the material world, all that is superlatively worthy of life still endures to claim an eternal share in the far-reaching sequences, in the inconceivable harmonies of the hereafter.

Beautiful and peaceful, in this mild, genial season of early winter, is the aspect of the lonely hill where once stood the honored structure that among a more imaginative people would have been cherished as the ancient temple of civil and religious liberty. It is one of those still gray days of an exquisite loveliness that seems infused with a deeper meaning, a more restful content, than is imparted even by the loving gladness of sunshine. In its surpassing harmony of melting hues, the atmosphere is like one great softened pearl. Along the changeful horizon, the veiled tints, the tender half-lights, are deliciously blending into purest amethyst that again passes into solemn depths of rich purple shadow, overhanging the leafless woods and the sad brown slopes, soothing the grief of the deserted landscape with a lingering memory of the warm autumnal haze. The near Atlantic owns the sacred influ-

The Old Friends' Meeting House

ence of the halcyon hour, forgets to chafe the rocks with harsh accustomed roar, and sends up a deep voice of music from the winding shore. Dare one dream of an unseen Italy, here in the fast gathering shades of a New England winter? Yet is not the sentiment of a southern scene suggested by the melancholy beauty of the tombs, by the fantastic forms of the strangely intertwined trunks and branches of the old forest trees, like ancient ilexes in some historic place of sepulchre? The purple-toned atmosphere, the mild brooding stillness, yielding only to the distant, softened sound of the surf,— are not these among the elements of the subtle spell that thrills our hearts and our imaginations, in contemplating the unfading pictures wrought by poets and artists, of a fairer land than ours? Yes, it is the heart that creates its own Italy; and beauty is no haughty sovereign, no remote angel vision, but a gentle, familiar deity, whose shrine is on every hillside, whose gracious words of response are borne to her worshippers on every evening breeze.

Suddenly the fast westering sun looks forth in a burst of transcendent glory; dispersing the soft, floating gossamer web of evanescent cloud. With the departing mists vanish all the wandering vaporous fancies that love to linger half revealed in the subdued tones, the quiet lights of a dreamy day. This is New England soil below; it is the clear, cold, stainless blue of a northern heaven that gleams above. No strange, distant scene is this, but the long-familiar, oft-visited spot, endeared to human recognition as the centre of the virtuous annals of a simple people. Where the stranger views but desolation and oblivion, the eye of faithful memory shall trace as fair, as bright a record as ennobles many a prouder site, graced by the art of the historian and the sympathy of the poet. The wintry brown hillside, long abandoned by man to the unforgetting ministry of nature, has been clothed by her in daily beauty. Now caressed by the last warm smile of the departing sun, it glows for an instant in full radiance, then, through gray gradations of twilight shades, passes into the solemn sphere of silence and gloom. Night descends upon the scene and wraps the tombs of the fathers in darkness. Shall we leave them to the deeper night of forgetfulness? In the brief moment that is ours, ere we too enter the fast falling shadows, may we not spare one thought of grateful remembrance to the humble, unknown benefactors of a nation, who here sleep in seclusion and neglect? To memories such as these shall we not yield the spontaneous tribute of an affectionate homage, inspired by the deepest, most earnest sympathy, gratitude, and devotion?

NEGRO SLAVERY IN THE COLONY OF RHODE ISLAND

THE comparatively mild and favorable conditions of negro slavery, as it formerly prevailed in New England, are well known. Rhode Island has been severely censured for her share in the iniquitous slave-trade; but her accusers have not infrequently been wanting either in ability to observe or in candor to acknowledge the truth, that the crime was never countenanced by her Legislature, or sanctioned by public opinion among her worthiest citizens. Although many merchants of Newport and Providence were deeply implicated in the guilt of the "Guinea coasting-trade,"— such was the euphemism devised by the uneasy mercantile conscience to veil the actual horrors of the traffic in humanity,—and although the later colonial laws permitted the holding of slaves, yet it does not appear that their numbers in this Colony were ever proportionately large, and it is believed that the degree of commendation which has been granted to the general course of Rhode Island legislation relative to this subject by those who have long enjoyed the most ample opportunities for a careful examination and comparison of the ancient records, has not been lightly or undeservedly bestowed.

The first act of the General Assembly referring to domestic servitude, and which bears the early date of May 18, 1652, should be familiar to all who are interested in shielding the good name of their native State from any unjust aspersions that may be affixed to her history.

"Whereas, there is a common course practiced among Englishmen, to buy negroes, to that end they may have them for service or slaves forever, for the preventing of such practices among us, let it be ordered that no blacke mankind or white, being forced to convenant, bond, or otherwise serve any man or his assigns longer than ten years, or until they come to bee twentie-four years of age, if they bee taken in under fourteen, from the time of their cominge within the limits of this Collonie, and at the end or terme of ten yeares to sett them free, as the manner is with the English servants, and that man that will not let them goe free, or shall sell them away elsewhere, to that end that they may bee enslaved to others for a longer time, he or they shall forfeit to the Collonie forty pounds." (The attentive reader needs no reminder of the fact that the stipulated fine was, in that age and country, a sum of much greater comparative value than at present, and its forfeiture a penalty probably sufficient to deter any colonist from the prohibited transgression.)

In this memorable enactment, who does not recognize the lofty spirit, the true manhood, so characteristic of the best days of the English Commonwealth and its noble Republican defenders? There is no forced assumption of strenuous virtue in the brief and plainly worded document. Its originators utter no pharisaical condemnation of the customs adopted in other colonies; they simply say: let such practices be put away from *us*. Let no black mankind, or white, be suffered to serve any master for a longer season than is the manner of English servants, from the time of their first coming within the liberties of this Colony. Could the provisions of this wise and humane law, worthy of a more enlightened age, have been generally enforced, they would naturally have been succeeded, in the progress of civilization, by still better forms of legislation, and Rhode Island might have presented the proudest example to her sister colonies, and to the world. Had the will of these early law-givers ruled our past, the history of our State would afford fewer pages darkened by the gloom of injustice and inhumanity. But they were merely commissioned to govern Providence Plantations and Warwick, and their authority could not be extended to other parts of the Colony, which was then, and long afterward, in an unhappy, distracted state, for want of a strong central government. Poor little Rhode Island! always the Cinderella of the colonial family — what leisure or opportunity had she for the inception and achievement of a thoughtful and judicious reform? Denied admittance into the celebrated "Union" of 1643, because of her spirited refusal to submit to the jurisdiction of Plymouth, she was thus thrown upon her own unaided resources for protection against the ever dreaded savage foe, from whom she was compelled to endure many assaults that were provoked by the harshness or temerity of her neighbors. The fiercely disputed claim of Connecticut to the Narragansett country kept her in perpetual rancor with that Colony, always the *bête noir* of the early Rhode Islander, and the long hostility was maintained on both sides with that unscrupulous energy by which a border warfare is invariably marked. Her stately sister, Massachusetts, calmly insisted upon certain fancied rights of government over Newport and Providence, even attempting to introduce her own code of laws into the latter town, which naturally proved somewhat restive under St. Botolph's officious patronage. The Saints of Plymouth, too, were not averse to share in spoiling the Philistines of the Plantations, and laid claim to Shawomet, now Warwick. As for heretical Rhode Island, her only patron saint was His graceless Majesty, King Charles II, of unblessed memory. Yet the tyrannical monarch was the best and earliest and truest friend of our State in a time of helplessness and need, and her historians have never forgotten the debt of gratitude justly due his name. To have been the friend of America, in her season of adversity and gloom; and, in after years, to share her hour of triumph — what a lofty privilege was that for nation or sovereign! What a rich and abundant harvest was to be reaped from that brief and unnoted seed-time! Has the Republic ever proved ungrateful? Do not the long and tried friendship with France and the cordial and catholic amity extended to Russia show that Americans have not ceased to remember

"Where was our friend when the world was our foe."

The citizens of this State may claim with just pride an honorable share in the merit of a recent graceful and appropriate national act. The unanimous order for the restoration of the monument erected by the King of France, late in seventeen hundred, in the cemetery of the chief church of our island city, in memory of a brave and faithful commander, was a fitting tribute from the representatives of the American people to the services and renown of a noble, gallant, and chivalrous ally. The words of a Rhode Island Senator are recorded in the national archives, and have become as imperishable a part of history as the spontaneous testimony of gratitude which they elicited — a gratitude that, in the felicitous expression of the Marquis de Noailles, has proved more enduring than the tomb of Egyptian granite placed over the remains of the Chevalier de Ternay.

Considering the many obstacles existing, in colonial times, to the formation of a firm government, it would not be surprising if internal affairs should not have received the closest or most judicious attention. The late Judge Durfee, in that glowing and animated apotheosis of his native State, comprised in the discourse delivered by him before the Rhode Island Historical Society in the year 1847, finds, in our primitive scheme of government by a union of separate sovereignties, the first outline of the plan upon which the early confederation of the States was subsequently formed. But it will doubtless be admitted that the system was a very imperfect one, and, in both instances, gave rise to many of those vexations, perplexities, and delays, which so often awaken the varying emotions of sympathy, impatience, or indignation in the interested reader of our Revolutionary history. With the question of conflicting authority pending between Williams and Coddington; with the powerful Gorton, whose influence over his followers was far greater than that of any nominal governor, long established at Warwick; with the extensive Narragansett country, comprising a third part of the Colony, erected, by His Majesty's especial command, into a separate dependency, to be called the King's Province, and ruled only by King's Commissioners; from all these varying and uncertain elements, how should unity of sentiment and action be attained as a natural result? The attention of the fathers was often drawn aside from those subjects which should properly have claimed their thoughts, to the vast and bewildering variety of theological opinions of which this little territory was the centre and stronghold. Anne Hutchinson and her disciples, whose "pernicious doctrines" had thrown the stable Colony of the Bay into dire confusion and dismay, had sought a refuge in hospitable Newport, while the avaricious and unworthy among the inhabitants of these towns were suffered to evade or openly transgress the statute law, in the interests of trade. Thus the usage of negro slavery gradually gained ground, without greatly alarming the consciences of our good ancestors, whose minds were fixed upon questions deemed by them to be of far greater moment. In those days the full force of human intellect was directed toward the solution of speculative doctrines of polemic philosophy. Doubtless certain mental qualities were thus provided with an excellent training, which has had its especial share in the development of the New England character; but did it open the way to broad views, or tend to increase the power of the benevolent feelings? Alas! while the founders of New England hesitated between the comparative merits of the Calvinistic gospel, as expounded by Edwards or Hopkins; while they jealously strove to eradicate the fatal errors of Quakerism or Familism, the common every-day interests of the race were strangely forgotten, and a more dangerous evil than any of those so much dreaded was fast approaching an unheeded maturity.

That Mistress Hutchinson was a grave and virtuous gentlewoman of remarkable mental endowment, a kind, charitable, and beneficent neighbor, a warm and faithful friend,—all this could profit her nothing while she wilfully clung to her "thirty erroneous and heretical opinions," even presuming to advocate them in the dread presence of reverend dignitaries. Persecution and banishment from her native colony and her home must inevitably follow in due course. Remembering these facts, and reflecting upon the hard fortunes of Williams, Gorton, and other so-called "firebrands," by whom their gloomy contemporaries were so greatly shocked and alarmed, we can but conclude that we should at least hesitate before dealing very severely with a recent somewhat startling assertion, that "practical Christianity, as a reality, began only with the nineteenth century." Its author probably would not deny that very much still remains to be accomplished by an age which has inaugurated and assumed responsibilities so solemn and so momentous.

The peaceful days of the Colony came at last and found slavery accepted as the universal custom. By evasion of law, and in defiance of opinion, it had finally acquired a sort of sanction from the influence of time and habit, and more especially from the considerate treatment generally received by the slaves. It is believed that there were but few exceptions to the prevailing rule of kindness to old servants, which is so eminently English a sentiment, and which was recognized by the early settlers of this State, and their descendants, as an obligation imposed by all the mandates of honor and humanity.

The Legislature, however, was not to be deterred from the passage of the very creditable act of July, 1715, prohibiting the importation of *Indian slaves*. This law was continued in force and reënacted in 1766. Those Indians who, up to this time, had been held in servitude were probably the survivors of the great battle of the Narragansett fort. They had been sold, not for life, but for *a term of years*. It was customary for New England authorities to sell their captives, even into West Indian slavery, but Rhode Island may rightfully receive a complete exoneration from the guilt of this charge. So highly honorable a phase of her history may in some partial measure redeem her less upright conduct toward another unhappy and more defenceless race.

In 1722, or perhaps earlier, Dr. MacSparran, rector of the Narragansett Church, in conformity with the instructions of the Venerable Society, to whose enlightened and judicious benevolence the country has owed so much, began a course of religious teaching among the slaves, obtaining their attendance to the number of seventy every Sunday morning. His example, commended by the excellent Berkeley, always a sincere friend to the best interests of America, was speedily followed by Mr. Honeyman, rector of Trinity Church, Newport, and by other Anglican missionaries. From religious to secular education, the transition was naturally effected with comparative facility. Accordingly, we find that in 1737, George Taylor, the Society's schoolmaster at Providence, admits two black children to his school of more than twenty pupils. "This, with Mr. Taylor's good life and conversation, comes attested

Negro Slavery in Colonial Rhode Island

by Dr. MacSparran." Twenty-six years later the Reverend Marmaduke Browne reports from Newport to the Society for the Propagation of the Gospel in Foreign Parts that he has opened a school for the instruction of negro children, to consist of fifteen of each sex, which is to be under his own inspection, and he trusts will answer the intentions of the charitable persons therein concerned. It is evident that the elevating influences to which the slaves were thus admitted were extremely efficacious in improving their general condition, and in preparing the minds of their masters for the scheme of gradual emancipation, which was afterwards to be introduced and adopted. Says the Bishop of London, in his Pastoral Letter of 1725, addressed to the "Masters and Mistresses of Families in the English Plantations": "Let me beseech you to consider your slaves as *men* and *women*, who have the same frame and faculties with yourselves, souls capable of happiness, and reason and understanding to receive instruction in order to it."

In June, 1774, the importation of *negroes* was strictly forbidden, by special enactment. The language of the preamble indicates the prevalence of republican ideas among the people of Rhode Island, who, in these early and ominous days of the long contest opening before them, were yet firmly resolved that the wards of the State should enjoy the same liberty for which its citizens were preparing to contend in the field. It runs thus: "Whereas, the inhabitants of America are generally engaged in the preservation of their own rights and liberties, among which that of personal freedom must be considered as the greatest, and as those who are desirous of enjoying all the advantages of liberty themselves, should be willing to extend personal liberty to others." All slaves thereafter brought into the State were to be free, with the usual exceptions in favor of persons travelling through the country, or coming from other British dependencies to reside here. Citizens were forbidden to bring slaves within the colonial limits, without giving bond to remove them in a year.

Must the slave importer or the captain of a slave ship be regarded as if excluded from the sphere of true charity? There was, perhaps, some excuse for the latter, in the theological beliefs of his time. Not that *he* presumed to inquire into such matters; his business being simply to obey orders and enable his respected employers to supply their customers, among whom reverend gentlemen were not infrequently numbered. All these learned and worshipful individuals must understand questions of conscience much better than he, and (unless possessing exceptional vigor of mind and will, in which case his crime would be indeed unpardonable) he could not avoid the dim, awe-struck conviction that all these poor heathen were inevitably doomed, in a future life, to a much severer ordeal than that of mere physical suffering, unless, perchance, they might be brought to the light and knowledge of Christianity. Why, even on board those ships where the captains were far enough from being humane (which of course *he* always meant to be, and tried to be, when the interests of the company did not prevent), what were the worst sufferings of the Middle Passage compared with that fiercer trial which had been so carefully wrought out in slow detail by the parson whose preaching he happened to hear the last time he was ashore? The merest shadow of a trifle! And had he not been told of late, and glad enough he was to hear it, that the shivering, fainting, exhausted child he had landed on Boston Pier, years ago, had lived, after all, to be known as "Phillis, the extraordinary negro poet," yes, lived to write, in gratitude—

> "'Twas *Mercy* brought me from my *Pagan* land,
> Taught my benighted soul to understand
> That there's a God, and there's a *Saviour* too;
> Once, I redemption neither sought nor knew."

And—and—his employers, the respected company—paid well—of course they did—they would not find many men who would look after other people's property as if it were their own. Come! my good fellows! our ship is waiting for us, the wind is fair, let us sail out into blue water, and as for all these troublesome questions, let us leave them to be settled by the landsmen; they are *their* concerns, not ours!

Such may have been the inarticulate parley of the slave-captain with his narcotized conscience and blunted sensibilities; nor should his defence be denied whatever degree of consideration a shrinking and averted charity may be induced to bestow. Shall a reverend historian of the Macedonian conqueror not only justify, but eulogize his career of terror and destruction among the peaceful and civilized nations of India, on the plea that the advantages of a true Greek culture followed in the wake of his armies, and, because the wrong-doing of a mere sea-captain presents no splendid or picturesque elements to command our admiration, shall he therefore be refused a hearing, nor allowed to demand whatever small amount of tolerance may be granted him if he show that he had been the means of transforming a little wandering savage into the well-taught, Christian young woman, the pride of cultivated Boston, the correspondent of Washington, who styled her "the favored of the Muses"? Ah! when we all are summoned to appear before that Higher Tribunal, it will be no source of regret to remember that, needing mercy ourselves, we freely showed mercy to others!

As for the landsmen, to whom their officer so vehemently appealed, they looked to their growing gains, and were not in the least unwilling to assume the disputed responsibility; especially as it could be so easily and neatly transferred to Ham, or Cain, or Adam, or whatever Scriptural sinner of an eligible antiquity and a pleasingly comfortable remoteness.

By the Revolutionary Act of February, 1778, slaves were declared free upon enlisting in the Continental army, a due compensation being provided for their owners. Many availed themselves of this privilege, and served with patience, courage, and fidelity, during the war.

It has been alleged that some States abolished slavery in so guarded a manner as to give the owners an opportunity to dispose of their slaves to the people of the south before the appointed time of manumission, thus gaining the credit of benevolence, obtaining relief from the presence of the negro population, and also profiting in no inconsiderable sum. A foreign traveller has pronounced this ingenious scheme a phase of "Yankee smartness," of which the Empire State did not disdain to avail herself. But no similar charge can justly be brought against Rhode Island. The law enacted in October, 1779, effectually prevented such a practice, by forbidding the selling of slaves out of the State, without their consent.

In February, 1784, the Abolition Act, long urged upon the people and officials of the State by Thomas Hazard, for forty years a preacher in the Friends' Meeting of Narragansett, and by other early advocates of universal freedom, was passed by the General Assembly. Moses Brown, the venerable Providence merchant, and a worthy member of the Society of Friends, was instrumental in procuring the enactment of this law, which was so great a triumph for the anti-slavery cause. The tenor of the preamble expresses a resolute, consistent, and generous acceptance of the final issues resulting from the agitation of the question, whose decision had so recently been referred to the fearful arbitrament of war. It is worded as follows:

"Whereas all men are entitled to life, liberty and the pursuit of happiness, and the holding of mankind in a state of slavery as private property, which has gradually obtained by unrestrained custom and the permission of laws, is repugnant to this principle and subversive of the happiness of mankind, the great end of all civil government," etc. By the provisions of the act, all future children of slaves were to enjoy complete freedom, and fitting regulations were made for their support. Also the importation as well as the sale of negroes in the State was forbidden.

The descendants of Thomas Hazard, of South Kingstown, have preserved a paper drawn up by him, which has lately been published, and which is entitled: "Essay of an Act to prevent the slave-trade in this State, and *to encourage the abolition of slavery.*" It proceeds thus:

"Whereas the trade to *Affrica* for slaves, and the transportation and selling of them into other countries, is inconsistent with the principles of justice and humanity, with the law of nature, and that more enlightened and civilized sense of freedom which has of late prevailed:

"And whereas the law of Congress in the year 1784 agreed and resolved that we will neither import nor purchase any slaves imported, after the first day of *December* next, after which time we will wholly discontinue the slave-trade and will neither be concerned in it ourselves nor will hire our vessels, our commodities or manufactures to those that are concerned.

"Nevertheless in violation thereof a renewal of the trade to *Affrica* has taken place.

"Therefore, etc.,"—the remainder of the document is occupied with the assignment and recital of penalties to be inflicted upon citizens who might hereafter, "directly or indirectly import or transport on his or their account any of the inhabitants of that part of the world called *Affrica* into any other country or part of the world whatsoever as slaves." The whole plan and language of this paper so closely resemble those of the Act of October, 1787, as to suggest the conjecture, if not positive conclusion, that the latter was originated by the same active and illuminated mind.

During the month of June, 1790, a society was formed in Providence and incorporated by the Legislature for promoting the abolition of slavery. Many of the best and ablest and most distinguished men of the State were included in this dignified body of early abolitionists.

"In conclusion," observes Judge E. R. Potter, of Kingston Village, whose report (upon anti-slavery petitions), submitted in 1840 to the Representatives of the Rhode Island Legislature, has been followed as authority for the facts detailed in the foregoing paragraphs, "it may be remarked that slaves were never subjected here to severer punishment than whites for the same offences, as has been the case in some States; and they enjoyed the protection of the laws for offences against their persons equally with the whites. And again, no law was ever passed to restrain the manumission of slaves, except just so far as was necessary to prevent their becoming chargeable to the towns where they lived. A master might desire to liberate his old and useless slaves with a view of getting rid of the expense of their support, and this the law interfered to prevent; but with this exception, there never was any restraint upon the power of manumission, and our town clerks' offices contain the records of numerous manumissions by slave-owners of their own accord.

"It is believed that while slavery existed in Rhode Island, the slaves were always treated with humanity, and that they were generally rather a burden than a source of profit to their owners. And the owning of them encouraged idleness and extravagance, and has been the cause of the ruin of many formerly wealthy families among us."

The memories of our forefathers are fast vanishing within the dark strongholds of unreturning, unrelenting time. But few and vague are the transitory glimpses afforded by fancy or conjecture of the inner lives of those who have gone before us. That they hoped, suffered, loved, rejoiced, and sorrowed — it is known — it is unknown. The long-foreseen, inevitable issues of each individual life — are they not traced in the wide invisible annals of humanity? Have they not forever faded from the special history of a race, a nation? But the solemn record of their public acts yet remains. In what spirit should it be approached by us, their descendants? While dealing in strict justice with aught of unworthy or ignoble that may appear, shall we not be cheered by each slightest indication of future progress, and bless the first faint dawning of the light that now guides our steps onward to higher, and still higher pathways? Let us give thanks for the promise of national integrity no less than for its fulfilment. The scroll of history is still darkened by many a crime, stained with many a tear; but we gather renewed constancy and courage from the immortal faith and patience of the silent generations, and we cherish the assured trust that coming time will bring the noblest triumph foretold in the counsels of the western world — whence universal illumination, a wiser justice, a broader charity shall prevail, and gladden the distant future of humanity.

TRADITIONS OF NARRAGANSETT SERVITUDE

ON many ancient Narragansett estates, once of great extent but now divided and alienated, may still be seen, on the brow of a bleak hill, or in the centre of some lonely field, a group of low, green mounds, unmarked, unless by rude native stones that bear no inscriptions. These the farmer spares, as he guides his plough in the spring, and perhaps repeats to his questioning boy the substance of the familiar tradition concerning them—that they are the graves of old negro servants belonging to certain powerful families once inhabiting the King's Province, but whose very names may, in some instances, have vanished from human speech or record as completely as those of their former slaves.

Waiving the more serious aspects of the subject, it will be the purpose of this, and of a succeeding sketch, to fix in a few brief paragraphs the fleeting memories of some of the old family retainers whose names are most familiar to the residents of our good "South County," as it is invariably styled by our Providence friends. Such simple traditions, slight and fragmentary as they are, may possess a passing interest for those who wish to trace with close attention all, even the minutest particulars pertaining to the history of society and civilization in our State, especially during transitional periods.

Scarcely one of these shadowy figures fills a more prominent place in the recollections of living persons than *Old Guy*, who gained his freedom as a volunteer in the Continental Army, having served in Colonel Greene's regiment, at Fort Mercer, or Red Bank. He was always a favorite with children, who were delighted listeners to his recitals of many famous battles, in all of which he had, of course, borne a distinguished part, and had saved the country on more than one occasion. But little is known, from any other source, of his achievements during the war. Indeed, it has been unfeelingly hinted that his courage might have been something less than Agamemnon's. Be that as it may, the government had certainly deemed him worthy of a pension, and who that observed his tall, erect, and really soldierly figure, always proudly conspicuous in the procession of veterans defiling through the streets of Providence on each recurring Independence Day, would willingly recall these unworthy reflections upon the fame of our South Kingstown hero?

He was also the principal personage on another anniversary — the summer festival of the Narragansett negroes, during which they held their mimic gubernatorial election. It was a genuine Saturnalia of New England bondsmen — such a season of exuberant mirth and feasting and jollity, as sensibly recalls the early days of Merrie England, or, rather, must seek its proper archetype in the congenial tropics, whence came the childlike race that so heartily enjoyed these rustic gayeties, evincing so immense a capacity for such a prolonged continuance of idleness and amusement as soon becomes an inexpressible weariness to the sterner Anglo-Saxon. In these, our hurried, anxious times, it is more than ever difficult to conceive of this imperious holiday occasion, with its curious exactions and its al-

Traditions of Narragansett Servitude

together astonishing customs, even when thus faithfully portrayed by a historian of Narragansett:

"In imitation of the whites, the negroes held an annual election on the third Saturday in June, when they elected their Governor. When the slaves were numerous, each town held its election. This annual festivity was looked for with great anxiety. Party was as violent and acrimonious with them as among the whites. The slaves assumed the power and pride and took the relative rank of their masters, and it was degrading to the reputation of the owner if his slave appeared in inferior apparel, or with less money than the slave of another master of equal wealth. The horses of the wealthy landowners were on this day all surrendered to the use of the slaves, and with cues, real or false, heads pomatumed and powdered, cocked hats, mounted on the best Narragansett pacers, sometimes with their masters' swords, and with their wives on pillions, they pranced to election, which began generally at ten o'clock. The canvass for votes soon commenced, the tables with refreshments were spread, and all the friends of the respective candidates were solicited to partake, and as much anxiety and interest would manifest itself, and as much family pride and influence was exercised and interest created as in other elections, and preceded by weeks of *parmaturing* (parliamenting); about one o'clock the vote would be taken, by 'ranging the friends of the respective candidates in two lines, under the direction of a Chief Marshal (usually Guy Watson, after the Revolution and until the annual elections ceased), with assistants. This was generally a tumultuous crisis until the count commenced, when silence was proclaimed, and after that no man could change sides, or go from one rank to the other. The Chief Marshal announced the number of votes for each candidate, and in an audible voice proclaimed the name of the Governor elected for the ensuing year. The election dinner corresponded in extravagance in proportion to the wealth of his master. The defeated candidate was, according to custom, introduced by the Chief Marshal, and drank the first toast after the inauguration, and all animosities were forgotten. At dinner the Governor was seated at the head of the long table, under trees or an arbor, with the unsuccessful candidate at his right, and his lady on his left. The afternoon was spent in dancing, games of quoits, athletic exercises, &c. As the slaves decreased in number, these elections became more concentrated. In 1795, elections were held in North and South Kingstown, but in a few years one was held in South Kingstown only, and they have for years ceased.

"The servant of the late Senator E. R. Potter, of Kingston, was elected Governor about the year 1800. The canvass was very expensive to his master. Soon after the election, Mr. Potter had a conference with the Governor, and stated to him that the one or the other must give up politics, or the expense would ruin them both. Governor John took the wisest course, abandoned politics, and retired to the shades of private life."

Silvy Tory was once famous in Narragansett, as a fortune-teller. She lived within the limits of a region commonly designated in phonetic phrase, as the old "Minstrel" (ministerial), but otherwise known as that tract of three hundred acres forming the debatable land

Traditions of Narragansett Servitude

so long the subject of a legal contest between Dr. MacSparran and Dr. Torrey, the representatives of the Episcopal and Congregational Churches, and which was finally awarded to the latter contestant. Sylvia may have been provided with a home in this district of country in consideration of her quasi-claim as the last of Dr. Torrey's slaves. She had long since survived her master and all his immediate family, and could now look out from the door of her cabin upon her greatgrandchildren, playing in the sunshine. Thin, and tall even in extreme old age, with small, erect head, and glittering, watchful eyes, her wild, uncanny, almost feral aspect was doubtless of good service to her in the pursuit of her occult *métier*. But (with whatever natural disappointment to narrator and readers) it must be owned that Sylvia's record was merely characterized by a most annoying tameness, not at all in accordance with the expectations awakened by her high tragic air. Though every commendable effort were to be made to invest her with the dim, uncertain atmosphere of romantic interest and mystery, she would still remain, perhaps, the most harmless, innocent, poor, good old woman that ever assumed the direful character of sorceress. Many of the young people of the neighborhood, with their visitors, frequently called at Sylvia's cabin, on the pretext of some charitable errand. At such times the sibyl, having been duly propitiated by a present of tea,—that luxury so dear to universal womanhood,—would graciously consent to unveil the mysterious events of the future. She did not place her entire reliance upon palmistry, but drew various auguries from an examination of the "grounds" in the teacup. Dismissing all members of the visiting party but one, she carefully steeped a "drawing of tea," with such obscure rites and ceremonies as she had brought with her out of African savagery. Shaking the cup and gazing at its slowly settling contents, she would gravely announce the decrees of fate to her listener, some half-amused, half-frightened girl, who then withdrew, giving place to her companions, who followed her in turn, and whose separate experiences were usually found to bear a marvellous resemblance to each other. Truth to tell, our ancient Narragansett oracle was no more prodigal in rich displays of inventive genius than other lofty seers, who (for a consideration) will condescend to reveal the secret courses of the stars. She was never known to depart from the brief and simple, but eminently pleasing and popular formula, which she had so often found to bring many a good silver half-dollar to cross her withered palm. To each questioning village damsel she foretold a swain of surpassing excellence, whose complexion, as the sibyl (with striking impartiality) declared, should be "dark, but fair!" The pair would meet with crosses and losses, certainly, but it would be a long lane that had no turning, and if they went right, they would be pretty sure to come out right, at last. "And," she generally added, by way of valedictory, catching her sole inspiration from the wild and lonely beauty of the picturesque spot where she had lived for many years, "and you'll live happy ever after, in a fine home on a high hill, with woods on one side of you and water on the other."

But Sylvia also received certain older, and, by courtesy, wiser applicants for the benefit of her hidden powers. Did a cow stray beyond boundaries, or was a horse stolen, the bereaved owner hastened to inquire of Sylvia, who would obligingly furnish him with various occult directions, by a strict adherence to which, the lost might be found. One seems to be describing the English peasantry of the eighteenth century, with their firm faith in the marvellous endowments and benevolent disposition of some "white witch"; but the place was the New England of schools and churches, and the time only about 1850. Must the poor old woman be held to a very rigid accountability for her chosen method of gaining a slender and precarious livelihood, through the easy credulity of her superiors, in which she probably shared? Have there not been many persons of a higher station and wider influence, who have by no means scorned to follow a similar course?

Sylvia had reached what was computed to be the great age of one hundred and four years, and was still in tolerable physical health, when her death occurred. A granddaughter who lived with her and cared for her went out on an errand to a neighbor's, and this short absence proved fatal to the unfortunate woman, who had been left alone and seated close by the fireplace, holding her trembling hands to the blaze. It was too late to save poor Sylvia from an agonizing death.

This granddaughter, Bridget by name, who was indeed fully old enough to look the character of soothsayer, in which she was ambitious to be known, claimed to have succeeded to the mystic arts and powers of her relative. But her prestige in the community was less, or the influence of rustic superstition was on the wane, for she obtained very little patronage, and the indignant descendant of the seeress was forced to accept the less dignified position of a mere charwoman.

Polydore Gardiner was a most important personage to society and a chief among the aristocracy of his own people. The favorite musician on all festive occasions, no country dance was perfect, or could be enjoyed with proper spirit, unless Polydore were present with his beloved fiddle, and followed, as it might sometimes happen, by an admiring group of friends and companions: Cato, Caesar, Plato, Primus, and others of classical fame, who hovered about him in awe-struck delight. His father had been a slave; but Polydore was a free gentleman, and a landed proprietor besides — a distinction of which he was not a little proud, owning, as he did, some acres of stony pasture-ground on the Matoonuc Hills, where he built his cabin, and whence he affably descended, when besought to lend the grace of his presence to each rustic ball or party.

Old Patience was well known to the inmates of many hospitable kitchens. Nothing about her was suggestive of her name. The unhappy woman was hardly aware of her bitter temper, for her mind had long been impaired, and thus it happened she had been a constant wanderer and a perpetual pensioner upon a charity that was always readily and cheerfully granted. But, crazed as she might be, she still retained a sharp tongue and a biting wit, wherewith to silence any thoughtless or unfeeling persons who might offer her annoyance. Of wild, morose, and haggard looks, she seemed always plunged in gloom and despair. Holding her own people, for the most part, in utter scorn, she kept aloof from them as much as possible, with one exception, her "Cousin Is'bel," with whom she was proud and eager to claim relationship, and who had long been a faithful servant in the family of Dr. George Hazard, of South Kingstown. This honored relative, Patience was pleased to treat with distinguished consideration, and made herself quite at home in the friendly kitchen over which she presided. Here she would remain for hours, crouched in the chimney-corner by the fire, without speech or movement, unless it were in uttering some tart reply to the curious questions of children, toward whom she was by no means gracious. At other times, her forlorn or defiant mood softened under the influence of kindness, and she would be more communicative, if the right chord was touched. Almost the only being for whom the bewildered brain and frozen heart seemed to entertain any but bitter emotions was a young gentleman—a certain "Master Isaac"— whose nurse she had been in his childhood, and whom she held to be the one unparalleled impersonation of all that was most excellent in youth. Of him she would always willingly talk, wherever she might be (but whether any of the young ladies, her occasional listeners, ever encouraged her to pursue the theme, discreet tradition saith not), frequently closing her eulogy with: "Now be a good girl, missy, and treat the old woman well, and maybe she'll speak a good word or two to Master Isaac!"

In the family of this admirable Master Isaac once lived *Rosanna*, who enjoyed the distinction of being a sister of the famous *Gambia*, of whose sayings and exploits what lover of old Narragansett lore, gossip, and tradition has not often heard? She, also, was remarkable, and especially in the manifestations of a singularly accurate memory, automatic, as it were, in its action, and not seldom occurring, as a compensation, among such individuals as apparently occupy the lowest grades of intelligence. The mind, being engaged with but few and simple objects, retains these with almost the tenacious grasp of mechanism. Totally innocent as Rosanna might be of any technical knowledge of almanacs, records, or calendars, she knew very well when Monthly Meeting dinners were to be prepared for guests among the assembled Friends. Accordingly, when members of the family applied to her, as they often did, in real or feigned perplexity concerning the exact date of any past occurrence, however trifling, she was able to reply that it took place so many days before or after the time of the last (or whatever) Meeting. Resting her forehead, shaded by its crisp white locks, upon her shrivelled fingers, she would pause for a moment, to take silent counsel with herself. As the bird flies, as the bee traces his unswerving course through the pathless air, so her instinctive recollection sped along its narrow darkened way until it touched the desired point of time, and the chain of association was completed. The result, arising from whatever obscure intuitive process, guided by this primitive count of days and seasons, was marked by unerring exactitude. How many persons, young or old, can accomplish as much so quickly, or so well, with all the supremacy conferred by mental training and discipline, and fortified by calendars, diaries, and one knows not what

Traditions of Narragansett Servitude

boasted and elaborate appliances for ensuring entire accuracy? It was the savage keenness of minute vision, transferred from the sphere of sense to that of mind; the arrested development of twenty faculties to nourish and stimulate *one* up to an overwrought degree of perfection.

THREE REPRESENTATIVE SERVANTS OF THE OLD TIME

IT was not unusual, a century ago, to bestow upon slaves the names of English cities. York, London, and Deptford were living witnesses to the prevalence of this humorous or fantastic custom. Thus, among others of equally ambitious nomenclature, *Rochelle* was waiting-woman to Madame Powell, a native of that city, who passed the closing years of her life in North Kingstown. The maid was once, at least, found guilty of adapting some articles of her mistress' wardrobe to her own use, and growing somewhat restive under the grave and perhaps prolonged remonstrance which ensued, she finally exclaimed, in her own irresistible dialect, and with an energy of expression that recalls the racy utterances of Mrs. Stowe's black heroines: "Laws, Missis, seems so 't was no use a-tryin' to be good. 'Specs *Rochelle will be Rochelle, allers!*" How many individuals of later days, and infinitely wider opportunities, have not too often had reason to echo poor Rochelle's sudden burst of passionate philosophy!

Among the old retainers of early days in Narragansett, *Gambia*, or rather, in full title, *Senegambia*, was easily eminent. He was included in the paternal inheritance of the late Willett Carpenter, of North Kingstown. But his new master, holding the usage of slavery in a just abhorrence, immediately set him free. Of the negroes formerly belonging to the place, all had, at this date, died or received their freedom, and sought other homes, with the sole exception of Gambia.

"The *last* of all the bards was he!"

Three Servants of the Old Time

who, in garret or hall, chanted their artless praises of the heroes of that feudal time, among whom, of course, the members of their masters' families were always sure to be conspicuous, in their fond, simple, and loyal estimation. But Gambia — whose distinguished name his fellow-servants never presumed to abbreviate, after their usual familiar and engaging manner, was not without his own superlative antecedents, and sang the Iliad of his noble family with endless particularity and intense enthusiasm. Like other hereditary bondsmen (who inhabit a certain glorious island), he was the avowed descendant of a race of ancient kings. He was no less than a Prince, and his royal father reigned sole monarch of all Guinea! He delighted to describe the state his father kept in his (Gambia's) own country: "Lived in a great palace, oh, ever so big; and you go in at the silver door, up the gold-iron *teppitones* [stepping-stones], and over the door was a pretty little gold-iron dog." "What *was* gold-iron, Gambia?" "Oh, better than iron, and handsomer than gold, gold-iron was. Well, and when you go up the teppitones, and pound with the knocker, the peart, sassy little dog, he bark! And then you go through long, *long* entries, till last you come to the gold-iron throne" (for the narrator stoutly averred the existence of his favorite metal) "and the king sitting on it, beautifully dressed in white man's clothes. British captains have made his father, oh, such fine presents; Gambia don't know *how* many!" It also appeared, from the veracious testimony of his son, that the Majesty of Guinea maintained a large fleet of gigantic ships on the river Gambia. "Great ships *they* were; no such ships anywheres in England; why, they the biggest ever was made!" In confirmation of these statements, the romancer forthwith related a story which bears a curiously modern air and is not a little suggestive of the facile extravagance of that style of humor which we may perhaps call Californian, rather than American: "Oh yes, one day the captain — he very nice, polite man, and one day he speak up loud to the little cabin boy, and he say, 'You scoundrel you, why for don't you get down in the ship's hold, and fetch up a mug of cider? quick! do you hear!' So the little boy he go, and he stay long, *long* time till the nice captain *most* get out of patience, he stop so long, and when he come up again, with the cider, he old man, and his beard all gray!"

Such were the fantastic relations so persistently repeated by our hero that they must finally have assumed an aspect of probability, even to himself. They were the rude outward manifestations of a kind of wild, grotesque poetry latent in the untutored, undeveloped soul, and transient gleams of heavenly light flashed across the thick darkness wherein a desolate mind was aimlessly wandering and groping toward the unknown possibilities of the future. Imagination owns no thraldom, and who shall deny her free presence and communings with the higher nature, even of the slave? Do we not remember that he is a poet who writes:

> "There breathes no being but has some pretence
> To that fine instinct called poetic sense;"

nor denies it to

> "The rudest savage roaming through the wild!"

Three Servants of the Old Time

His transparent "riddles," as he was pleased to call them, were an unfailing source of delight to his companions, as formerly to young master, by whom they had, of course, been highly applauded in the early, happy, uncritical days when he innocently thought no society could be so enchanting as Gambia's. One of these memorable fancies doubtless originated on some winter's day, when whirling snow-flakes filled the air, and Gambia shrank shivering into the chimney corner, intently watching the unfamiliar, supernatural scene. It was in some such moment of inspiration that he suddenly exclaimed: "What that dance 'round the house, 'round the house, and fling in a white glove at the window?" What immense glee pervaded the childlike soul at this triumphant achievement, and how natural a circumstance it was that another "puzzle" should be immediately constructed on the model of so surpassing a success! Accordingly, rain was presently personified as "A woman dressed in gray, that goes crying 'round the house, and throws her black veil in at the window!"

Like all the sons of genius (of the popular and conventional type), Gambia entertained an unconquerable aversion to hard work. It was almost impossible to make him useful in the field; and even when relegated to the lighter labors of the house and farm, he found these equally repugnant to his lofty tastes. No such thing as a *churn*, he said, was ever seen in *his* country. "How did you manage there, Gambia?" "Oh, the king my father have great large round trench [?] made" (turning the crank of the churn with a rapidity quite surprising, and inspired by the inventive ardor of his Munchausen-like narrative) "and lined all with white shining stone. Then pour in cream, and fill all up to top. Then the king's beautiful white horses — twenty trained horses they were — they just go down the steps, and prance round a little, and in three-five minutes butter come!" And, at this juncture, it would not infrequently be found to have made its appearance even in the humble New England churn over which the African gentleman had condescended to preside, while uttering this magnificent protest.

A long day's idle fishing was naturally much more to Mr. Gambia's taste than any active occupation whatever, and he often deserted the field for a more congenial resort — a large pyramidal rock, situated on the shore of his master's farm, and still known as the "Gambia rock." Few other fishermen continue to frequent it, for it is somewhat difficult of access, and is nearly submerged at high tide. Its adventurous occupant once narrowly escaped drowning, while visiting this favorite spot. Surprised by the returning tide, his retreat was cut off while he was either asleep or absorbed in poetic meditation; and he was forced to cling to the abruptly shelving summit of the rock, drenched and blinded by the spray, and expecting each moment to be swept away by some wave higher than the last. He finally gained the shore, at the falling of the tide, and ran home with ashen face and rolling eyes, clamorous for sympathy, and eager to relate the thrilling particulars of his late danger and escape in his own graphic and forcible language.

Such are a few of the perhaps trivial traditions concerning the well-known Gambia, which have been long

Three Servants of the Old Time

preserved in the family by whom his memory is still held in a half humorous, half kindly regard.

But how to describe *Aunt Ibby?* If "H.,"[1] whose persistent silence, during the past months, the readers of the *Providence Journal* find it hard to forgive, should, in some fortunate moment, consent to give us her portrait from his own ever ready recollections, we should indeed possess her genuine presentment — the work — no, rather the simplest and lightest touches — free, yet faithful — of a practised and masterly hand. This obviously incomplete sketch can but offer a few outlines, which some readers will be able to enliven with the subtile coloring infused by memory.

Aunt Ibby (her full name, fine enough for the heroine of a young lady's novel, was Isabella Remington) had been one of the slaves of Edward Hull, but, unwilling to avail herself of the opportunity conferred by freedom of seeking another home, continued to live with his daughter after her marriage to Dr. George Hazard, of South Kingstown, and remained in this latter family (excepting a short period of service in Newport) until her death, many years later. She was the "Cousin Is'bel" so highly esteemed by Old Patience, the unhappy woman described in a previous paper, and for whom her kind-hearted relative had always a friendly welcome. Dressed in a black gown, over which she wore a short neat dark blue calico sack, and with a snowy "mob-cap" surmounting her pleasant features, Aunt Ibby was a cheerful figure of contented tranquillity, as in her leisure moments she plied

---
[1] This was Miss Carpenter's uncle, Edward Hoxie Hazard, a veritable mine of local history, who wrote with a delightful garrulity.

her swift knitting needles, seated in her accustomed corner by the kitchen fire. This was often the chosen resort of all who wished to be instructed by good judgment, and sound, if quite unconscious, philosophy; or to enjoy acute and racy observations upon people and things. It is a curious fact that some of these sayings, long proverbial in the small circle of individuals who retain a distinct recollection of "Aunt Ibby," are identical with such as are attributed by George Eliot to her memorable creation, the inimitable Mrs. Poyser, of the trenchant tongue and the ready reply. But our good old Aunty possessed a far warmer heart than that of the prim English wife, and a radiant charity was her chief characteristic. In the staunch household ways of frugality, industry, energy, her soul took delight; yet she was slow to blame those who were less willing than she to part with ease and comfort to satisfy these requirements. Never was she heard to utter a harsh word in censure of the absent, but did others enter upon a malicious or thoughtless course of remark, she had always some kindly suggestion or apology to offer. Not Burns, the great poet of human charity, could have been more sincere in the fulness of universal sympathy than she who, in the gentleness of her spirit, would have extended a free forgiveness to the crimes of a very Legree. Nor would the wonderful "monarch-peasant" have disowned whatever fortuitous likeness of soul might subsist between his rarely endowed nature and that of a member of a lowly race, whose sole glory, whose only greatness was her singular depth of goodness. For is it not the highest truth that —

Three Servants of the Old Time

> "We love him, praise him, just for this,
>   In every form and feature,
> Through wealth and want, through woe and bliss,
>   He saw his fellow-creature!"

Regarded more as a friend than as a servant, respected no less than loved by the children, who, in their play or in their transient grief, always counted upon her quick and tender sympathies; still she never presumed upon the consideration with which she was invariably treated, or manifested those opinionated humors, or that obstinate self-will, which so often render a really valuable servant simply intolerable, and are such qualities as have converted the very name of a staunch and trusty old family retainer into a sort of household terror. All the humble, modest, gentle virtues pertaining to that station in life which she so worthily filled, were hers. Care, faithfulness, diligence, honest pride, mingled harmoniously in her singularly perfect character. With her habits of sunny contentment, she always clung fondly to the dear familiar presence of common blessings, and enjoyed them with a hearty gladness which was the pure and spontaneous effluence of a sincere and enduring gratitude.

She entertained no uneasy apprehensions of supercilious usage, for the native elevation and simplicity of her truly dignified character was its own surest defence, and no one could have treated Aunt Ibby otherwise than with respect. She was a living witness to the truth that a genuinely noble soul can elevate its assigned position, and needs no earthly dower to sustain the impressive influence of a goodness that is from above. The often quoted lines of humble George Herbert are no figment to those who know how beautiful was the indwelling spirit that guided the thoughts, and words and acts, of this good and loving old negro woman. Nor can that place in life, the toils and trials of which she so meekly accepted, ever prove other than a most arduous one. How many of us expect to merit a loftier title than that of good and faithful servant? What is the life of such a one but a long, untiring course of patient, systematic, entire self-abnegation? And what is this but an effort toward the very highest fulfilment of the distinctive principles of Christianity, difficult of attainment as they are, even by the best and most enlightened classes of society? Then what right have people to demand of their servants that they shall display a brighter virtue, a more deeply spiritual life, than all the saints of all the ages? And again, if the occupations of a servant really afford scope for the quest and achievement of the noblest moral obligations, the most unselfish goodness, we shall, if we are true men and women, offer no less recognition and reverence to Virtue when she chooses to dwell with poverty and obscurity than when she sits at the rich man's table and fares sumptuously every day.

In Aunt Ibby's extreme old age, it became the duty and privilege of her mistress and friend to provide her with the quieter comforts of a separate home, and there, still surrounded by familiar scenes and faces, she passed away in a peaceful and happy tranquillity. A fitting burial-place was found for her in the grounds of the ancient Meeting House so long occupied by the humble and consistent Society of Friends. There, in that quiet spot, the centre and sanctuary of so much unconscious, unpretending excellence, rises many a silent memorial sacred to the righteous names of true and honest worth. The snows of many winters have piled their drifts high above *one* secluded grave; but with the flowers of each returning spring, the gracious memory which it recalls blooms afresh in living beauty; and when it shall have ceased to be known on earth, it will still be bright in the unfading records of heaven. Human sympathy inspires a thought, a prayer, of affectionate remembrance, over the low ridge of earth faintly marking the place of repose of her who was the meek impersonation of trust, affection, fidelity, and all gentle, true-hearted womanliness.

A TRAVELLER IN OLD NARRAGANSETT

IN the few copies now extant of the "Life of the Rev. Jacob Bailey,"[1] who was a frontier missionary of the English Church in this country, and whose journals have been edited by a member of the Historical Society of Maine, may be found the statements that form the groundwork of this paper.

To make the acquaintance of our authority: He is of New England birth, but is deeply imbued with Old World ideas. In his revolt from the principles of a Puritan education, he has striven to become thoroughly English, deriving all his opinions in religion and politics from British sources; but he still remains a true Yankee in that independence, quickness, and shrewdness of observation, which gives no small value to his narrative.

His life yielded him better opportunities for acquiring cosmopolitan breadth of view than could be enjoyed by many of his fellow-provincials. Although born to poverty, he was enabled, through the kind offices of his pastor, to enter Harvard College, not, however, before he had reached the age of twenty. While a student of divinity, he supported himself by teaching. Not long after his admission to the Congregational ministry, he adopted Episcopal opinions, having been influenced by the persuasions and arguments of the Rev. Dr. Caner, rector of King's Chapel, and Dr. Sylvester Gardiner, an eminent Boston physician, a native

---

[1] In Miss Carpenter's lifetime this family name was represented in Rhode Island by Mr. William W. Bailey, of Providence, the accomplished botanist.

of South Kingstown, Rhode Island. After various discouragements, the most painful being his unkind reception by the president and other officers of the university, when he desired to obtain from them the certificate of good moral character, which was at last ungraciously granted him, he sought and received Episcopal ordination abroad. He enjoyed much "condescending notice" from dignitaries on both sides of the water, and also had the opportunities, naturally less appreciated by him, of hearing Whitefield, and making the acquaintance of his "ingenious countryman, Mr. Benjamin Franklin."

On his return, he married, and became rector, from time to time, of several parishes in Maine. Continuing to pray for the King after the awakening of the Revolutionary spirit, he was mobbed and driven from his home in Pownalborough. In his absence his wife and children suffered many hardships, but finally joined him in his flight to Halifax.

Mr. Bailey continued his missionary work in Nova Scotia, and died at Annapolis, in that colony, in 1808, aged seventy-six.

His early journals were reviewed by him in mature life, and he never lost the habit of noting the events of the year, adding occasional reflections. A keen, practical observer, in a limited range, of men and affairs, his curious studies of contemporary provincial character are piquant and interesting. According to his own judgment, he read the Yankee nature profoundly, sharing it as he did, saving only the thin polish acquired in his English travel. But the higher qualities of his countrymen, those larger traits of colonial character which were fast developing into a national maturity, wholly escaped the quick, but narrow, intellectual vision of the Tory parson. In his officious ridicule of the social environments from which he had but lately emerged, he was like his friend and model, that free lance among churchmen, the Swift of America, as he would have chosen to be called, Dr. Peters, English missionary at Hebron, Connecticut, and author of a bitter, satirical history of that province. The silhouette of Mr. Bailey, prefixed to his biography, is more suggestive of character than more ambitious efforts at likeness often are. As was said of a pencil sketch of Boswell, "busy self-importance and dogmatical good-nature were never more strongly expressed."

Jacob Bailey's birthplace was in the obscure township of Rowley, Massachusetts. Here the Puritan influence was all in all, and society was primitive to rudeness. The centres of civilization in the New England of that day were but few, nor was their influence extensive. Boston was graced "with far-off splendors of the throne, and glimmerings of the crown"; Newburyport, Portsmouth, and Newport enjoyed a free communication with the outer world, and the life of the eighteenth century in familiar places like these is tolerably clear to our retrospective glance. But where, save in family records, or traditions, or in obscure pages such as these before us, shall we find the story of life in a town like Rowley, remote from the capital, holding no direct communication with the sea, isolated from the visits of strangers, and inhabited only by descendants of the Puritan settlers? What a void that life might be, what a triple wall of prejudice, ignorance, and suspicion divided this valley of very moderate happiness from the exterior world, our young student shall tell us. We will follow his brief recapitulation of the elements of his early life, as they appeared to him when later years had accustomed him to other scenes.

"In my tenth year [1741] I found myself an inhabitant of a place remarkable for ignorance, narrowness of mind, and bigotry.... Any divergence from the received mode of thinking and acting drew upon the unfortunate innovator the full battery of village blame and ridicule."

Doubtless many soaring spirits have prided themselves on a scorn of eminently wholesome restraints, and the complaints of our student might pass for the sorrows of a young Werther, were they not thus repeated and emphasized later in life, and by a person who could never have been found guilty of cherishing a morbid sensibility. We find the youth not over-exacting in his dislike of the Dutch tenacity with which these villagers clung to the traditional customs of their fathers. "As for all politeness, and every kind of civility, except what their great-grandfathers taught them, it was considered a crying sin. Thus, I have known a boy to be whipped for saying 'sir' to his father, when he came home from school. This stupid exactness might be observed in the field, at home, in the town, and even in the meeting-house. Every man planted as many acres, ploughed with as many oxen, and gathered in his crops on the same day as his grandfather."

And yet, when the alarum of the Revolution sounded, these routine-hardened men responded to the newly asserted claims of country, while the educated New Englander, who so coolly analyzes his early associations, could not free himself from the rule of habit, and was found among the most bitter Tories. Whether the fault were in his nature, or in his surroundings, it is too evident that the home of his childhood, and the country to which he owed the allegiance of his manhood, never inspired him with sentiments of love or devotion.

But it will be thought that although the soil of Rowley might be barren in the graces, it was surely fertile in the more hardy growths of the virtues. On this point hear Mr. Bailey: "Of a lecture-day you might see fathers of families with a becoming gravity in their countenances, flocking from the house of devotion to the house of flip." As to the worth of this devotion: "When the sermon begins everyone has the privilege of becoming drowsy, about the middle many catch a nod, and many sleep quietly thro' the application. These honest people would esteem it a great hardship to be denied a weekly nap in the meeting-house."

But the village life had other elements than such as may be viewed in a half humorous light. Not only were refinement and elegance foreign to provincial manners, but the morals of the period were of a very low order. Yet the veil of respectability was cast over all. Inward purity of heart and life might be sacrificed if a strict observance of the outward forms of religion was still preserved.

"Upon the ringing of the bell on Sundays, everyone repairs to the meeting-house and behaves with tolerable decency till prayers are over. As to singing, some continue to place such sanctity in a few old tunes, that they either hang down their heads in silence, or run out of the meeting-house while their neighbors are singing one of more modern composition. The character of the New England Saints is to worship the Sabbath while they disobey the laws of the God of the Sabbath."

Mr. Bailey received much flattering notice from Sir William Pepperrell, when, in 1754, the baronet was waited upon by the student, who was making the tour of Portsmouth and its environs, soliciting from persons of distinction the means of continuing his college course. *Mais, nous voyons en plein moyen age!* If we are thus reminded of the mediaeval students, who, in their foot journeys, sought largesse of each richer traveller, the notes of a later journey of Mr. Bailey's through Connecticut and Rhode Island transport us to feudal times by the proofs they give of the gross, the all but savage life of the people of that day. Of the citizens of Providence, where he found entertainment at "Capt. One's [Olney's?] tavern," he gives a dark description. "The inhabitants are, in general, very immoral . . . and famous for contempt of the Sabbath. Gambling, gunning, horse-racing, and the like, are as common on that day as on any other."

He admires the "two streets of painted houses on the northeast side of the bridge which graces the town," but he finds the country between Pawtuxet and Warwick "a desert," in which the people seen were "almost as rough as the trees." In riding through "a great wood" he "came to a house about the bigness of a hog-stye. The hut abounded in children, who came around to stare at us in great swarms, but were clothed only with a piece of cloth about the middle, blacker than the ground upon which they trod. I made no doubt that these people enjoyed themselves as much as we in our elegance and plenty.... At length, being very dry, we came to another house, where we lit, and, coming in, found five or six women in a little room without any floor or ceiling. Two or three of them appeared to be young. One of the wenches made haste to draw us some water, while another made search for a drinking vessel, and the last gave us water in an old broken mug, almost as ancient as time."

At Major Stafford's, in Warwick, "the daughter of the house came to wait upon us ... barefooted and barelegged, with a fine patch and a silver knot on her head, with a snuff-box in one hand and a pinch at her nose in the other."

The Greenwich people are described as "very profane and impolite." In North Kingstown, at "Thomas the Quaker's," the traveller found "the dirtiest tavern-keeper that ever was made. All the time I stopped I could scarce get a word out of him."

In the village built on Tower Hill, in South Kingstown, Mr. Bailey discovered some of the finest gardens in New England. "The people here live in better position than in most parts of the government." He put up at Squire Case's tavern, frequented by Franklin, and well known, as his host did not neglect to inform him, to all gentlemen travellers on "the road from South Carolina to Piscataqua." According to the custom of the time, mine host met the traveller and his companions outside the door, bidding them welcome to Tower Hill, serving out wine to them, and doing the honors of his table at dinner, while entertaining his guests with an account of the murder of one Jackson, an itinerant dealer in skins, by Captain Thomas Carter, of Newport, his chance travelling companion. "We found the Squire to be a most prodigious loquacious gentleman. He offered to wait upon us down the hill to see the murderer as he hung there in gibbets ... we beheld the sorrowful sight. The man had been there three years already, and his flesh was all dried fast to his bones, and was as black as an African's."

The next object of note in the journey is "the great Quaker meeting-house, an odd-built thing, having a kitchen and chimney at one side." In Charlestown "we lodged five miles from the place where the great Narragansett battle was fought, in which so many soldiers expired. Their king is now a young man of eighteen, at school at Newport. ... We passed his house—of late miserably fallen to ruin—and had a sight of two of his sisters, who came to the door as we rode by. Westerly is a miserable, poor, unpopulated place ... yet near the river there are divers good farms." Few changes seem to have been wrought in the aspect of Westerly, and other early settled parts, in the forty-five years that had passed since they had been visited by Madam Knight, whose descriptions are in much the same tone as our traveller's. It is the New England of a day which knew nothing of the civilizing influences of commerce and manufactures that these observers show us. Would that the unreflecting *doctrinaires* who declare that "serfdom is inseparable from the factory system" might cast a glance upon this picture of the miseries of an agricultural serfdom!

One perceives in following the course of this narrative, that New England had once a native peasantry, and of a dangerous sort; a neglected, illiterate, immoral class. The work of the Revolution, which, by preparing the way for the prosperity of the whole people, finally obliterated many arbitrary distinctions, was still in the future. Indications of the diarist's humble origin often appear in remarks like the following: "Had an interview with Col. Gibbs, who behaved towards me with a degree of complaisance, tho' I have had my share of extraordinary caresses from several persons in exalted stations."

Mr. Bailey kept a school in Kingston, New Hampshire, where he found the people "hardened and vile." All vices prevailed. On preaching his first sermon, his style is admired to a degree which, in his *naïve* manner, he pronounces, "a little disagreeable," and he piously ejaculates, "Good Heavens preserve me from the mighty swellings of pride!"

It seems that his probation as a divinity student had not hindered him from sharing in such amusements as amateur theatrical performances given in public places, playing cards in doubtful company, and drinking deep of punch, perhaps chosen for the same reason that Parson Adams preferred it, "the rather that there was nothing said against it in Scripture." These worldly tastes called out no censure from his contemporaries. But at old Plymouth, where his earlier ministrations were conducted, one Deacon Foster, styled by Mr. Bailey "the famous," was apprehensive lest the young preacher should be no better than "a North Shore man," otherwise Arminian.

His voyage to England to obtain Episcopal ordination is graphically sketched by his fearless pen. His passage was by steerage in an English merchantman. The narratives of Swift and Defoe afford no darker scenes of vice and degradation, no more revolting details of misery and squalor, than those described by the young American traveller, who, on entering the ship, found himself "in the midst of the most horrid confusion, and in a spot but little better than the infernal abodes." The ship's officers, though herding in foulness and vice, yet assumed a superior tone toward the unhappy passenger, freely ridiculed his provincial accent, and subjected him to every annoyance, for which their position of tyrants in little gave them opportunity. Mr. Bailey thus indicates the traits of his *compagnons du voyage:* "John Tugg, midshipman, good-natured, honest fellow, but profane. Captain's clerk, who would drink very hard. One of the mates, an ingenious, obliging young gentleman; what I most valued him for was his aversion to swearing. Ship's carpenter, who drank excessively, and swore roundly. One Butler, English parson's son, descended from the Cavalier poet, stiff Jacobite; his language shockingly profane. Lisle, lieutenant of marines, fifty years old, gigantic in stature, distinguished by the quantity of liquor he drank and the oaths he swore. Irish midshipman, the greatest master of profanity that ever I knew."

Such were the congenial companions to whose society the young student was restricted during the long voyage. This nightmare group of personified vices forcibly recalls the similar assemblages depicted by Cervantes or Le Sage. "Lisle, lieutenant of marines," is a figure worthy of a place in the recitals of Gil Blas.

Here is one scene from the horrors of the passage: "At nine we began to think of supper, and a boy was called in. Nothing in human shape did I ever see so loathsome. . . . He brought us our dish, beef, bread, potatoes and onions, stewed together and served in a wooden tub. The table furnished with two pewter plates, one knife, one broken fork, two broken metal spoons. Carousing continued until two, when I mounted into a sort of canvas bag, hanging from the beams. Here I had no rest, other than a few uneasy snatches, and awoke in the morning with ten thousand dismal apprehensions ringing in my ears."

The hideous voyage was over at last, and the young American soon found himself taking part in scenes of a widely different character. He was suddenly transferred from the surroundings of squalor to those of splendor. "To-day dined with the Bishop of Rochester. The dining-hall, vast and composed of marble arched above, and twenty feet high. We [the company of candidates for orders] sat down with his Lordship, the Bishop of London's lady, and others, being twenty-one, and were served with twenty-four dishes, dressed in such an elegant manner that many of us could scarce eat a mouthful."

The excited fancy of the untravelled young provincial transmuted the Bishop's heavily plated dinner service into "solid gold." One readily divines that this memorable occasion of awful honor was often described by the worthy participant in later years, and that his parishioners of the backwoods of Maine or Nova Scotia may have had as much reason to complain of the recital as the retainers of Scott's Lady

Margaret had to dread her references to the visit of His Sacred Majesty to Tillietudlem Castle.

The minister is no sooner comfortably settled at Pownalborough, on a goodly glebe, with a roomy house, and with one of the finest gardens in New England, planted and cultivated by his own hands, than the summons of the Revolution sounds, bringing dismay and alarm to the quiet fireside. Comfort, elegance, domestic security and tranquillity, disappear in a moment. The respected clergyman has become a hunted exile. He expresses very genuine feeling in very artificial verse, sending it to an English friend. The following stanza of the poem was read in a London coffee-house, and drew tears of admiration and sympathy from the assembled wits and politicians.

> "Once more with heavy parting sighs,
> We roll around our misty eyes;
> My partner calls to mind
> Her babes beneath the heaving ground,
> And mourns and weeps with grief profound,
> To leave their dust behind."

The Parson's flight to Halifax was not without an occasional touch of adventure. A curious incident vividly illustrates certain phases of New England character. Stopping for dinner at a house on the Maine frontier, "Mrs. Bailey was dressed with a small roll upon her head, which induced the mistress of the house and her father to exclaim vehemently against the wickedness of the times; and when they perceived that she was a minister's wife, they conceived the wearing of the roll to be an unpardonable crime."

Another incident *en voyage*, from the deck of a

schooner: "A sailor put over a line and caught two codfish; when the two brothers in command, coming on deck, reproved him sharply for his wickedness in profaning the Sabbath, and when they could not restrain him they swore a multitude of oaths. Thus the New England Saints worship the Sabbath."

The boldness of the American privateers in their repeated attacks upon the coast, almost under the guns of Halifax, arouses the admiring indignation of the expatriated Yankee. The exploits of his hardy countrymen might well have reminded him of the daring deeds, so dear to English pride, of Drake and Hawkins, when, "in great Eliza's golden prime," a like spirit of adventure was abroad. But time had mellowed the lurid colors of Protestant piracy; it had not yet gilded the acts of American Revolutionists. Few mortals are gifted with insight that penetrates even the near future, and the vision of our honest narrator was no dimmer than that of his neighbors.

"I am persuaded," he says, " that my countrymen exceed all mankind in a daring and enterprising disposition. Their bold and adventurous spirit more especially appears with distinguishing *éclat* when they are engaged in any unjust or vicious undertaking; and their courage commonly increases in proportion to the badness and villany of the cause they seek to support. Let a New England man once throw off the restraints of education and he becomes a hero in wickedness, and the more strict and religious he has been in his former behavior, the greater will be his impiety in his present situation. It has often been remarked by foreigners who have been engaged in commerce with our Puritans, that when they first come abroad no people alive have such a sacred regard for the Sabbath, and none have such an aversion to profanity, yet they quickly become the most docile scholars in the courses of vice, making the greatest proficiency in every kind of profanity. They openly ridicule their former devotion; are very expert at framing new and spirited oaths, and when they have any extraordinary mischief to perform they always choose to perpetrate it on Sunday."

Mr. Bailey's remarks upon certain traits of his travelled countrymen are in the same vein with those of his friend Dr. Peters, but his judgments on these innocents abroad, though expressed with no lack of emphasis, are not marred by the extravagance of the satirical Doctor's gibes. Our authority finds his opinion concerning Puritan character confirmed by the observations of an English acquaintance, who "made several shrewd remarks upon the behavior of my countrymen who formerly used the Halifax trade. Some he found to be as honest and fair dealers as ever he met with, but in general he found them to be the profoundest hypocrites in nature, and the cunningest knaves upon earth, for though men advanced in life were averse to swearing, and would pucker up their mouths, and roll their eyes towards Heaven, at the mention of an oath, yet they would not scruple to lie, and deliberately appeal to the Almighty in confirmation of a falsehood. He had known some young fellows from Boston government, who, upon their arrival in Halifax, would not swear, upon the greatest provocation, but when highly exasperated, would only exclaim, 'I vow, you are a sarpently Satan, a'most!' And yet in a few weeks these very conscientious travellers would free themselves from all the restraints of education, and exceed the most abandoned sailors in bold impiety. They would take the Sacred Name in vain, practice the most horrid oaths, and even make a public scoff and ridicule of all religion."

But why, it may be asked, should we inquire so closely into the weaknesses and follies of the darkened past? Why let in light upon those traits of New England character that a generous forgetfulness would conceal? A New England poet shall give the answer; and in Whittier's words we shall find a fit authority for our strictures upon the provincial spirit.

> "And will ye ask me, why this taunt
>   Of memories sacred from the scorner,
> And why with ruthless hand I plant
>   A nettle on the graves ye honor?
>   .   .   .   .   .   .
> Not to reproach New England's dead
>   This record from the past I summon.
>   .   .   .   .   .   .
> No—for yourselves alone I turn
>   The pages of intolerance over;
> That in their spirit, dark and stern,
>   Ye haply may your own discover!"

Are those discordant traits which were noted by our acute diarist so completely things of the past that we shall find it altogether unprofitable to review them with an application to the present? The town of Rowley, as it was in Bailey's day, no longer exists; but certain qualities of character which marked its men and women still survive in villages more favored by time and circumstance. Unhappily, intolerance, uncharitableness, and ignorance are not yet extinct. Generous culture and cosmopolitan advantages must remain the portion of the few; but the influences of free thought in religion and free government in the State should shed such fulness of light upon the obscurest hamlet that, in the time to come, the typical New England village shall have left a record far different from that which perpetuates the shame of Rowley.

THE PIOUS DREAMER

THE record of a vision which has been preserved for more than a hundred years is prefaced by the seer's letter, or, rather, the fragments of it now remaining. The circumstances of its preservation indicate that it was addressed to some member of a certain North Kingstown family. Of this household the "Lillis" affectionately referred to in the letter was an inmate. A young Connecticut woman, coming to Rhode Island as a teacher, she never returned to her early home, but was interred in the farm burial-ground, among the family with whom she had lived. The letter, as it now remains, opens thus:

I wish I could write you better news than at present, although if I go back a year and a half past I could write you blessed news, when God did marvels amongst us, which I imagine you have heard of and rejoiced at; but alas! the gold is become dim and the most fine gold changed, although I hope there is some movings on the minds of some few, yet I think the saints are not so active for God and the good of souls as in months past; but iniquity abounds amongst us, and the love of many waxes cold, for which the Lord is frowning. He is sending His armies of insects that are cutting off the fruits of the earth. It is thought that in general where they expected 50 bushels they won't have one. Seth Wetmore is one of our greatest farmers. He sowed 14 acres of new ground, expecting a large crop; plowed it up and planted it with corn. Deacon Bacon told me the other day he did not expect half a bushel this year. And O!

that we, as a people, now the judgments of God are evidently abroad in the earth, might learn righteousness.

I am removed from the farms, and live at widow Bacon's, in Westfield, where I hope to receive a letter from you soon, and don't let it be long. Your friends would be glad to see you here. I and my wife send our kindest love, not only to you, but to your father and mother and all the family, not forgetting my Lillis. And now I conclude, wishing that the good-will of Him that dwelt in the burning bush may dwell in all our hearts, is and shall be the prayer of your affectionate friend, and I humbly hope, your brother in the best relation.

ZACCHEUS BEEBE.

Middletown, June 16, 1787.

I send you enclosed a copy of a vision I had the same day that I wrote this letter, soon after I finished it, and if it may refresh your soul as much as it did mine you will bless God for it all the days of your life.

The Vision—It is written in the Word of God that in the last days He will pour out His spirit upon His servants and handmaidens, and old men shall dream dreams and young men shall see visions. I had been writing a letter to a friend at a distance, and being weak and feeble I lay down on my bed with my face toward the wall, to take repose, and soon fell into a sound sleep, when I thought I was amongst a charming number of saints worshipping the living God. I thought I never saw a greater union and sweeter agreement among a people in all my life, the power and love of God seemed to be evidently among them. I thought I cast my eyes toward heaven and saw the blue vault of heaven split asunder, through which I thought I saw a stream of light and love proceeding from the throne of God, clear as crystal. To give you my idea, as the rays of the sun in the firmament at its first rising shine into a door or window so the stream through the whole house will be lighter than anywhere else, so the whole stream of light from heaven to where I stood shin'd with light and love. Never did I see anything so strait, and on either side the stream it were decked with thousands of little rays of light, all pointing one way, even toward heaven. I thought that every drop of light and love that God bestows is to be returned to Him again, and while I stood wondering at the sight, I thought I saw the fiery chariot of God's love come through a gap that was in the vault, coming through the midst of the stream a hundred times swifter than I ever saw an eagle fly. I thought it was all over glorious and in color like to a rainbow, and was carried on wings of love. In a few moments it was just by where I stood and turned short about with the fire part toward heaven, and rested on its wings, keeping its wings in a slow motion to bear it up, and waiting for me to come in. I thought my soul was transported; I thought I stood with my heart and hands extended to heaven, crying "Glory, glory to God in the highest!" and just as I was about to mount into the chariot I turned to my brethren, crying, "Glory, glory to God; I am going to glory in the fiery chariot of His love! and I as much believe I shall see you in glory in a little while as I believe I ever had an existence." While I was thus speaking to them I thought

The Pious Dreamer

I saw three lads among the people making mouths and mocking at what I said. I thought I spoke out to tell them the consequence of so doing, and awoke out of sleep. But O! the disappointment. My wife sat near the bed, and, seeing me all in tears, asked what I had been dreaming about. "O!" said I, "I had the most glorious news since I lay down that ever I had in my life. O! that I had been suffered to take my flight. O!" said I, "if one view of the glory and love of God will fill a soul with such joy even in a dream, what will the open vision and full fruition be in glory?" I don't know that the thoughts of it has been out of my mind when I have been awake since that time.

The writer, a rude worthy of our primitive time, has left in this characteristic letter a sufficient indication of his mental personality, with its stern and rugged features and the gloom of its environment. He unconsciously sets forth a map of his narrow spiritual territory, manifest in all the limitations of its poverty, the stubbornness of the soil, and the harsh nature of its growths. A mind like his, unenlightened and arid, resembled one of his own rocky pastures, never penetrated by the genial powers of sun and dew. But as the brief New England summer sees the magnolia come into bloom on the stern coast of Cape Ann, so the hard and prosaic nature of the Puritan had its fervid flowering time of religious emotion. The higher elements of that experience are not wanting in the pious vision of our untaught mystic, and his crude imagery appeals to such as hold the sentiment more Christian than heathen, that to man nothing is alien that belongs to humanity.

There is a week-day and a Lord's-day side to this double epistle. The more familiar half of the missive is the sufficient explanation of the record which follows it. One is the natural complement of the other, and in both we trace the traits of the same undeveloped intelligence. The confused strivings of a mind oppressed by the grievous conditions of nature, as interpreted by the harsh spirit of Calvinism, are evident in the narrative, and in its style. Not that "cant" is a just reproach to the ignorance which delights in the special speech that it accepts and esteems as a savor of godliness. The craving after a mystical phrasing in which to enshrine spiritual truths is no less natural than the use of an exact terminology in physical science. The writer of this pious epistle seems to have been an earnest, honest man, unwittingly nurturing and cultivating such blemishes of character as harsh judgment, spiritual pride, and pietistic narrowness, while laboring to form himself on such imperfect models of manhood as he took for exemplars of sanctity. He strives after the habits of thought suitable to the "saints," and takes their language on his lips, hoping some day to be counted among them, not only, as we may guess, by the Recording Angel, but by his near friends and neighbors. Some touch of egotism, some frailties of self-seeking, must be pardoned to humanity, even in its most cherished types. In these secret weaknesses of the soul our old worthy was not much more guilty than many of his superiors in wisdom and culture.

How irreverent the "ingenious dreamer," as Cowper called Bunyan, would find the plain, modern way of accounting for his sacred vision! His feeble health and lack of wholesome air and exercise; his daily meditations, and the influence of the godly men whom he studied from books or report; the unhappy dissensions in his church, the existence of which we may safely assume as suggesting the contrast of the "charming number of saints in sweet agreement"; the exalted opinion of his own holiness, which summoned a fiery chariot for his translation; the occasional disrespect shown him by reckless youth, which evidently so rankled in the good man's breast as to call up the disturbing sight of the "three lads among the people making mouths and mocking," so effectually as to destroy the frail air-woven tissue of the dreamer's self-pleasing imaginations—these bodily and mental conditions surely afford material for the vision strangely preserved through the chances of a century which has swept away many records of greater worth.

The story of his visionary transports is certainly conceived in a higher tone than the reader of the preceding letter would readily have expected. The pietist now emerges from the bounds of sectarian cant into the large speech of the Hebrew writers, whose words recur naturally to his awakened imagination. Strong feeling creates its own style, and the dreamings of the unknown Puritan are told in a manner not below that of the learned Swedish seer. The mysticism of the Book of Revelation had permeated the mind that conceived of "the stream of light and love," the "throne as clear as crystal," the "chariot coming a hundred times swifter than ever I saw an eagle fly," and "in color like to a rainbow," with "its wings in a slow motion." The realism of the writer mingles forcibly with the lofty Eastern imagery, and brings us within the range of his actual experiences, as in his homely illustration of the sunbeam shining "into a door or window," and in that quiet, unconscious touch by which we share with him the sight of the eagle of our lonely coast.

But whence did the musing yeoman evolve a thought like this: "Every drop of light and love that God bestows is to be returned to Him again." Before Emerson taught the absorption of the spirit in the ocean of infinity,

"Lost in God, in Godhead found";

before the craving for Nirvana had found expression in the western mind, or pantheism had become a word of common usage, the solitary and unlearned pietist, brooding over the mystical speculation that set his mind free from the sordid round of his dull labors, had arrived at a dim dream-reading of metaphysical subtleties.

But what said his brethren in the church of his mysterious vision? Found they aught unorthodox in its dark sayings, and did they bid him go dream by rule another time?

Let them dispute as they would, they could not shut out this provincial Bunyan from the one source to which he looked for authority, and whence he unconsciously derived that Oriental fervor of his dreams which contrasts strangely with the hard routine of his working hours. The Scriptures were the sole origin of whatever elevation of thought, tenderness of emotion, or poetry of expression was cultivated by the Puritan. Sternly rejecting all worldly learning, he dwelt within the influences of an unrecognized culture, which softened the atmosphere in which he moved, and enriched it with an unsuspected beauty.

SUNDRY SAVORY RECIPES TO CURE DIVERS DISEASES

THE credulity of our Puritan ancestors was not wholly expended upon matters of religious superstition. The belief in witchcraft was natural enough to people who put faith in the repulsive recipes which were not confined to household medicine, but were the prescriptions of the most learned physicians of the time. But perhaps it should not surprise us, in view of the inexact nature of medical science, that inert substances and injurious practices should long have continued in credit. The average custom of dispelling an eclipse by an energetic beating of drums and sounding of gongs is a perfectly rational one, from an empirical point of view. It is certainly a sovereign method of abating the infliction, for no sooner has the ceremony been piously performed than the threatening phenomenon yields to its efficacy. It is no wonder that a scheme always crowned with success should be commended by tradition and endorsed by practice. So, not unlike the exorcist, the leech diligently strove to affright the evil spirit of illness by exhibiting his most villainous compounds. Finally, the patient, if strong enough to overcome both the disease and its treatment, recovered—glory to Esculapius! Or he, perchance, died, in which case glory was still due, of course, to Esculapius and his pious servant, but maledictions dire were poured upon those baffling agencies, the malignant humors and the critical days.

Does not medicine still suffer more from solemn pretension and ignorant meddling than any other profession? Not only is it wounded in the house of its friends by the followers of "yon gentle bird, that rides upon the stream, and is the patron of their noble calling," but it suffers from the self-sufficiency of patients, nurses, and their friends, for everybody claims to know something about medicine. New Englanders have long since lost their Byzantine zest for theological speculations. Those metaphysical niceties which once engaged in endless controversies the Greek artisans and their spiritual successors, the Yankee farmers, are now left to professional disputants. Law has lost its attractions for the popular mind, since it has disused those fine, manly practices of the Middle Ages, by which a knotty point might be settled at small expense of brain power, and the weight of the plaintiff's arm, rather than the weight of his arguments, gained him his cause. But medicine continues to be the prey of that general interest with which it must always be regarded as long as the touching story of his aches and ails shall be dear to the heart of the valetudinarian. No doubt there may be good as well as harm in that most common form of "scientific curiosity" which appears in the interest we take in our neighbor's ailments, and especially in our own. If medicine is, as its teachers sometimes style it, the common-sense profession, it cannot wholly repel the claims of its laity to a certain right of private judgment.

Some curious illustrations of the practice of household medicine in New England more than 200 years ago may be gleaned from family manuscripts such as the notes of John Saffin of Boston, son-in-law of Captain Thomas Willett, the early settler of Plymouth, and

Savory Recipes for Divers Diseases

first mayor of New York. Saffin's quaint language has furnished the heading for this article, and a few quotations from his pages will serve as indications of the regimen of his time.

Under the note "this is a receipt procured by Mrs. Wyng from a skilful physician and communicated to my wife October third, 1675," we find the heading of "An eye water for salt rhumes, chataracts, or felmes." The ingredients are "faire running water, white sugar candy, white copperis, white rose water," "the herb eye bright," with the "oyle of snailes." The living ingredients are to be kept one night in a "basket of sweet pott herbs, or grape leaves." The mixture is to be strained through lawn, and exposed to the sun in "a single glass bottle." The application is made by dropping in each eye, "though both be not injerure."

Another remedy for the same ailment is marked *probatim est*, and consists of a mixture of "winter wheat and raisen white wine, steeped for six days in a copper vessel." Afterwards the liquor is to be strained and the wheat "brused in a morter." Then the standing and straining process is to be repeated until, at the end of a week, the water is ready for use, " and will smart a little, but in a short time it will recover the eyes."

"Almonde milke" is the name given to a concoction of stewed chicken, mutton broth, blanched almonds, and rose water, "cinemon and loafe sugar," precisely as if it were a dish of Persian luxury prepared for "the Sultan Shah Jehan, when he goes to the city Ispahan." It is to be served on "a chaffeing dish of coales," and it is "good against a consumption."

"A golden water" may be prepared from "unslake't

lime" and spring water, and is intended for a lotion. This also is a *probatim est.*

"An excellent medicene" for "a patient grieved" is the external application of "an egge boyled very hard, then pill off the shell, and use it hot as you can . . . and it will cure." This is at least a more available remedy for acute attacks than some of the receipts given in these pages, not a few of which call for processes of twelve hours' duration.

A salve is made from "sallett oyle," white lead, red lead, and beeswax, stirred into white vinegar with an alder stick. When ready to drop like syrup "on a pewter dish," it is time to "take it off, and keep it for your use," and so long as it was carefully kept locked up it was no doubt a harmless thing to have in the house.

"To prevent infection or cure pestilential diseases" is a receipt which enumerates "an handful of rue and a handful of sage," to be "boyled in a quart of sack or muscadine," adding "a nutmeg and as much ginger or long peper well beaten small together, then boyle it againe a little more, and add about two spoonfuls of balme water, and half the quantity of a nutmegg of mitridate, and of treacle, of all which take a spoonful to prevent and two to remove ye malady."

Another prescription for the cure of the same class of diseases is associated with an historical name, having been "experienced by George Monk in ye West Indies." The instructions are to "take the thigh bone of a gamon of bacon or that bone of a swine, burn it to a powder white, then take a nutmeg wrapt in paper and a little of said powder of bone and put into a small quantity of brandy and let the patient drink thereof, fasting in ye morning, and at other times, often long after meals."

"An excellent medicen against obstructions" is made from "the moss that grows upon the outside of an oyster-shell that is of a brownish, and some of a scarlet colour, dry it well in an oven, then rubb it to a fine powder, then let the party grieved take thereof about the quantity that will lye on a shilling or poynt of a knife, in a glass of wine or syder, in the morning, fasting, and so three or four times a day or two following."

"An ach in the shoulder or elsewhere" may be cured by an application of "oyle of marsh mallows, raisons of the sun, and figgs," with mustard seed. When ground in "a mustard quarn, with good wine vinegar, spread it upon a lamb's skin and lay it on the place grieved, and it will cure"; after which hopeful statement it seems superflous to continue with:

"Another for the same, etc." This consists of "a pint of pure malmsey, and four or five onions peeled and sliced, with beaten peper," and " strained threw a cloth, and at two or three times dressing it will help, as hath been proved."

"For sudden and epidemical attacks," Rev. Samuel Lee, deceased, father-in-law of the writer, and first minister of the Bristol Congregational Church, furnishes the following recipe. He was English, and a graduate of Oxford: " Take the roote of tormentill, dry it well, then beate it to a fine powder, wich mixe (at discretion) in wine or brandy, a small quantity, let it soak 24 hours at least. Drink thereof two or three times in 24 hours, and it is an excellent medicine." Saffin's note to this runs to the effect that after the herb has steeped at least 24 hours in the liquor it should be taken "according to discretion."

Saffin also furnishes from his domestic experience "a medicine to cure the rickitts." It is a mixture of white wine, "two nuttmeggs greated," with white sugar candy, saffron, and the shells of "two new layd eggs." Of this "give the child that is grieved a spoonful or two every night and morning, according to the strength of the child.

This is followed by "Another for the same disease," which has evidently been copied from an original receipt and preserved with especial care as a family treasure. It is a copy made by John Saffin from the manuscript of John Eliot, who was a connection of Saffin's, being his wife's brother-in-law. Savage says that John Eliot, son of the Apostle to the Indians, married Sarah, third daughter of Thomas Willett, and John Saffin married her sister Martha. The signature included in this copy shows that the original writer (Eliot) sent the receipt to one of his wife's parents, presumably her mother. We may, if we like, fancy it to be an excerpt from the Apostle's own book of domestic medicine, and it is believed by descendants to be the only personal memorial of his wife, Ann Mumford (or Mountfort), who was betrothed to him in England, and followed him to America the next year. She was the mother of one daughter and five sons, of whom but one survived his parents, and died in 1687. In her husband's words spoken of her at her funeral, three years before his own death, she was "a dear, faithful, pious, prudent, prayerful wife." Unusual honors were paid to her memory.

Savory Recipes for Divers Diseases

Her recipe is, in full, as follows:

Take an oxe gall, a like quantity of fresh butter, mingle them, and boyle them together with wormwood, rue, feather few, of each a like quantity, as much as the s^d leekquor will containe, over a gentle fire, for the space of three or four hours, straine it, and keepe it for yor use. With this anoynt the child all down the brest, and cross the short ribbs, bathing it well against the fire; this doe every night for a moneth together, in the spring, as soon as the said herbs may be had; in the meantime frequently give the child water wherein a handfull of currants have been boyled.

This is my mother's *probatim est,* wch she hath cured many with, and it seldom faileth.

Yo^r very son,

JNO ELIOTE.

With this graphic indication of the state of medical science in the Puritan household, and the accompanying glimpse of the neighborly duties of the Puritan matron, we will close the list of such extracts as could properly be taken from the old note-book. They may serve to instruct us in the domestic habits of a people whose traits, notwithstanding our hereditary claim to comprehend them, strike us with a new sense of strangeness as often as we try, by the help of manuscript remains, to reconstruct their extinct personality.

AN OLD BOOK OF HOUSEHOLD MEDICINE

THIS neatly written, carefully indexed manuscript was doubtless regarded as a curiosity even in 1793, when it was bought by Benjamin Waite Case, a young Newport physician, of John J. Rhodes, shopkeeper, of Exeter. The book, which seems to have been compiled in Newport, is the work of two or more persons. The original owner was evidently a credulous, painstaking simpler and empiric. His manual opens with a careful list of definitions of such recondite terms of medical science as "stimulate; to prick; to provoke"; and the characters used in prescriptions are fully explained. Several passages on hygiene are scattered through the volume, and are generally transcribed from authors who, notwithstanding the barbarous and superstitious notions by which the profession was then ruled, do occasionally manifest glimpses of good sense. When " ye Physician to ye Duke of Saxony" cautioned his professional brethren against the excessive use of medicine, "for moderation must be used with ye Stomach," he announced a principle which, unhappily, has not yet been reduced to practice, but which is equally applicable to states of sickness or health. The virtues of apples are warmly described in an extract from such an authority as the "Compleat English Dispensatory." An instance is given of "one who used to eat thirty every day for his breakfast [!], and Dr. Baynard highly cries *ym* [them] up as a most noble Pectoral; having twice cured himselfe of a confirm'd Consumption by their use." Physicians will be interested in learning that consumption can be cured a second time. Our compiler having sundry personal reasons for desiring to understand the treatment of gout finally inquires into the means of prevention as well as cure, quoting "A Treatise of ye Goute," which recommends "hot Salads, such as Salary, but all Spiritus Liquors to be avoided as one would avoid a Mad Dog, and afternoon Sleep to be shunned as a fierie Serpent. Cyders are admirable good for goutic people, and Cremor tartari with their meat instead of comon Salt." The benefits to be obtained by a free use of cold water are set forth in sundry extracts from Sir John Floyer and other lights of science; while the transcriber reinforces theory with practice; keeping a diary in these pages, from which we learn that cold bathing afforded him great relief from the attacks of his old enemy, the gout. He also relates that "Mr. Allen was so lame in his arme that he could not proceed on his jarney home. I put his arme into a tube of cold watter and gave him about a quart of cold water to drink & in ¾ of an hour he said his arme was well, and proceeded on his jarney"—possibly in search of some less rigorous form of hydropathic treatment. Members of our amateur practitioner's family could not escape so easily: "*Mem.* July 1, 1725. My Jeny was Sez'd with a fever and had a Soar Throat. I sent her to bed and gave her a dose of Cold Water, and she went to sleep. I tended her with water only, sometimes cold and sometimes with a tost, and she was quite recovered in about three days." Tar water was held in great esteem by the compiler, and he quotes from the *South Carolina Post Boy* in proof of its efficacy in cases of small-pox. The use of this "infallible remedy" seems to have encouraged the people to employ pure water in fevers; and we find in a quotation from "Sir John Floyer's Book, Print'd 1722," the following statement: "I could give a hundred such instances, where People of all Ages have been lost by being deny'd drink; and in Small Pox it has been of fatal Consequence." There would seem to be but little excuse for the physicians who refused water to their patients down to a date within the memory of middle-aged persons, if even one distinguished member of their fraternity had learned a better method so early as 1722. Some sensible remarks upon the uses of buttermilk are also taken from this author: "I am now upon ye grand elixir, and Physician's Anti-Interest, ye renowned Liquor Buttermilk. I must assure ye Reader y^t several to my own Knoleg, have been cured of preternatural heats and Som of confirm'd Hectics by ye much use of Butter-milke; both Sower and Sweet are good, and with whay, and milk meats of all sorts, keep ye blood calm and quiet, and in a true state of Health." The subject of "cold beathing" is a favorite with the transcriber, and he multiplies quotations from his most revered authorities in praise of this custom. "Cold baths will procure good rest," says one of these hygienic teachers, and "The Country Parson's Verses on Cold Bathing" teem with enthusiastic praises of hydropathy. With regard to other rules of health, Dr. Colebatch announces: "We live more by air than by meat." For drink he advises "ye smallest and thinnest wine or beer, and even with that to mix a small quantity of water." The passions must be duly regulated. "People ought to be very nice in ye Regulating Angar, fear and

An Old Book of Household Medicine

Mallincholy, which must be avoided, and chearfulness to be kept up as much as possible, for passion has drove some into headach, some into Collick." The conclusion of the whole matter is found by the compiler in these choice lines:

> "Drink what is clear,
> And eat what is new;
> Conceal what you hear,
> And speak what is true."

We will now examine a few of the sovereign receipts contained in this invaluable manual. Gout seems to have been the disease for which a panacea was most eagerly sought. Directions "to cure ye jaunds" run as follows: "Take a piece of Casteel Soape and slice it into thin pieces and put y^m into half a pint of water and let it dissolve and drink it 2 or 3 times." This prescription is simple, cleanly, and doubtless may be confidently commended to such as have faith in its curative agency. "A Receipt to make Swamp Cabbag Salve," possibly learned from the Indians, may not impress the modern mind very favorably, but it is herewith submitted, with all due reverence: "Take ye Cabbag and pound it in a mortar and boil it in hogs fatt, and strain it and put ¼ of a pound of bees-wax to a pound of hogs fatt and 1 ounce of turpentine to a pound dito, and if it is not hard enough add a littel Roosom and put it all up in an Earthen Pott. The first we made was May ye 16-1741." A certain highly esteemed "*Aqua Opthalmica* (Ey Watter)" is thus compounded: "Take white vitriol and bay salt." But perhaps the reader will hardly care to inquire further into the merits of this soothing preparation. The *American Magazine* for September, 1743, is the authority for the statement that "in ye yallow Fever at Phila., 1741, those y^t drank fresh lime or lemon Punch ordinarily Escaped ye Infection; Tho constantly attending ye Sick." A certain elixir described by our skilful simpler must have been much sought after, one would think, since its properties were such as to "comfort ye senses, revive ye spirits, bear up ye heart, and make ye sick pleasant. *To be taken in wine.*" Ah, this is an elixir we have heard of before. That standard work, "The Druggists Shope Opened," is quoted to prove that "Powder of Earthworms taken fasting before and after ye change and full of ye moon cures apoplexies and epilepsies," as indeed it ought to. It possesses another valuable quality, in that it "glews together broakn bons." Also, "A Precious Salve compounded by that famous Chirurgeon, Jerem of Brunswick, hath healed many that had their members out of joynt." It seems that "A plaster of Burgundy Pitch" was successfully applied by our amateur practitioner in the case of "a Parson complaining to me of a Grief in their Stomach of about seven years duration, and they expected it w'd caus their End." Rue is to be eaten with bread and butter by nervous patients, as it has the admirable quality of "bridling those inordinate notions which affect the whole Constitution." A receipt for Daffy's Elixir as it was given by the original compounder to Sir Richard Ford, when lord mayor of London, is taken from "The Accomplisht Lady's Delight." Close upon this follows "Mrs. Dyer's Recept," for what, we are not told, but among the ingredients are "2 ounces of Liquorish," with "Pruents," and "one pound of Reasons,"—which last would seem to be

An Old Book of Household Medicine

strangely out of place in a prescription. A more familiar part of the compound is the quart of "good olde Rum," in which the solids are to be steeped. No recipe seems complete to our skilled authority unless it contains wine or spirits, indispensable ingredients of his never failing remedies, "than which nothing can be contrived more effectual, though there are innumerable Pretentions *made to it by Quacks and imposters.*" If the worthy writer could only have looked forward to the time when the "quacks" who dared to reject from their practice the earthworms, and the swamp cabbage, and the quarts of rum, with other noble medicines of undoubted potency, should be held in more respect than all his devotion to the healing art could gain for him, he might have despaired of the future. How should he, while writing out with great satisfaction his sovereign recipes, so unquestioningly accepted by our ancestors in the eighteenth century, conceive that the sentiment with which they would one day be regarded, would find its natural expression in the following lines, which the careful hand of our compiler has piously traced on these pages, little dreaming of the application which the present reader gives to them, after scanning the various nostrums which fill the book:

> "My Soul, come meditate the Day,
> And think how Nigh it stands,
> When Thou must Quit this house of clay
> And fly to unknown Lands."

THE CONFLICT OF COLONIAL AUTHORITIES IN NARRAGANSETT

THE jurisdiction of the Narragansett country was long disputed between Rhode Island and Connecticut. Its fertile lands and extensive sea-coast were regarded as colonial prizes. But stronger than the desire of gain was the spirit of rivalry between colonies that from their earliest years had been accustomed to think harshly of each other. It seems a strange and ill-timed burst of Anglo-Saxon obstinacy and aggressiveness — this hand-to-hand struggle between two infant communities that would have had enough to do, one would think, to fight common enemies and provide against common evils.

By the Connecticut charter of 1662, the possession of Narragansett was secured to that Colony. As the region was settled by Richard Smith (1639) and Roger Williams (1642), subjects of Rhode Island, a petition was addressed to Charles II by the colonial government. The question was submitted to referees, of whom at least one, William Brenton (who has given his name to Newport landmarks), was friendly to the interests of Rhode Island. They adopted a middle course; making Pawcatuck River the boundary between the rivals, and giving the inhabitants near Richard Smith's trading-house the privilege of deciding to which Colony they would belong. They assembled and chose Connecticut; doubtless desiring the protection of a firmer government than that of Rhode Island in those early times. But their action naturally gave great offence to the authorities of Providence and Newport.

Conflict of Colonial Authorities

"Under which king, Bezonian? speak, or die!"

was a fulmination which may well stand for the tragic attitude assumed by the threatening colonies.

New bickerings began, and matured in hostile acts. In March, 1664, twenty armed men, crossing the sacred boundary of the Pawcatuck, entered the house of a citizen who owned allegiance to Rhode Island, and forcibly removed him to Connecticut. This invasion provoked reprisals, and in May, the Rhode Island authorities seized John Greene, of Quidnesit, an adherent of Connecticut, confining him in Newport, and threatening similar offenders with arrest and imprisonment. Border controversy was fast growing up to the stature of border war.

Meanwhile (April, 1764), the King had appointed four Commissioners, of whom the chief was Colonel Richard Nichols (commander of the fleet that reduced New Amsterdam the same year), with Sir Robert Carr, George Cartwright, and Samuel Maverick. These gentlemen endeavored to secure a suspension of hostilities by setting apart the disputed territory as neutral ground. They thus created an independent jurisdiction, styled the King's Province; the government to be administered for one year by Rhode Island magistrates, these submitting to the Commissioners, as representatives of royal authority. So easily did the gentlemen Commissioners dispose of Rhode Island affairs when met to hold informal council at their favorite Boston tavern, the "Ship." Nichols, who had served under Turenne, and had conquered the New Netherlands, was prepared to deal summarily with these few poor provincials. Rhode Island, now a dismembered commonwealth, vainly petitioned the King (1666) for the restoration of her territory.

Connecticut was forced to relinquish the prosecution of her claims during the years of King Philip's War (1675–76), but took advantage of the first breathing space after the destruction of the Narragansett tribe by her forces at the "Great Swamp Fight," to claim the whole region, as a conquered country! Rhode Island, despairing of justice, would have compromised by the cession of half her unfriendly neighbor's demand. The offer was not accepted. Each community scorned to avail itself of the armistice obtainable by acknowledging the neutral rule of the Commissioners. The scenes of 1664 were repeated. Hot proclamations were issued by both governments, bidding their devoted adherents stand or fall by the true cause. Arrests, captures, incursions of troops of horse, followed in quick succession. John Saffin, a citizen of Boston, but holding his Narragansett lands subject to Connecticut authority, was convicted at Newport, of adhering to "a foreign jurisdiction." Such was the height of indignant feeling against the sister Colony and her well-wishers, that this worthy Boston merchant met the treatment of a very Shylock. Not only were his lands "confiscate unto the State of Venice," or her modern representative, the doughty little republic of Rhode Island, but he was, with superfluous severity, also sentenced to pay a fine. In return, sundry Rhode Islanders were seized and imprisoned in Hartford and New London. Again (1680) Rhode Island made a fruitless appeal to the King, but no respite from hostilities was sought by either of the high contending parties.

Conflict of Colonial Authorities

In April, 1683, the King commissioned Edward Cranfield, William Stoughton, Joseph Dudley, Edward Randolph, Samuel Shrimpton, John Fitz Winthrop, Edward Palmer, John Pyncheon, Jr., and Nathaniel Saltonstall, giving them full authority to decide this long-vexed controversy. They met at Smith's Block-house, near Wickford, attended by the agents of Connecticut and Plymouth. The legislature of Rhode Island assembled within a mile, denied the right of the King's Commissioners to settle the pending claims, and ordered the sergeant-at-arms, with his trumpet, at the head of a troop of horse, by loud proclamation, "to prohibit them from keeping court in this jurisdiction." This blowing of horns around that miniature Jericho, the contumacious hamlet of Wickford, failed to level its walls. The injured dignities of the Assembly having been appeased, that body continued its session oblivious of the fact that the Commissioners maintained a show of authority, spending two days at the block-house taking the depositions of aged inhabitants. They then hastily adjourned to Boston, and, at that convenient distance, of course decided that the "King's Province" belonged of right to Connecticut. A prompt remonstrance from the Rhode Island authorities prevented a royal confirmation of this decision.

The King's third Commission, relating to this question, was issued in 1685, and appointed Joseph Dudley, president of Maine, New Hampshire, Massachusetts, and the *King's Province*. He held his council at Smith's, and, as autocrat of the region, even gave new names to the townships subject to his brief authority. But his fall from power soon followed that of Andros.

Both sought safety in the Colony which they had oppressed. Dudley was concealed at Smith's for a week, but was captured by Massachusetts men and imprisoned in Boston, shortly after Andros had met with similar reverses. Rhode Island, crushed, but not subdued by arbitrary rule, now strove to resume her jurisdiction over the Narragansett country. The contending colonies made some unsatisfactory attempts to terminate their controversy.

In 1720, Rhode Island, in a letter to Connecticut, spiritedly declares that "as you have rejected all endeavors," she is resolved to appeal again to royal authority. A new dynasty reigned in England, but the fiery contentions that had burned in colonial breasts during the rule of the Stuarts were still unquenched in the times of the House of Hanover. Joseph Jencks, Lieutenant-Governor of Rhode Island, was appointed her agent at London. Jeremiah Dummer, agent for Massachusetts, was empowered to represent Connecticut.

In 1726, George I announced the final decision of this ancient quarrel; making Pawcatuck the western boundary of Rhode Island (thus reverting to the course adopted by referees in 1663) and terminating the existence of the King's Province, an independent State for half a century. Both colonies, exhausted by the disputes and struggles of eighty-three years (for the controversy arose in the second year of the settlement made by Roger Williams), were glad to yield, and sign an honorable peace.

But a root of bitterness remained; and the shallow waters of the Pawcatuck flowed between neighbors who showed as ready a talent for misinterpeting each other's qualities as though the "mountains interposed," of which the poet writes, had "made foes of brethren." These colonies, so widely differing in their schemes of civil and religious administration, so strongly contrasted in their ideas of public and private duty, were long in coming to an attitude of mutual understanding and appreciation. The Pharisee of Connecticut uttered his thanksgivings that he was not as those other men were, with needless loudness and fervor; while the Publican of Rhode Island showed a graceless reluctance to be edified by these outpourings of pious respectability. The old enmities, involving temporal as well as spiritual causes of strife, were in part the foundation of the Rhode Islander's hereditary ridicule of the excellent colonists across the water; and the traditional feud perhaps lent its acerbity to the Connecticut citizen's orthodox horror of his free-thinking neighbors. The jest and the anathema are now alike the harmless shadows of an obscure memory, and one who follows the course of colonial affairs may well wonder that the old quarrel should have been so tenacious of life. Observing the perpetual wrangles about territorial possessions that agitated the saints of Connecticut, one remembers the satirical-charitable words of Roger Williams concerning them, that "the geography of the country being hardly emerged into any tolerable light, instead of ascertaining their boundaries on earth, they fixed their limits only in the heavens."

AN OFFICIAL PAPER OF 1727

WIDE-MARGINED, many folded, time-stained, thin-worn and creased with use, but with the good black ink not yet faded from its yellowed surface, the old paper has still its voiceless story, not without meaning and suggestiveness for the present time. The choice precious relic! The true antiquarian treasure! Hold it up to the full stream of sunlight pouring through the window. Comes into view the faint tracery of the elaborate water-mark, bearing the signature of the maker. Britannia, a large lady, with very stern and strongly emphasized features, which are fitly surmounted by the helmet of a Roman soldier, seated in her car of victory, triumphantly points with her sceptre to this no doubt eminently respectable name. But its long forgotten letters, almost obliterated by time, remain a recondite mystery, to the solemn solution of which, Britannia, in her novel character of Sphinx, perpetually invites. The document is drawn up (or shall we say drawn out?) with much prolixity, and is transcribed in a large, fair, clerkly hand. On a folded corner of the outer leaf a neatly written endorsement briefly indicates the purport of the contents, dated 1727. Sole copy now existing in all probability. Signed (with true official haste) by Joseph Jencks, Governor of the Colony of Rhode Island and Providence Plantations.

That mighty potentate, doubtless ambitious of a wider rule than fate had allotted to him in the fractional colony that owned his sway, seems to have sought a stern compensation in a rigid tyranny over his mother tongue; entering upon such merciless dealings with the

King's English as would drive any modern governor, however modest his accomplishments, to absolute despair, did he detect similar deviation from literary rectitude in any paper bearing his hand and seal. In the year of our Lord 1727, the chief magistrate of Rhode Island was a ruler indeed. He speaks (or his secretary speaks for him), and syntax is annihilated; he writes (by the same subaltern), and affrighted orthography retires aghast before him. In truth it must be confessed that the literary execution of this state paper is not such as to inspire much awe for the erudition of the worthy colonial fathers. An examination of this astonishing manuscript, totally innocent of punctuation, written as if to be read in a single breath, leaves the bewildered reader plunged in a chaos of melancholy musings upon the confusing variety of opposing interpretations of which His Excellency's oracular text might have proved susceptible, had not the individuals composing the little official circle cherished a loyal willingness to do his respected bidding.

Nor would his contemporaries, in general, think the less of Captain Joseph Jencks, our worthy Baptist governor in the year of grace 1727–28, for his occasional trifling literary lapses and omissions. Our good colonists set but small value on the acquirement of a correct orthography. Many of them would perhaps have scorned an over-careful particularity in such matters, as partaking of the spirit of the infinitely little. A letter more, or a letter less, pray what could it signify? Had not every freeman the privilege of his own inkhorn? Were he but a true citizen, and a good neighbor, sure he was welcome to spell as he pleased. (Those were the good old times. What a sad abridgment of our sovereign prerogatives since then! *Est-ce notre liberté?* we may well ask, with the French of 1793.) So the flax fields were planted in season, the dismal wood cleared, the hideous swamp drained, and the "Pagan Salvages" kept from the door, above all, so that the roughly squared timbers of the rude meeting-house were securely placed, minor matters might be left to care for themselves. Thus thought the fathers of the Colony, under the pressure of sternest cares; braving the rigors of the climate; struggling with the demands of a newly organized government. They were not posing for effect in the eyes of future ages, after the morbid manner of the Gaul; but were merely plain, God-fearing men, striving in the long enduring courage of patience to acquit themselves bravely in life and serve their king and country well and truly. Learning was good; it would come in time; a happier generation should enjoy the fruition of its benefits. For us (we seem to hear them say) the dreary march, the wasting bivouac, the deadly battle. For you the joy of victory, the glory of conquest, the assured possession of the captured town, the hard-won field,

> "The shout of them that triumph;
> The song of them that feast."

Among these our predecessors were many who were, of necessity, men of action rather than of contemplation. Let us follow the artless record of their steadfast purpose, in its original expression. Let it stand confessed in the full halo of its serene antiquity. Lay no rash correcting hand, O Printer, upon its innocent ec-

An Official Paper of 1727

centricities of diction. Forget, O Proof-reader, the mysteries of thy craft, nor presume to invade its blank simplicities with presumptuous punctuation, unknown to the scribes of those easy-going, uncritical days. In the name of antiquity, in the name of all the antiquarians, forbear! Suffer the "most honored and worshipful Mr. Governor"—or rather, his clerk, for our mind misgives us that we may have spoken ill of gubernatorial dignities without just cause, and that the paper in question may never have passed under His Excellency's revision—suffer his clerk, then, to lay waste the English language, "as in his wisdom he shall think propper." So prays the humble transcriber of the following document:

Colony of Rhodeisland

Worthy & Esteemed Friends
    Francis Willett & William Robinson
 These Comes to Jnforme you that wee haue persuant to ye Gen'l assemblys order wrote to the agent Concerning the affaire which was Laid before ye last assembly as you uery well know Relating [to] ye young Sachim and John Checkley Wherein they that were the authers of them writing so Unfairly Laid down the state or Surcumstances of the aforeSaid Jndian Sachims & his people upon which wee took occation To lay before our agent at home a true state of the afores^d Jndians in this Colony first that ye said Sachim was but a youth of about Seuenteen years of age Secondly that he Speaks tolerable good English thirdly his people ware but few and scattered and lieuest at Seruice by the month or year with English Marsters

all which wee haue incerted in our Letter a coppey herewith you will Receiue and wee would Send Depositions to Proue the same

These are therefore to authorize you forthwith upon Receipt hereof to go to the Town of westerly in this Colony and there take such and so maney Depositions as you Jn your wisdom Shall think propper in this affair only J would aduise you to take majr Joseph Stantons Euidence and also Capt John Babcocks and if you Can tak all of such as are willing and free to giue their Euidence Jn the Nature of an oath for that may be more agreeable To those before whome it appear than an ingagement and Likely to giue less Grounds of Disafection and you are farther Directed to make all the Dispatch you possiably Can for it is Designed home by Charles Bardin and Capt Joseph Whipple tells me he will undouptedly Sail the begining of the Next week so that time will be Pretieus therefore To Conclude Shall subscribe yours to serue nothing doubting But that you will do all and Euerything that Shall be by you thought Needfull for the Honneur & Jntrust of this Colony Jn this affair

Giuen under my hand in Newport this
     24th day of may anno &c 1727
       Joseph Jencks Govr

[*Endorsement, in the handwriting of Francis Willett.*]
Gov'r. Jenks' Order to take Evidences in Westerly, Concerning Ninigreat.

Who will offer a full elucidation of the facts of minor Colonial history, dimly indicated in the foregoing paper?

An Official Paper of 1727

Who can identify the "John Checkley" inculpated in its vague and uncertain charges? John Checkley, who became rector of St. John's Church, Providence, was in London in 1727, but could hardly have been the author of these indefinite accusations of "ye young Sachim," which so deeply stirred the indignant sense of justice in the minds of his protectors and guardians.

The "Colonial Records," as published, are silent concerning the Assembly at which "this affair" was debated and the resolution adopted that full information and suitable instructions be forwarded to Richard Partridge, our Quaker agent "at home." He shall set this matter right, before his Majesty's Council, if need be, divesting it of all the falsities wherewith it hath been so maliciously involved, by certain ill-wishers to the welfare of this Colony. He shall prove to their lordships that this simple Indian lad is as far from assuming any show of sovereignty, on his poor three thousand acres, as we, the King's most loyal subjects, should be from sparing so idle a delusion. Mere conjectural hints, these! little else may be evolved from the record, strangely reticent, with all its affluence of detail. The endorsement of Esquire Willett alone preserves to us the name, or rather title, of the young sachem (since all the descendants of the first Ninegret continued the style of aboriginal Caesars), who speaks "tolerable good English," possibly having enjoyed the freedom of that centre of learning, the office of our worthy Secretary of State. His name might otherwise have remained unknown to later readers of the governor's informal, gossippy public order. From Judge E. R. Potter's "History of Narragansett," a work of patient industry, pervaded by a humane and liberal spirit, it appears that the Ninegret of this period was Charles Augustus, whose guardians and trustees were Captain Thomas Frye, William Wanton, Esq., and Major Joseph Stanton, gentlemen known as trusty friends to the interests of the tribe, and regarded by its members with much loyal and faithful esteem. It was this young sachem who gave forty acres of his land as a church site and glebe, to be occupied by clergymen of the English Church: ("For he loveth our nation, and hath built us a synagogue.") The grant was confirmed by his brother, George, who succeeded him in the tribal honors, and who was the father of "King Tom Ninegret," of Charlestown and Newport tradition. The Indians "at service with English Marsters" may have been the survivors of the "Great Swamp Fight," with their children. Many of the captives were thus disposed of by the authorities of Rhode Island, but their enforced servitude was for a term of years only. Among minor points of local interest, we may note the name of the ship Charles Bardin, after a Newport merchant of those days, and probably her owner.

The instructions relating to a judicial oath indicate the presence of Quaker belief and education in Westerly. The Assembly, therefore, judiciously appoints William Robinson, of South Kingstown, a member of that sect, to take the affirmations of the Friends; while Esquire Willett, of Boston Neck, in North Kingstown, can more fully receive the depositions of the world's people. Such are the implied directions of the governor, who, like editors, kings, and other great men, and indeed as the representative of the royal authority, employs in this paper the majestic plural pronoun; showing no false dignity, however, in descending from its heights, as a sudden thought strikes him, and he drops the character of sovereign. The quaint air of homeliness and rusticity pervading His Excellency's leisurely style is more readily perceived than its more creditable characteristics, and the casual statement that "time is Pretious," is the sole intimation conveyed by the document that its originators had any conception of that fact.

The personages whose outward presentment and mental habits are so vividly recalled by this old-time paper, which brings them before us in their little round of daily occupations — whither have they vanished? The well-meaning governor; the prolix clerk; the dark, silent Indian youth, and his mysterious accuser; the stout sea captain, who would not delay his voyage for any trifling land affairs when his good ship was tugging at her anchor and the breeze set fair for "home"; Willett, the Churchman; Robinson, the Quaker; where are they?

>"Gone like a wind that blew
>A thousand years ago."

Yet what strange remote influence is breathing forth from these faded lines, traced upon umbered and crumbling paper! Has some wizard impressed it with the lasting magic of his spell? Some sudden palingenesis evokes from their sleeping dust these long buried forms, once so active in the busy little drama of their day. The scenes of an obscure past, escaping from the relaxing grasp of oblivion, rise and pass before us. We see the Quaker official, in the traditional garb of his sect; his friend and companion, the Squire, who is of the world's people in dress and manner, both well mounted and amicably pacing together while on their way to execute the commands of the governor, in the ancient township of Westerly — meeting but few persons on the quiet road, at the early morning hour of their appointment, unless some of their humbler neighbors may be astir, by whom they are greeted, as the poet tersely sings:

> "With mute obeisance, grave and slow,
> Repaid by nod polite,
> For such the way with high and low,
> Till after Concord fight."

We watch them drawing a hasty rein at the ever open door of the rude inn of colonial times, dismounting beneath its swinging sign affixed to the tall buttonwood that overtops the low-pitched roof of the wide, rambling building. The halt is no less for their horses' refreshment than their own. When these have been fed, and led up and down the green by the black hostler, the gentlemen pursue their way within the Westerly boundaries, dutifully seeking the appointed witnesses, not forgetting good Major Joseph Stanton, the tried friend and counsellor of three generations of the short-lived descendants of the first Ninegret, the Nestor of the Narragansetts. Then homeward, to part company at Tangatucket Ford. Friend Robinson has now reached the borders of his estate, and is within easy distance of his own gates. But the Squire has to ride seven miles further, before, seated at his "walnut tree" desk, in the "Haul" (*vide* town-officers' inventory) of his late hon-

An Official Paper of 1727

ored father's house in Boston Neck, he can make out the papers desired by the colonial authorities, directing them, in his flowing and elegant chirography, to "His Excellency the Governor: At his house in the Towne of Newport: These with Speed": or in words of similar import. He delivers them at a seasonable hour the following day to a trusty messenger, by whose hands they are committed to the governor, who soon forwards the all important packet to the staunch ship Charles Bardin, Whipple, Master, who "will undouptedly Sail" by early dawn. In his careful keeping it must surely arrive in safety at the capital of our Sovereign Lord, George the Second—possibly to arouse some slight notice and discussion among the wits and philosophers of his polite court.

But whatever fate attends the unstudied record of official wisdom above transcribed, wherever it may go, whatever company it keeps, at least the honest document makes no pretensions; resting upon its genuine foundations in truth, justice, and integrity. Its curiously unconscious phraseology is appealingly suggestive of the good provincial folk by whom it was planned and written. Its artless and unpremeditated wording may call a smile to the lips of some merely critical reader. Not thus the historian. With more philosophical breadth of view, he marks purport rather than execution; the spirit of the record and not its form. True, this relic of colonial times is not a monument of learning. It is far from being an able state paper. Perhaps it may not be even business-like. Yet, to a loyal reader, the sense is plain, and the diction, if familiar, at least free from the burden of legal circumlocution. Does it not speak with the power of purpose springing from the influences of sincerity and rectitude? Are not its eccentricities and provincialisms thus redeemed from ridicule? Did not justice approve the intent; kindness smile upon the words; and grave determination affix the seal? There is a worthy meaning latent in its homely form, struggling with the rude and insufficient terms of expression, now overlaid with the gathered dust and dimness of many years. But these do not conceal the better qualities of this forgotten memorial, this long-silent witness to the justice of the colonial fathers. In their grave honesty of aim we recognize such innate dignity as exalts this poor record of their worthy deeds to a place higher than it could claim by its rough execution, its homely and rustic strain. For there is a higher sphere than that of mere learning; and the most brilliant results of a scholarship or of a statesmanship that has not taken counsel of heart and conscience, are, when weighed in the just balance of Heaven, less than the least of those simple acts prompted by an unswerving morality. Is not this the lesson taught by this obscure historical fragment, and has not this faint echo from the fast receding spaces of the past a living meaning for the present?

THE END

Index

INDEX

Abolition Act, passed by General Assembly, in February, 1784, 207, 208.
Adams, Rev. Samuel, 114, 240.
Alden, Captain (son of John Alden, of Plymouth), 162.
Alden, John, of Plymouth, 162.
Allaire, ———, 22.
Allen, John, 50.
Andros, Sir Edmund (governor of Massachusetts), 17, 18, 50, 51, 73, 270, 271.
Anne, Queen, 57, 160.
Antilles, the, forced emigration to, 11.
Arabella Letter, the, 55.
Archibald of the Hass, 88.
Arnold, Benedict, 171, 172.
Arnold, Samuel G., historian of Rhode Island, 31.
Arnou, ———, 27.
Atherton Company, the, 12, 13, 18.
Atherton Purchase, 45.
Aunt Ibby (slave; full name Isabella Remington), 219, 227, 228–230.
Ayrault, Daniel, 30.
Ayrault, Dr. Pierre, 15, 19, 20, 21, 22.

Babcock, Captain John, 278.
Bacon, Deacon, 248.
Bailey, Rev. Jacob, 232–246.
Bailey, William W., 232.

Baird, Rev. Dr. Charles W., 20, 25.
Ballou, ———, 24.
Barbut, ———, 22.
Bardin, Charles, 278.
Bass, Rev. Edward (afterwards Bishop), 123, 125.
Beauchamps, ———, 22.
Beebe, Zaccheus, 249.
Belcher, Rev. Joseph, 15.
Bellamont, Governor Richard, 46, 52, 139.
Berkeley, Bishop, 83, 96, 202.
Bernard, Sir Francis (governor of Massachusetts), 98, 116.
Bernon, André, 27.
Bernon, Gabriel, 25, 26, 27, 28, 31–34, 36, 159, 160, 173.
Bernon, Mrs. Gabriel (Hester or Ester LeRoy; first wife), original owner of famous gold rattle, viii, 160.
Bernon, Mrs. Gabriel (Mary Harris; second wife), 160.
Bernons, the, of La Rochelle, 26, 27, 28.
Bernonville, 26.
Bondet Hill, 21.
Boston Neck, North Kingstown, 46, 69, 80, 135, 141, 142, 144, 148, 283.
Bours, Rev. Peter, 115.
Boyle, Robert, 55.
Bradstreet, Rev. Dudley, 77.

Index

Charles II, 198, 268.
Charles IX, 3.
Charles Augustus Ninegret, 280.
Charles Bardin (ship), 280, 283.
Checkley, John, 277, 279.
Church, Captain, 157.
Church of England, the, 10, 31, 34, 55, 92, 94, 113, 117, 123.
Clap, Thomas, 83.
Coddington, Anne (wife of Andrew Willett), 141.
Coddington, Content, 82.
Coddington, Nathaniel, 155.
Coddington, Colonel William, 82.
Coddington, Mrs. William, 82.
Coligny's colony in Brazil, 10.
Collier, William, 138.
Collin, ——, 22.
Collins, Mrs. Abigail, 61.
Cooke, Dr. Elisha, 69.
Cooke, John, 164.
Copley, John Singleton, 115, 124.
Cowper, William, 114, 252.
Cranfield, Edward, 271.
Crassons, Joseph, 27.
Crusaders, descendants of, 6.
Curtis, ——, 179.

Danforth, Rev. Daniel, 57.
Davids, the, 22.
De Bernon. See Bernon.
De Marigny, ——, 22.
Decatur, ——, 24.

Dedford (slave), 80.
Deptford (slave), 222.
Dickens, Charles, 128.
Dickinson, Charles, 82, 155.
Dickinson, Phillippa (wife of John Case), 82.
Dimmis (slave), 80.
Dinwoody, ——, 82.
Dochmore, ——, 57.
Dudley, Governor Joseph, 43, 46, 49, 52, 54, 71, 137, 139, 271, 272.
Dummer, Jeremiah, 272.
Durfee, Judge, 199.

East Greenwich, 12, 13, 15, 19, 45.
Eddy, Mrs. ——, 63.
Edict of Nantes, Revocation of, 3, 4, 27, 29, 35, 160.
Edwards, Jonathan, 200.
Eliot, John (son of the Apostle to the Indians), 260.
Eliot, Mrs. John (wife of the Apostle to the Indians), 56.
Ellsworth, Mrs. Grace. See Saffin, Mrs. Grace.
Emerson, Ralph Waldo, 254.

Falkland, Lord, 55.
Faneuil, Benjamin, 160.
Faneuil, Peter, 28, 160.
Faneuil Hall, 28.
Fayerweather, Samuel, xiv, 83, 94, 98, 99, 112, 113, 114, 115, 116, 117, 118, 119, 120, 122–131, 146, 165.

Index

Bradstreet, Governor Simon, 77.
Brenton, William, 268.
Bridge, ——, 77.
Bridget (slave; granddaughter of Silvy Tory), 217.
British State Paper Office, 22.
Brown, Anna (wife of Hezekiah Willett), 135.
Brown, Rev. Daniel, 160.
Brown, John, 107, 132.
Brown, John, 2d, 135.
Brown, Mary (daughter of John Brown and wife of Thomas Willett), 134.
Brown, Moses, 207.
Browne, Captain John, 93.
Browne, Rev. Marmaduke, 115, 116, 180, 203.
Browne, Thomas, 93.
Bull, Jireh, 157.
Bull's Block-house, 14, 85.
Bunyan, John, 252.
Burgundy, Counts of, 25.
Burns, Robert, 228.
Burr, Aaron, 135.
Byfield, Judge, 66.
Byles, Rev. Mather, Sr., 123, 125.

Cade, Jack, 72.
Caesar (slave), 123, 128, 218.
Calvin, John, 7, 9, 21.
Calvinism, 7, 8, 74, 252.
Caner, Rev. Dr. Henry, 117, 232.
Carpenter, Ester, 173.

Carpenter, Esther Bernon, vii, viii, ix, xvi, 111 n., 146 n., 227 n., 232 n.
Carpenter, Francis, viii, 146 n., 173.
Carpenter, Mrs. Francis (Esther Helme), vii, 172.
Carpenter, Rev. James Helme, viii, 173.
Carpenter, Mrs. J. H. (Mary Hoxie Hazard), viii.
Carpenter, Joseph, 142, 173.
Carpenter, Joseph, Sr., 142.
Carpenter, Mrs. Joseph (Anne Willett; first wife), 142.
Carpenter, Mrs. Joseph (Mary Willett; second wife), 142.
Carpenter, Willett, 46, 161, 173, 222.
Carpenter, Mrs. Willett (Elizabeth Case), 173.
Carpenter Place, 148 n.
Carr, Sir Robert, 269.
Carré, Rev. Ezekiel, 21, 22.
Carter, Captain Thomas, 239.
Cartwright, George, 269.
Case, Dr. Benjamin Waite, 164, 173, 262.
Case, Elizabeth (wife of Willett Carpenter), 173.
Case, John, 82, 93, 94, 164.
Case, Mrs. John (Phillippa Dickinson), 82.
Case, Joseph, 173.
Cato (slave), 218.
Channing, John, 120, 123.
Charles I, 117, 143.

[288]

Index

Fayerweather, Thomas, xiv, 112, 124.
"ffones, Sam'l, Town Clerke," 155.
Flint, Dorothy (wife of Edmund Quincy), 136.
Flint, Rev. Josiah, 136.
Flint, Mrs. Josiah (Hester or Esther Willett), 136.
Florida, colony in, 10.
Foix, Counts of, 6.
Ford, Sir Richard, 266.
Foster, Deacon, 240.
Fox, George, 179, 181.
Francis I, 26.
Franklin, Benjamin, 111 n., 176, 177, 233, 238.
Friends' Meeting House, first, in Kingstown, 175, 230.
Frontbeck, Rev. Mr., 117.
Frye, Captain Thomas, 280.

Gage, General, 117.
Gambia (slave; full name Senegambia), 219, 222, 223, 225, 226.
Ganeau, ——, 25.
Gardiner, Colonel John, 83, 94, 107, 142.
Gardiner, Samuel, 104.
Gardiner, Dr. Sylvester, 83, 92, 93, 104, 105, 106, 108, 232.
Gardiner, William, 104, 106, 108, 142.
Garfield, President James A., 24.

Garrett, John, 41.
Gedney, Judge, 162.
George (slave), 123, 128.
George I, 110, 272.
George II, 107, 109.
George III, 145.
Gibbs, Colonel, 240.
Glebe, the, 83, 85, 92, 95, 96, 98, 99, 145.
Goodfellow, Robin, 72.
Gorton, Samuel, 199, 201.
Graves, Rev. John, 123, 125.
Grazillier, ——, 22.
Great Swamp Fight, the, 14, 45, 84, 157, 202, 270, 280.
Greene, Colonel, 212.
Greene, John, 269.
Greene, "King Richard," 114.
Griffin, Mrs. Winifred, 61.
Grignon, ——, 22.
Grimm, Bess, 55.
Grinnell, ——, 25.
Griswold, Fort, near Groton, Connecticut, 171.
Gurney, Joseph J., 189.

Harris, Mary (second wife of Gabriel Bernon), 160.
Harris, William, 160.
Harrison, Captain Joseph, 104.
Harvard College, 112, 143, 232.
Hawthorne, Nathaniel, 55.
Hazard, Alice, 84.
Hazard, Edward Hoxie, 227 n.
Hazard, Dr. George, 219, 227.
Hazard, Joseph, 84.

[290]

Index

Hazard, Mary Hoxie (wife of Rev. J. H. Carpenter), viii.
Hazard, Penelope, 84.
Hazard, Dr. Robert, 116.
Hazard, Governor Robert, 84.
Hazard, Mrs. Robert (Esther Stanton), 84.
Hazard, Sarah, 84.
Hazard, Thomas, 79, 83, 115, 184-189, 207.
Helme, Bernon, 172.
Helme, Esther (wife of Francis Carpenter), viii, 172.
Helme, Gawain, 159.
Helme, Judge James, 129, 162, 165, 166, 167, 169, 170, 171, 173.
Helme, James (son of Judge James Helme), 172.
Helme, James (great-grandson of Judge James Helme), 172.
Helme, Mrs. James (Esther Powell), viii, 83, 162, 168, 173.
Helme, Mary, 172.
Helme, Nathaniel, 172.
Helme, Powell, 172.
Helme, Rowse, 83, 162, 171.
Helme, Samuel (son of Judge James Helme), 172.
Helme family, the, xii, 156, 161.
Herbert, George, 130, 229.
Hill, James, 117.
Holmes, Rev. Abiel, 136.
Holmes, Mrs. Abiel (Sarah Wendell), 136.

Holmes, Mary Jackson (wife of Dr. Usher Parsons), 136.
Holmes, Dr. Oliver Wendell, vii, viii, ix, 136; letters from, to Esther Bernon Carpenter, ix-xv.
Honeyman, Hon. James, 116, 202.
Hooker, Rev. Samuel, 135, 143.
Hooker, Mrs. Samuel (Mary Willett), 135.
Hopkins, Dr., 130.
Hopkins, Samuel, 200.
Howard, Martin, Jr., 163.
Huguenots, the, 3, 4, 7, 9, 11, 16, 18, 19.
Hull, Edward, 227.
Hull, John, 60.
Hull, Madam, 61.
Hunt, Eliza (wife of James Willett), 135.
Hunt, Lieutenant Peter, 135.
Hutchinson, Anne, 200, 201.

Isle de France, 6.
Isle de Ré, 21, 26.

Jackson, Edward, 136.
Jackson, Mrs. Edward (Dorothy Quincy), 136.
Jackson, Jonathan, 136.
Jackson, Mary (wife of Judge Oliver Wendell), 136.
James II, 14, 57, 63.
Jefferson, Thomas, 144.
Jencks, Governor Joseph, 272, 274, 275, 278.

Index

Jerauld, ———, 25.
John (slave), 214.
Johnson, Augustus, 163.
Johnson, Dr. Samuel, 114.
Josias, Charles, Sachem, 49.
Jowett, Professor, 182.
Julien, ———, 21.

KING Philip's War, 14, 85, 135, 157, 270.
"King Tom Ninegret," 280.
King's Chapel, 77, 116, 117.
King's College, New York, 119, 122, 124.
Knight, Madam, 15, 176, 239.

LA BERNONIÈRE, manors of, in Poitou, 26.
La Rochelle, historic Huguenot city, 4, 6, 7, 10, 21, 22, 25, 26, 28, 29, 33, 159, 160.
Lamb, Charles, 191.
Lechford, ———, 59.
Lee, Rev. Samuel, 44, 51, 56, 139, 259.
Le Moine, Möise (now corrupted to Mawney), 21.
LeRoy, François, 160.
LeRoy, Hester *or* Ester (first wife of Gabriel Bernon), viii, 160.
Le Sage, Alain René, 241.
Lee, Rebecca (third wife of John Saffin), 43, 139.
Lefèvre, ———, father of the French Reformation, 7.
Legaré, ———, 22.

Leverett, Governor John, 45, 70.
Leyden, Pilgrims of, 10, 133.
Lidgett, Mrs. Elizabeth (second wife of John Saffin), 139.
Lidgett, Peter, 43.
Limrick, Rev. Paul, 88.
Limrick, "Cousin Tom," 88.
Little Rest (now Kingston Hill), 80, 116.
London (slave), 222.
London, Bishop of, 77, 78, 98, 99, 203.
Longfellow, Henry W., xiv.
Louis XIV, 3, 5, 14, 16, 17, 18, 57.
Lucas, ———, 24.
Luce (slave), 80.

MACSPARRAN, Archibald, 105.
MacSparran, Rev. James, 78, 79, 80, 81, 83, 85–90, 92, 95, 96, 97, 102, 108, 110, 112, 113, 125, 162, 179, 180, 181, 202, 203, 215.
MacSparran, Mrs. James (Hannah Gardiner), 83, 92, 97, 98, 103, 104, 105, 106, 108.
MacSparran, James (nephew of Rev. James MacSparran), 105.
MacSparran Hill, 92, 111.
Macaulay, Thomas Babington, 17, 29, 150.
Marchant, ———, 25.
Margaret African (slave), 80.
Marot, Clément, 29, 173.

[292]

Index

Mason, Anne, 123.
Mason, Thaddeus, 123.
Massacre of 1572, the, 4.
Massom, ——, 104.
"Master Isaac," 219.
Mather, Cotton, 49, 55, 67, 68, 69, 136.
Matoonuc Hills, 218.
Matoonuc Tavern, 176.
Maverick, Samuel, 269.
Mawney, Pardon, 36.
Mazarin, Jules, 5.
Merry Mount, 62.
Miantinomi, Sachem, 80, 143.
Miantinomi's Rock, 143.
Middle Passage, the, 204.
Milton, John, 72.
'Mint (slave), 80.
Moffatt, Dr., 163.
Monk, George, 56.
More, Sir Thomas, 55.
Mornay, Duplessis, 26.
Mumford *or* Mountfort, Ann, 260.
Mumford, Peter, 107.

NARRAGANSETT, 12, 13, 14, 15, 17, 18, 19, 21, 22, 23, 46, 77, 78, 80, 81, 87, 88, 89, 92, 93, 94, 113, 115, 118, 143, 145, 160, 165, 184, 268.
Narragansett Bay, 143.
Narragansett Church, the (St. Paul's), 77, 78, 79, 92, 93, 94, 95, 103, 111, 112, 113, 118, 131, 145, 155, 160, 162, 202.

Narragansett Ferry, 135.
Narragansett Glebe. *See* Glebe, the.
Narragansett Rock (formerly Pettaquamscutt Rock), 156.
Narragansetts, tribe of, 14, 80, 282.
Newbarry, Walter, 13.
Newbarry Plantation, 13.
New England Yearly Meeting, 178.
"New Haven College," 83.
Nicholls, Colonel, 133.
Nichols, Colonel Richard, 269.
Nicholson, Sir Francis, 78.
Noailles, Marquis de, 199.

OLDHAM, ——, 59.
Old Guy (slave), 211.
Old Patience (slave), 218, 219, 227.
Orson (slave), 80.
Oxford colony, the, 21, 29.
Oxford massacre, the, 12.
Oxford University, 130, 259.

PADDY, William, 159.
Palmer, Edward, 271.
Papillion, ——, 24.
Parker, Bishop Samuel, 96.
Parsons, Dr. Usher, 136.
Parsons, Mrs. Usher (Mary Jackson Holmes), 136.
Parton, James, 144.
Partridge, Richard, 279.
Pawcatuck River, 268, 269, 272.

Index

Pease, Simon, 142.
Penn, Governor, 55.
Pepperrell, Sir William, 237.
Pequot Path, 175.
Pequots, 59.
Peter (slave), 80, 161.
Peters, Dr., 234, 245.
Pettaquamscutt, 81, 97, 143.
Phillis (slave), 122, 128.
Phillis (negro poet), 205, 206.
Phipps, Sir William (governor of Massachusetts), 52.
Pineau, ——, 24.
Plato, 80, 218.
Polydore Gardiner (slave), 218.
Potter, Judge Elisha R., 12, 35, 36, 74, 172, 209, 214, 279.
Powell or ap Howell, Adam, 160, 162.
Powell, Elizabeth (wife of Rev. Samuel Seabury), 162.
Powell, Esther (wife of Judge James Helme and daughter of Adam Powell), viii, 83, 162, 168, 173.
Powell, Madam Hester (wife of Adam Powell and daughter of Gabriel Bernon), 82, 159, 160, 222.
Primus (slave), 218.
Prince of Orange, the, 57.
Pyncheon, John, Jr., 271.

Quague, Rev. Mr., 123.
Quakers, 76, 78, 177, 180, 181, 185, 191.

Quincy, Dorothy (wife of Edward Jackson), 136.
Quincy, Edmund, 136.
Quincy, Mrs. Edmund (Dorothy Flint), 136.
Quincy, Josiah, 136.

Raleigh, Sir Walter, 55.
Randolph, Edward, 271.
Rawson, Grindall, 64, 139.
Redwood Library, Newport, 124.
Reformation, the, 3, 6, 7.
Renaissance scholarship, 9.
Revocation of the Edict of Nantes, 3, 4, 27, 29, 35, 160.
Revolution of 1688, the, 8, 27.
Rhode Island Assembly, 12, 18, 49.
Rhode Island Historical Society, xv, 35, 36, 142, 152, 199.
Rhodes, John J., 262.
Richelieu, Cardinal, 5.
Robinson, Matthew, 83, 93, 119, 120, 123, 124, 128, 171.
Robinson, Rowland, 141.
Robinson, William, 184, 277, 280, 281, 282.
Rochambeau, Comte de, 177.
Rochelle (slave; waiting-woman to Madam Powell), 80, 222.
Rohan, Duchesse de, 10.
Rome, George, 165.
Rosanna (slave), 219, 220.

Index

St. Bartholomew's Day, 3, 48.
St. John's Church, Providence, 31, 160, 279.
St. Paul's Church (Narragansett Church), 77, 78, 79, 92, 93, 94, 95, 103, 111, 112, 113, 118, 131, 145, 155, 160, 162, 202.
Saffin alias Ellsworth, Mrs. Grace (wife of Simon Saffin), 41, 42, 140, 141.
Saffin, derivation of name, 39.
Saffin, John, viii, 16, 40–73, 134, 136, 137, 138, 139, 140, 141, 148, 256, 257, 260, 270.
Saffin, Mrs. John (Martha Willett; first wife), viii, 43, 62, 63, 65, 69, 134, 136, 260.
Saffin, Mrs. John (Mrs. Elizabeth Lidgett; second wife), 139.
Saffin, Mrs. John (Rebecca Lee; third wife), 43, 139.
Saffin, John (son of John Saffin), 63, 64, 65, 138, 139.
Saffin, Simon (son of John Saffin), 64, 65, 70, 136.
Saffin, Simon (father of John Saffin), 40, 138.
Saffin, Thomas (son of John Saffin), 134.
Saltonstall, Nathaniel, 271.
"Sarah, Queen Dowager" (Indian), 80.

Seabury, Bishop, 36, 96, 162.
Seabury, Rev. Dr. Samuel (father of Bishop Seabury), 36, 162.
Seabury, Mrs. Samuel (Elizabeth Powell, granddaughter of Gabriel Bernon and stepmother of Bishop Seabury), 36, 162, 167, 169.
Senegambia (slave), 80. *See* Gambia.
Sewall, Judge, 47, 48, 51.
Sewall, Rev. Dr., 117.
Sewall Fund, 157.
Shawomet (now Warwick), 198.
Shippen, Edward, 47.
Shrimpton, Samuel, 271.
Silvy Tory (slave), 214, 215, 216, 217.
Smibert, John, 83, 96.
Smith, Richard, 268.
Smith Block-house, the, 46, 271, 272.
Society for the Propagation of the Gospel in Foreign Parts, the, 31, 34, 78, 93, 106, 113, 162, 202, 203.
Society of Friends, the, 178, 181, 184, 190, 207, 230.
Sons of Liberty, 163.
Squire, Philip, 55.
Stafford, Major, 238.
Stanton, Esther (wife of Robert Hazard), 84.
Stanton, Major Joseph, 278, 282.

Index

Staples, Judge, 74.
Stepney Churchyard, 63.
Stiles, Dr. Ezra, 112, 133, 135, 142, 143, 144.
Stoughton, Governor William, 51, 271.
Stowe, Harriet Beecher, 144, 222.
Stuart, Gilbert, 87.
Stuart, Gilbert Charles (second son of Gilbert Stuart), 88.
Swift, Dr., 85, 125.

TANGATUCKET Ford, 282.
Taunton Iron Works, 54.
Taylor, George, 202.
Taylor, Mary (wife of Francis Willett), 142.
Ternay, Chevalier de, 199.
Thatcher, Rev. Mr., 65, 138.
Torrey, Dr. Joseph, 88, 89, 156, 215.
Tour de la Lanterne, 29.
Tourtellot, ———, 22.
Tower Hill, 80, 156, 157, 162, 163, 171, 172, 173, 176, 238.
Trevett vs. Weeden, 171.
Trinity Church, Newport, 31, 78, 115, 116, 145, 180, 202.
Tugg, John, 241.

UPDIKE, Lodowick, 93.
Updike, Wilkins, 18, 133, 171, 173.
Usher, Bishop, 55.

WALKER, Rev. Robert, 108.
Wanton, William, 280.
Ward, Henry, 163.
Warren, ———, 47.
Warwick, 197, 198, 199, 237, 238.
Washington, General George, 111 n., 166, 177, 206.
Watson, Guy, 213.
Weeden, William, 74.
Wendell, Judge Oliver, 136.
Wendell, Mrs. Oliver (Mary Jackson), 136.
Wendell, Sarah (wife of Rev. Abiel Holmes), 136.
Westminster Abbey, 90.
Wetmore, Seth, 248.
Whale or Whalley, Colonel Theophilus, 143.
What Cheer Rock, 160.
Whipple, Captain Joseph, 278, 283.
Whitefield, George, 233.
Whittier, John G., 75, 246.
Wickford, 13, 45, 46, 80, 145, 160, 271.
Wilkinson, Captain Philip, 104, 105, 106.
Willard, Rev. Mr., 65.
Willett, Rev. Andrew, 132, 133.
Willett, Andrew (son of Thomas Willett), viii, 69, 134, 141, 142, 148, 151, 155.
Willett, Mrs. Andrew (Anne Coddington), 141.

Index

Willett, Anne (first wife of Joseph Carpenter), 142.
Willett, Edward (son of Samuel Willett), 135.
Willett, Francis, viii, 93, 142, 143, 144, 145, 146, 173, 277.
Willett, Mrs. Francis (Mary Taylor), 142.
Willett, Hester *or* Esther (wife of Rev. Joseph Flint and daughter of Thomas Willett), 136.
Willett, Hezekiah (son of Thomas Willett), 134, 135.
Willett, Mrs. Hezekiah (Anna Brown), 135.
Willett, Hezekiah (uncle of Thomas Willett), 85.
Willett, James, 134, 135.
Willett, Mrs. James (Eliza Hunt), 135.
Willett, Colonel Marinus, 132, 135.
Willett, Martha (first wife of John Saffin), viii, 43, 62, 63, 65, 69, 134, 136, 260.
Willett, Mary (second wife of Joseph Carpenter), 142.
Willett, Mary (daughter of Thomas Willett and wife of Samuel Hooker), 135.
Willett, Samuel (son of Thomas Willett), 134, 135.
Willett, Sarah (daughter of Thomas Willett and wife of John Eliot), 135, 260.
Willett, Thomas (first mayor of New York), viii, 43, 45, 84, 98, 99, 116, 132, 133, 134, 141, 142, 148, 149, 151, 152, 256, 260, 279, 280.
Willett, Mrs. Thomas (Mary Brown), 134.
Willett, Thomas (son of Andrew Willett), 142.
Williams, Roger, 13, 156, 160, 162, 179, 181, 199, 201, 268, 272, 273.
Wilson, Samuel, 106.
Wilstead, ——, 47.
Winslow, ——, 41, 140.
Winthrop, Hannah, 120, 122.
Winthrop, John, merchant, 120, 123.
Witchcraft delusion, stories of, 161, 162.
Woolman, John, 187.
Wolsworth, Rev. Mr., 55.
Wordsworth, William, 108.
Wotton, William, 55.

YORK (slave), 80.

www.ingramcontent.com/pod-product-compliance
Lightning Source LLC
Chambersburg PA
CBHW060554230426
43670CB00011B/1818